Gullibles' Travels

The Whistling Girls & Crowing Hens Series

Book 2

Jan Anthony

ISBN: 979-8-8692-5691-1
Library of Congress
Preassigned Control Number 2024906928

Gullibles' Travels

The Whistling Girls & Crowing Hens Series

Book 2

*A creative memoir based on Bea Lindberg's
and Jan Anthony's letters,
prose, poetry, journals, diaries and imagination*

Jan Anthony

Mother Courage Press

Publisher, Jeanne Arnold

The Whistling Girls & Crowing Hens Series

Two straight married women risk families and careers, leave society's compulsory heterosexuality in 1972, and boldly thrive in an unchartered, intimate relationship. Jan and Bea experience historic events in the women's movement and gay/lesbian world in their 39 years together. Each book presents deeper levels on major topics and adventures.

The stand-alone books in this Whistling Girls & Crowing Hens Series will appeal to:

- young adults to appreciate what has come before them,
- elders to remember and respond to what they've survived,
- all readers to experience straight and lesbian lives, and
- women-loving-women who may have defied society's rules.

DEDICATION

Dedicated to the women in my life,

*especially Bea for her love and her poems
and journals,*

and for those who love her and our stories.

"Magnetic tension made it inevitable that we'd become more deeply involved. The energy held in each of us could not be contained—a power surging to envelop us. "What could it hurt if we just let it happen?" I whispered.

"As if electrified, she answered, 'Oh no! We can't do this! It could hurt you and it could hurt me and everything we've lived for. You're not strong enough for this—and neither am I!'

"While we stood silent, still embracing, I kissed her lips that were kissing me in return. A lifelong need too long repressed electrified both of us. There is no going back now.

CHAPTER 1

Jan on May 1, 1974

After one of our interludes, Bea sat across my kitchen table while I mixed martinis on the rocks. I turned to her and asked impulsively, "Will you marry me?"

"Yes!" without hesitation. I was shocked at my irresponsible proposal and stunned by her reaction. We touched glasses together and laughed nervously at the prospect.

"Jan, I'm overwhelmed by my feelings for you," as she raised her frosty glass toward me. "Each day I'm amazed at the depth that deepens daily." She paused, toasting and drinking from her martini as I did mine, "Instead of filling up with familiarity, we discover each other over and over again."

"I toast you again, you eloquent one." We sipped from our icy cocktails, gazing at each other over a soft hint of green olive juice.

"I love you. I love you."

Never has anyone spoken to me like this. "When I'm with you, Bea, I'm cherished like a child, yet I feel strong and free."

Stunned again at her shifting mood, "Jeez!" She startled me! "Look at the time! I've got to run to get the kids. Reality always breaks into our space, doesn't it? And I'll see you again as soon as I can, as soon as we can. I love you." And she downed her martini, planted a generous kiss on my lips, put the olive in her mouth and ran down the stairs and out the back door to her car.

I've not thought of myself as an adulterer. "Adulterer" sounds seedy. Perhaps I don't acknowledge that label because I love another woman rather than another man. But that rationale isn't justifiable because that diminishes both of us—as women are less valued than men. Bea makes me feel like a natural woman. What we've discovered is a completely new dimension so deep and fulfilling that it can't be wrong.

What is unsettling is not the "adultery" factor. I think I can handle living a double life, especially with my husband gone so much of the time. Rather, it's the fear of losing my children and making them suffer ridicule from their peers and having society shame them for having a bad mother, a lesbian, being poor, or having people look down on their mother for breaking the "last taboo," as if I'm even worse than a pedophile—or a cannibal.

Perhaps it's society's negative reaction to loving another woman that accounts for the high voltage that charges our relationship. Nothing equals what Bea creates for me, whether it's sexual, intellectual, emotional or spiritual. Actually, my compulsion to be with her is a fraction of how much I truly value her spirit of adventure, her multi-dimensional genius, her quick-witted flair and her courageous love that thrills and accepts me even though she's more fearful than I am of what may happen.

I'm bisexual. Heavens! I never thought I would even think about alternatives. Fairy. Queer. Lesbo. That's how my teenage peers used to taunt each other. But this is real. Sex with Alex is real and frequent. When I'm in the mood for it, I enjoy it. When I'm not, I make the best of it.

But I'm also a multi-lover, to coin a word. In the last two years, I've fallen in love with two women. My friend Marge continued to be my friend but she politely rejected my intense infatuation. My friend Bea and I alternatively affirmed and rejected our potential for being lovers until we let it happen.

And I love my husband, Alex Carnigian. And my children, family and many friends.

My calm, quiet husband's career is stimulating for him as a pioneering computer systems executive working incredibly long hours with six other men. Now he's reorganized order processing with fifty women keypunch operators and billing clerks working two shifts. One could assume that all this dedication was for the government, the military or landing more men on the moon. But he's modestly introducing a totally new computer operating system in one of the largest commercial printers in the US that employed over 2,500 full-time employees working at sites around the country.

In my internally angry reaction about being confined as are traditional wives, I considered his work to provide the world with comic books, paper-doll cutouts, Chinese Checker games and Betty Crocker cookbooks. And he never tells me differently.

Since they were infants, Matt, now 15, and Jenny, 12, and I shuttled their dad to and from the airport for business trips to New York City, New Jersey, Toronto and Nevada and who knows where. And now he's added his time away on many Sundays to find a suitable new minister for our relatively small Unitarian Universalist congregation. On other winter Sundays, Alex and Matt go ice-fishing.

Alex is a fine fellow and well-respected but quiet and reserved when he's at home. I have to interview him to stimulate conversation. I interview people all the time on my job. He wants me to be involved with his work, like listening to him read from some spreadsheet so I could double check it. Being a word person, I didn't understand nor had the patience for his tedious octal-on-the-basis-of-eight data processing techniques.

Words are my calling. I was a successful high school English and journalism teacher before being a full-time wife, mother, homemaker and volunteer. I use words now as I return to a paid writing career working part-time at two places: as a feature reporter for *Bay View Times* and now I've become the only designated but low-level communications person at Lakeshore Medical Center. With my mother being in mental hospitals for decades, I never imagined working at a hospital and I'm loving it and the staff and patients.

Our Unitarian friend Nick Dixon, who's Lakeshore Med's new executive, must trust me to produce positive publicity and print a variety of brochures and magazines with a fresh approach. He wants me to work part time. Plus, I can be in my office or work from home. It will take time to learn to understand hospital competition and politics and how to adapt negative news into positives while maintaining the hospital's integrity, but those challenges are beyond my salary range.

However, Nick may be trying to lure me away from my part-time newspaper reporter's job by offering a terrific trip to a graphic arts seminar in San Mateo, California. This trip was my business trip. This time I was flying on business and I took my husband along with me. The airlines challenged my request for a spousal rate always given to wives when they accompany their husbands on business but I finally talked them into that rate for Alex.

There I was in San Mateo for three days while Alex visited wineries and did exactly what he wanted to do, like visiting wineries. Our King Arthur-style motel had turret rooms with round beds covered with plush, red velvet spreads with matching swags and draperies. I imagined forged chains and wrist cuffs hanging on the wall to complete the medieval atmosphere.

We extended the trip to include two weekends and spent the first night at an authentic first-class Japanese hotel in San Francisco. Those Japanese really know how to take a bath, and I serviced my husband as his humble and obedient geisha girl—in and out of the tub and mattresses on the floor.

In our rented car, we drove 1200 miles north and south along the coastline to Monterey. With his William Saroyan mustache on his Armenian face, Alex was treated like a native, or "Fresno Indian." A stranger even spoke to him in Armenian.

The kids and Pepper stayed with the Dixons during the week and Alex's Sister Var and niece Sona took over on the weekends.

We travel well together. Alex and I spent from three weeks in Greece via a charter flight with the Chicago Foreign Relations Council. Except for our first night's reserved hotel room in Athens, we were on our own, starting and finishing in the Athens airport with its alert military surveillance and security checks. We saw bullet holes in the airport walls from two weeks earlier when a suicide squad attacked and killed three civilians and injured fifty-five.

We signed up for day trips at Tourism, tromped around Athens a lot but for sure, we visited the Acropolis on our first day. One lasting impression on us was an elderly couple with canes and a crutch struggling to climb up the path to the Acropolis. That's when we realized that travel lovers shouldn't wait until their children are through college before fulfilling their own travel dreams—too old and infirm to leave home. At the end of its evening "light show," I almost fell to my knees when pressed by rude crowds finding their tour buses in the dark shadows over ancient rubble.

We found places in Arthur Frommer's budget guidebook where the Greeks go, like Daphne's wine festival. Making it there via a public bus was challenging, but getting back was more so after savoring varieties of robust red wines, fruity clear roditis, sipping resiny retsina drawn from the barrel spigot and almost inhaling breathtaking, lusty ouzo.

Understanding Greek signs was hopeless. Rather than taking a comfortable tourist-type island cruise, we chose a Greek ferry heading south to stop first at Mykonos. When we got there, we followed practically all the passengers down the gangplank. Large families visiting grandparents? Could it be Greek Mother's Day? From the local Greek-style phone bureau with others waiting in line, Alex tried to call for hotel accommodations. The phone clerk was surprised that he wanted to call for a hotel in Mykonos. The conversation was hopeless too, and it took him a long time to make several frustrating calls.

I waited at the ferry dock and noticed several women limping with bloody knees. I made a mental note to be careful where I walked if so many stumbled and fell. Alex joined me, smiling a bit sheepishly because we had landed on the wrong island and would stay on Tinos until the ferry came the next day.

We discover what it was in Tinos that drew all those Greek families that we, like sheep, followed off the boat. It was the annual festival with young families bringing their newborns for a sacred blessing from the Virgin Mary at the cathedral up the hill from the dock. They climbed a double-wide paved boulevard of steps rising a half-mile up a great hill topped with a brilliant white, sun-drenched Greek Orthodox cathedral that looked more like an embellished Victorian government house—except for the cross.

That's why women had bloody knees. They crawl on their hands and knees to the top doing penance for sin or praying for something they desire. Some husbands or friends walk next to them, holding flowers, giving them water—but I didn't see any men on their hands and knees as a sign of devotion.

It was difficult getting a hotel room and lucky to find a house with one room for tourists—underprivileged tourists. We learned how to use an outside Greek toilet in a corrugated outbuilding. At least it had a seat. That night the old iron double bed sagged so much that we hung on to the headboard railings to keep from sliding in a heap into the center.

A weather-worn man collected the room fee and planted a fuzzy kiss on Alex after he gave the elder his worn jacket that wouldn't fit in the one canvas bag, a piece that we each toted for three weeks. We travel in old clothes.

Though happy that we experienced 24 hours in Tinos, we thought it best in the future to have Alex, our computer expert, ask directions in pidgin English so they can point to a direction.

After that memorable mistake in Tinos, I almost missed Mykonos. Because of high winds and waves, we boarded a tender to get from the ferry to the dock, but that wind and those waves pitched the tender just as I tried to step out of the boat. A muscular shore man grabbed me when my footing failed and set me down on the concrete pier, otherwise I could have fallen in the rough sea and probably squished between the dock and the tender. Of course, I gave him a thankful hug before he let go of me. When Alex shook his hand, he transferred drachmas to him. He did that for our tender's mate too. My potential accident must have scared him.

The extraordinary white ambience of Mykonos captivated me. Window boxes on each side of narrow streets bloomed with red geraniums and poppies flashing with green vines and less bodacious flowers. I morphed into an imaginary "Jet Set" woman looking for a nude beach, appreciating the simple, sweet, white orthodox churches capped with bluebird blue domes with silver crosses, and making a grand entrance onto an inviting taverna balcony serving moussaka, pastitsio, dolmades and ouzo. The extraordinary music, watching the dancers, breathing the sea air.

Alex told me he wants us to retire in Greece.

Finding a comfortable resting place on the crowded, nine-hour ferry trip to Santorini was a challenge. We finally landed after dark and were tossed with our canvas bags onto a tired donkey for a rainy ride up the zigzag climb to the town at the top. The handlers whistled and hollered commands to their donkeys that rubbed our legs against the short walls where we could look down the crater into darkness.

Dismounting at the top of Santorini's abyss and with wobbly legs, we each carried our bag along a brightly lit, one-lane street. With hotel reservations we found in our travel guidebook, we were warmly greeted after knocking on a standard Greek wooden door. Our welcoming host led us down a narrow corridor to our simple but adequate room. I opened the window shutters and gasped when I gazed from the unexpected edge of the volcanic crater out to the full moon and its rays floating toward us on the Aegean Sea.

By daylight, we could see the donkey path where they slip and slide on dung to skid down the crater's path, but what's the choice? (When we showed our slides at home, a friend told us about less stressful ship ports elsewhere on the island. But what fun is that?)

Two mornings later, we boarded another ferry to Crete and joined a tour to the remains of the ancient Palace of Minos at Knossos, once Europe's largest city.

Wow! Anthropologists analyzing samples of Minoan art found many Goddess images, including the Snake Goddess holding a snake in each hand, her arms raised in pride. Other frescos showed women, men and bulls: a woman figure grabs the charging bull's horns, a man figure vaults on the bull, and the woman lands upright and stands in victory. Our Greek woman guide toured us through the Palace with a royal room emblazoned with red and she pointed out that the throne is obviously small with a carved-out seat that could only fit a woman who governs.

And all this, she emphasized, showed women were not mere keepers of the home and children but were Mother Goddesses, rulers and leaders in the Minoan culture that influenced other cultures, including Greece.

Our Knossos host and restaurant owner regaled us and all his guests at a family-style table with Grecian menu delights and Gift-of-the-Gods goblets of his fermented fruit to drink under a king-sized ancient arbor filled with lush clusters of ready-to-pick purple grapes.

Alex wants us to retire in Greece.

We flew back to Athens so swiftly in a small Greek plane shuddering its metal wings over the sea, that we were convinced the pilot had a hot date in Athens and was making record time to fly and land without doing cartwheels.

After an easy day, we flew to Istanbul, Turkey, where Alex's canvas bag was lost with all his clothing. He was certain some Turk took it because it had his Armenian name printed on it. We spent hours in the famous marketplace and little stores looking for men's jockey underwear. Of course, our empathy for Alex's parents and millions of Armenians who died or survived the brutal Armenian genocide by the Ottoman Empire during World War I, was always present but unspoken.

Seeing men kissing each other on the mouth surprised me.

We experienced the magnificent St. Sophia Mosque, a former Greek Orthodox church with its massive, unsupported dome having one remaining Christian painting of Saint Sophia. Muslims converted it to a mosque with gigantic Turkish symbols replacing the human images. I kept hearing a tune bounce in my brain, "Take me back to Constantinople. No. You can't go back to Constantinople. Now it's Istanbul, not Constantinople. Why did Constantinople get the works? It's nobody's business but the Turks!" and I couldn't turn it out.

We had to take off our shoes to enter any mosque. That spooked Alex thinking they'd be stolen too, especially after he lost his shorts and the rest of his clothing. I laundered over- and underwear too frequently in a lavatory basin to hang from a rubber travel cord from whatever pillar to post we could find across a room.

Later we boarded a dusty local ferry to cross the Bosporus to meander around the harbor marketplace and claim we had been in Asia Minor.

Three weeks of travel made me edgy, especially when Alex wanted to have sex at every major place we stayed. The hot and gritty Istanbul hotel with noisy building construction, yelling and crashing all night next to our open window made me mean enough to refuse him. That caused me to think of a dog having to mark the spot wherever he went—especially in Turkey.

On our return to Istanbul's airport, we sited Alex's bag intact on top of a pile of lost luggage, and we flew out of Turkey to Athens as fast as we could.

Greece was an intellectually enlightening experience but, I'm sorry to say, my travel companion got to be boring after three weeks. I suppose I was boring, too. Often I'd spend late night hours staring out hotel windows with Cat Steven's songs playing in my heart and wondering what mischief my friend Marge was up to.

Thankfully we met two Jewish American sisters on their reunion, with one sister coming from Connecticut and the other from Israel. They'd been hit on by some Greek men and were looking for a safe escort. When they saw Alex get on the bus, they snatched us up as their companions, entertained us with their stories, showed us how to eat sensuous raw figs and choose the best wine at the tavernas. As independent, well-educated women, we enjoyed our shared sense of humor plus respect for the environment. While touring together at an ancient temple on a barren rock, an American woman with a sad husband bent down to pick a frail, budding plant from a crevice and, in unison, the two sisters and I shouted, "Don't pick the flower!"

Though we travel more than most parents, I'm always happy to get home to my children and my friends. Var and Sona took care of Matt and Jenny; they're at our house all the time anyway. Oh yes, when we landed from the flight home, crowds circled around airport TVs to watch the last game of the third set as Billy Jean King whipped Bobby Riggs in straight sets in the much ballyhooed "Battle of the Sexes." And we missed it, ballyhoo and all. After that, the United States Tennis Association announced it would award equal prize money to women and men in the U.S. Open Tournaments, a goal that King fought for.

Bea on March 11, 1972

I worked my ass off, did eleven loads of wash, changed beds, cleaned the house, and helped Jake clean the garage. We backed the boat out of the garage, swabbed The Dollar Sign's decks, and installed a new horn and letters on the bow. I cut Jake's hair and nurtured the kids after supper. Whew.

I remember my years managing a teen madhouse while I struggled to regain my self-esteem, maintain my weight-loss program and finish my UW-Milwaukee degree. But tons of rejection slips for my novel and my freelance submissions kept coming in.

The teens loved the Lindberg house. I'm Mrs. L. to this great bunch of teenagers who hung around my house because they have fun and did exciting things like scuba diving, boating, water skiing, building stock cars in the garage and on the driveway, making music, dancing, playing poker, partying. Some of them are even my own children.

But I became more and more dissatisfied with my marriage to Jake, frustrated with the roles I was expected to play and what I perceived as my lack of success. I did so much in so many creative ways and I had nothing to show for it. I managed to accomplish artistic endeavors, which gave me some satisfaction. I'm still writing and illustrating a children's novel and another novel that has never seen publication. I learned to play the guitar, write music, sing, and my creativity grew; yet something was still missing for me.

Of course, my husband didn't appreciate all those talents, returning to college, and establishing myself as a person.

In one argument, he said, "You and your goddamn college education."

He never even finished his first year of high school. I'd gone to Wright Jr. College and graduated with a two-year liberal art associate degree. At Wright, I studied theater and had a small part in a play as a cockney maid. I belonged to the Delta Eta Beta sorority. I also went to Chicago Teachers College for one semester. Fortunately, my credits transferred over to UW-Milwaukee.

Staring him down, I shook my head for emphasis and said back, "I'm one hell of a broad! I'm an artist, a writer, and a musician!"

"Yes, But I never wanted any of those. All I wanted was a wife and mother for my children."

And that's where we both are at this stage of our lives. I want to be a whole person. As a wife and mother, I don't feel that wholeness, and that creates a vacuum that needs to be filled somehow. No wonder I'm drinking more than Two-Beer Jake and with all the partying going on with the kids.

I'd do anything to get him to do something besides being "Poor Pop" to the kids, sitting in his chair acting like Archie Bunker with his damn poodle in his lap. I've got an agreement with that dog that if she doesn't sit in my lap, I won't sit in hers.

Last March, Jake and I took our kids to Florida to practice scuba diving. I wanted to surprise them at dinner with a totally new image, so I put on a blond wig that I brought along for the occasion. As I sauntered into the motel restaurant with my new body, blue sunglasses, and my wig, no one said a word, not one word.

I wonder, whatever happened to that wig?

That reminds me of my daughter's best friend Sandy, a strawberry blonde who attracted everyone's attention at my house. Everyone loves her, my sons, my husband, maybe even my daughter, but I was the one who was stone-ass bananas in love with her—and I didn't know what to do with those feelings for this "incendiary blonde."

Jan on March 19, 1972

While journaling details of our week of driving to the East Coast to see if Adele's daughter was okay in Boston, I realized how much I loved being free and having fun with my friends, especially Marge. I started planning ways to be with her, her sons and her mother.

One morning I woke up and realized that I might love others beyond my family—and that may include women. Exciting memories of the young woman I loved when I was in my teens resurfaced from that secret place I've hidden. Those emotions burst out again and landed on my dear friend Marge.

I wrote in my journal: "It was a morning in May when I exploded to wake up and become a new person. The sun had again burst into flame and I caught the sparks that were to ignite another with my happiness. I realized that I was in love and I gave myself permission to explore its depths. Exhilarating, breathtaking, joyful secrets that I love. I give love. I'm ready to share my love."

We usually sit around her kitchen table with a bottle of wine or vodka, but this time I edged her to sit on a sofa across from her grand piano that almost filled the living room. Strange! I never noticed how big that piano was, but it took so much room and it was hard to catch my breath.

"Marge, I want to tell you a secret that's hugely important to me."

She took my hand as if I were going to tell her of my fatal disease. "I'm listening, Jan."

I straightened my spine as I twisted toward her. Shoulders back. Chin firm so as not to cry, "I hope you won't be shocked, Marge, but I've fallen in love—with you."

She's a cool one, as if that happens every day or at least once a month.

"Jan, I love you too," in a flat, stone tone, "but not in that way, dear."

"I figured you'd say that. And I guess it's okay because I don't know what to do next if you return my feelings."

"I will always love you, Jan, but like a friend—a sister friend."

"OK, but I'll always be near when and if you need me?"

"You must be thirsty."

"I'm so parched I can't describe how dry I am."

"Well, you deserve a drink. Come on into the kitchen and I'll pour you a glass of ice water and—How about a martini?"

Jan on April 11, 1974

From the windows of Emerson House on this April afternoon, Bea and I could, if we chose to do so, look down on the park through the green leaves of a mature maple that grew close to the second-story apartment in a house that had been converted to Emerson House, our church school office and classroom space.

Cool breezes blowing through the open windows refreshed us as we embraced and kissed—friends for years but lovers now, committed in love despite husbands and families.

The scratchy, lime-colored fabric of the old-fashioned hand-me-down sofa rubbed red, raw patches on our arms and legs. The intense urgency of discovering and refining each new maneuver in lovemaking took us ultimately to the faded green carpet on the floor. In this relatively safe and spacious nest, we could move freely, with abandon, yet silently, as silently as possible, because we must remain alert to the outer world whose noises could shatter our existence should we be discovered in this condition in this secret place.

Our other senses surged. The touch of skin, fingers, lips, and tongues. The taste of life's juices. The heady smell of sweat and sex. Our vision is beholding our beloved's face—a mirror image here—this celebration of oneness, of equality, of power to initiate and to please the other to quaking orgasm. We were two women learning at intensifying levels how to love each other and, at the same time, love ourselves to deeper fulfillment.

In the blessed relaxation that followed, Bea slowly raised herself from the floor to sit next to my bare body, so prone on my stomach that I seemed almost to have melted on the rug.

"I learned to do this to my kids when they're hyper," said Bea who started to stroke my back gently with one hand, following the other hand in a line, moving from my brain stem toward the base of my spine. She kept one hand touching my spine at all times. In a few minutes, the currents of Bea's softness on my vertebrae touched my emotional nervous system. I let myself go again, but this time there were sobs of release, of letting go of the chaos of my marriage, the tension of my job and the anxiety caused by falling in love with a woman, Bea.

"Why are you sobbing?" asked Bea as she helped me get off the floor. We dressed each other in the midst of my tears, and the process was interrupted only by comforting hugs and gentle kisses before we curled up together on the little love seat with its high back hiding us from the window. We were not afraid here. We could not be seen.

With my heartbeat pounding, I answered, "I have never experienced this complete love for another human being. It is what I have been searching for, this love that totally envelops me with joy."

Focusing on reality, we talked for timeless hours. Finally, our eyes' lenses zoomed back from our faces to expand our view, seeing the leaves and the park and the cars in the street below. Time to part for a while. But we would meet again for a church school party hereafter, we prepared supper at our homes and cared for our families. We separated for that afternoon, tenderly unraveling our bodies and souls as we went our separate ways for now in bliss.

Mildred's undated letter from Winnebago

Please Barney,

Come on and get me. How much longer do I have to stay here? I feel fine and then they give me another electric treatment. Can't you take care of me yourself?

Crying and carrying on isn't going to help me and I don't know what can help me get well so I can leave here. Will you write me a letter anyway and let me know what to expect? I've been sleeping without pills for a week now.

Please come and see me. I'm getting lonesome.

Perhaps I'm getting a lesson in discipline. If that's what you want, I can be that way too. I would much prefer you would work with me and not be so quick to send me away. My heart has been broken ever since you have been so quick to send me away. What are you afraid of? Have I hurt someone? Do you think I will?

Jan on May 6, 1974

Back when I was a college student in 1950, I looked forward to taking my sophomore psychology class to try to understand more about mental factors that influence behavior, but I was disappointed that it was mostly about nerve endings and science. We were to write a term paper but when I told my instructor about what was happening with my mother, he excused me from that task, saying that I had greater experience and understanding than any term paper could give me. He was especially sympathetic when I told him that my father must decide whether to have surgeons perform a prefrontal lobotomy on my mother. She'd had so many electroshock treatments. They thought this next step would be appropriate.

He scanned a reference book and summed up the main points for me. The prefrontal lobotomy, developed in 1935 by Edges Moniz, claimed it was a perfect treatment for mental illness. In his experiments, he would bore into an individual's skull with a surgical pick and sever the prefrontal cortex. This would make the most troublesome patients docile. The procedure became so popular that Moniz won the Nobel Prize.

I told him, "My mother, when she's well, is a wonderful person—creative, spontaneous, humorous, and intelligent. She always struggled for equal rights and equal pay. I had a good role model when she was well. She's a part of me and she's taught me more than books and school. My father and I have to determine my mother's future. It's not easy. What do you think we should do? What's ahead in her future? What's ahead in ours?"

"I'm sorry, Jan, I can't give you an answer."

"A letter arrived from doctors at the Winnebago Mental Health Institute on May 6, 1950.

"We wish to inform you that the prefrontal lobotomy on the above patient has been scheduled for Thursday, May 11. Should there be any change in these plans, you will be notified."

The next Sunday, my father and I followed a Winnebago staff person outside and across the grass to see Mother in one of the little stucco cottages within the grounds. We entered this cell-like room with one white metal frame bed supporting her sheet-wrapped form, her head bulging in gauze. If I felt despair, how must my father have felt? He held her hand, his face close to hers. I stayed sitting at the foot of the bed.

We said nothing. I heard only our breathing and hers. A clean, leafy smell wafted through the open windows as the spring breeze made the thin white curtain wave at us. She opened her eyes and smiled and then went back to sleep. Had he made the correct decision? Too late now. She'd never be the same, even when she'd be well. She'd be passive, irreversibly dehumanized. No more vitality and determination—but no more madness.

After her recovery and after she healed and her hair grew back, we waited for those changes. But there was no transformation.

Thinking that Mom would recover from her surgery as a new woman able to come home to us before Christmas, Dad used a new design device, a black light, and he spray-painted a glowing chartreuse live Christmas tree and we decorated it with the sprayed red, orange, and yellow fluorescent plastic foam stars snowflakes and balls the size of grapefruit. We set it up in the front window and it became a traffic hazard when drivers' eyes would be mesmerized by its glaring radiance that seemed to leap out of the window and onto the snow. What a show we put on that Christmas, but my father and I exchanged our presents alone again on Christmas Eve under the glowing tree ablaze in color.

Dad sent her New Year's card to Winnebago, adding "Best Wishes on our 21st anniversary, January 1, 1930, to January 1, 1951. Love, Barney.

We moved the dazzling tree from the front room in our hope to have Mom see it and slid it into the dining room where it stood until Easter. We hadn't watered it for months; the needles, held on by the paint, stayed on their branches.

Twelve years later on April 4, 1962, Dad and I went to the University of Wisconsin Hospital in Madison because my mother was to have a hysterectomy. I was surprised that my high school friend OB/GYN Dr. Gloria Stevens, was her surgeon. We met with her in a dark office lit only by the light on her desk. After I gave her a welcoming greeting and maybe even a hug, Gloria was professionally reserved and unresponsive other than to recognize me and say hello. I didn't intrude. Later I found out she was in a long-term relationship with a nurse she met when they were both Lakeshore Med's nursing students and that probably prompted her to keep a low profile. But most importantly, Gloria told us what had happened to my mom years before.

Her medical records indicated that surgeons at Winnebago had started the pre-frontal lobotomy but aborted the surgery because

Mom was bleeding so much that they stopped the procedure—and no one ever told us.

Dr. Stevens seemed okay about my mother's lobotomy not being completed, and she quietly remarked that the procedure's popularity has expanded to make good American citizens out of "society's misfits like radicals and homosexuals."

CHAPTER 2

Jan on April 4, 1974

In addition to Sunday services, our UU church offered sessions on important new trends like Transactional Analysis or TA, sex education for our youth, assertiveness training, weekly meditations and feminist consciousness-raising groups, plus non-trendy folk dancing. After some consciousnesses were raised, a committee "neutering the hymn books" by crossing out male pronouns and penciling in gender-free alternatives.

Bea on April 11, 1974

This consciousness-raising session took on how being women affects our current family relations. One even wondered how lesbians make it work in a marriage-type relationship. Curiosity stimulated questions created fantasies. We must be careful not to behave like we know anything about that. Besides, we're not in a marriage-type relationship. I wonder if that will happen? How could it? If Jan were a man, I'd divorce Jake right away and marry her. I wonder if she would do the same?

Though we're all college grads, we've been full-time homemakers waiting for their kids to grow up so they can find a good job. They wouldn't be able to come to our morning rap group if they were working. Not everyone's lucky to have a job like Jan, who comes and goes almost as she pleases.

A minor fiasco happened last week after we met at our favorite remote rendezvous for some nurturing and on the way home, we stopped for a freight train. Jan's VW van was behind me and when she saw how long the train was, she jumped out of her car, ran to my open window and started kissing me as the train rumbled by. She would not stop for me to tell her that a guy in a car on the other side of the track was waiting and watching us from the undercarriage of the passing boxcars.

Another incident was when Jan woke up one night to find herself lying flat on Alex's body in bed, kissing him and saying, "Have you ever kissed a man with a moustache?" He woke up wondering what she said and what she was doing. "Oh, Just a dream. I'm sorry I woke you," and she quickly turned over and away from him, stifling her giddiness.

Jan on April 18, 1974

Thursday's consciousness-raising group talked about pregnancy and child-rearing issues, self-image, loss of self, and how we felt about our mothers. Mothers seemed to be blamed for everything that went wrong with so many of the women's lives. I guess that will be our fate when our children get to be our age, but I was able to say that no matter how my mother raised me, when she did, I knew she loved me. And she couldn't be blamed for any problems in my life and my decisions because, in fact, she was diagnosed as schizophrenic—and how can you blame a crazy woman for her actions?

Jan on April 25, 1974

"How do you feel about aging? About menopause?" Those questions started our circle of women in their mid-forties, mothers who live a comfortable life yet with normal concerns for the future and what they expect for themselves, especially when their husbands are gainfully employed and their marriages seem secure.

Susan referred to coloring her hair to disguise the aging process. I don't consider that as an option. What a bother. When I turned thirty-five, my doctor told me that now I'm on the downhill side of life. I disagreed with him, but I actually went to a beauty parlor and succumbed to a Merle Norman facial and a hairdo. Ha! For my birthday party date that night, Alex took me to see Katharine Hepburn in *The Lion in Winter* at its premier showing in a Milwaukee movie house. When I went to the ladies' room, I saw someone familiar in the mirror. I almost said Hi until I realized it was me.

Adelle tried to show me how to apply eyeliner, which took me several more minutes to arrange myself for work, and I stopped that quickly. Once, I caught Adelle without her customary layer of pancake make-up and she looked so old and wrinkled. That convinced me that my face would be what it is, with a little lipstick applied once or twice a day. Bea, with her fifty-some lost pounds, is proud of that, and she is a make-up artist; but she's an artist anyway so she has the talent. I guess my growing-up years with simple braids and without a woman role model to inspire me to cosmetic beauty left me retarded in those skills. And I don't care. But I don't want to end up like my mother in her condition, with no teeth and wearing institutional clothing. I guess I'll be more likely to end up looking like my father.

Our rap group moved on to discuss the concept of race and how it affects women.

I'll always remember personally relating to Malcolm X in his autobiography when he wrote about using lye to straighten his hair. When it was time to rinse off the lye, the water pipes in his run-down flat ran dry. He had to submerge his head in the toilet to wash the burning lye from his scalp. That was the last time he subjected himself to fit in with others' standards.

Perhaps that's another reason for supporting the concept of racial justice, which I acquired so long ago from my parents. Two

Black bachelors are neighbors at my dad's shop downtown and they are so gentle and kind. I watched in horror at events in Selma and Montgomery and grieved so deeply at the deaths of those little girls in the bombed church and the assassination of Martin Luther King, Jr. Of course, anyone with racial prejudice wouldn't be comfortable among Unitarians anyway.

Bea commented again on having an Archie Bunker for a husband, and that her father used racial slurs. Even her mother had called people "kikes" and other pejoratives so commonly used among their friends and neighbors. "It's hopeless to change them," she said, "but I'm getting sick and tired of it."

I can honestly say that I never heard any of those prejudiced words come out of either of my parents' mouths, even if my mother was crazy, and I added that I knew that my children have never heard those words from us. Sometimes I worry that they may become justifiably prejudiced because of some bullying by Black students at their inner-city schools. I hoped that wouldn't be true.

I added that I have empathy with civil rights struggles because I, too, am victimized because of our situation as women, abused by senseless power over others, including government edicts that unfairly control our decisions and our status. Feminism is creating awareness of injustice for women even among liberal and racial groups dominated by men. In speaking out that way, I let off some pressure that lives in me because of my evolving lifestyle. I wondered what would surface next in the struggles for equality for all—and where will I fit into the action?

Bea on May 1, 1974

May Day! May Day! May Day! Jan! Some of my words about acceptance echo what I really feel but don't say—about being totally accepted and loved by you, and loving you and totally accepting you. I love you without reservation. I don't care to have you change one jot of yourself or your personality for my benefit. What you are is what I love, totally. What you think, or what you do, or what you decide in the future, all will come from the total person that I accept and that I love. I put no restrictions, no conditions, no reservations on our relationship. Whatever you are is what I love, whatever you have been is what I love, and whatever you will become is what I love. Total acceptance.

Bea on May 2, 1974

Today's rap group was especially sensitive, but I was able to regale them with a few of my stories about early childhood experiences with sex. I'd spoken of them before, so I didn't take over the morning and gave others a chance to talk. But I must add that what my experiences did to my view of sex and of myself as a woman made me feel insecure and powerful at the same time. My varied experiences as a "rowdy girl" let me proceed with sexual episodes because I had nothing much to lose; yet withholding sex gave me control. But now I am so frustrated with my husband's rejection of me. What I want in my mid-life rush is to experience life to the fullest. I should have known after twenty years that my husband wouldn't be the one to do that with me.

Jan has frequent, good sex with Alex; I think she brags about it. Some of the others passed on speaking about their sexual issues. I would guess that they're like me—frustrated as hell with their husbands, but they may think they're not desirable anymore. That's not my issue since I've recreated myself.

I'd been faithful to him until I couldn't bear the boredom of our bed.

Almost all of the twelve women in the circle had been molested as a child in some way. It's up to them to define how seriously it affected them. Even minor touching may affect a woman in a major way. The trauma of prolonged sexual abuse came up, but no one discussed her personal story, probably because it could hurt too much. That's another secret for some women to bear.

Jan's mother told her that her first husband forced her to have four abortions after she had her Richard, who was hit by a car and died when he was eight. Those abortions left scars and wounds so deep that she almost died when she gave birth to Jan by caesarian section. One woman remembered the Unitarian woman in the early 1960's who had severe morning sickness and took thalidomide that her husband brought home from England. The fetus was threatened, a media blitz exploited her decision to go overseas for an abortion and she was condemned.

Another bared her soul to release her grief. After she divorced and lost her husband, she felt depressed and lost her sense of worth. When another man paid attention to her, she allowed him to have sex with her. It felt good being with someone again, except that they didn't take precautions and she got pregnant. The man wasn't interested in her anymore; perhaps he was even married. She didn't say. A single parent, newly divorced, pregnant with nowhere to go, she did what millions of women have done. She stepped into her bathtub with a hanger and performed an abortion on herself. Fortunately, she did it without physically harming herself, but her bloody physical and emotional experience was devastating. She said she's come out of this a stronger person. She asked that everyone keep her story secret. That agreement was part of the basic rules of the consciousness-raising group from the start.

Jan said she was lucky to have a guardian angel with her as well as her using practical alternative means of sexual gratification with her husband-to-be for the many years before her marriage. She called herself "a technical virgin" when she was married and has had sex with only her husband. (She looked at me to acknowledge that our relationship was her only other sexual experience, and my body twitched, my clit flipped, and my eyes almost rolled back in my head.)

I wasn't lucky during one of my pre-marital encounters. Once, on a date with a guy who had too much to drink—I probably did too—he got violent with me when I stopped him from having sex in his car. He pulled me out and raped me against the car and then he collapsed. That's when I walked away, ran actually, but he got in the car to look for me on or off the road using the car's spotlight. When he finally found me, I realized how far I still had to go, got in his car and he drove me home. The next day, he actually called me and asked me to marry him, for Christ's sake.

Of course, we had so much to talk about, we carried that subject over until next week. As usual, Jan and I had lunch somewhere and went to comfort each other before we had to return to her job and to our families.

I asked Jake to come to bed early. The kids were all out somewhere. He said something about how strange it seemed to have me home before dawn. In spite of his unskilled sarcasm, we turned off the TV, put the dog out and in, and went to bed, but I couldn't get a rise out of him. He said he didn't like the smell of alcohol on my breath, and he actually fell asleep on me. It is hopeless. Rejection! I got up to write for hours into the night.

He deserves to be hurt. He deserves to be shafted. He deserves it for what he's done to me over and over and over again, yet I'm too soft, too kind, too sympathetic. I can't do that to him, the soggy, soft wishy-washy person that I am, hurt by inference—and he never appreciates how I struggle for his affection.

Bea on May 3, 1974

I left for Algonquin to visit Angie Murak and talk with my good old friend—over a bottle of wine, of course. Steve took us out for supper at the Moose Club, where he tends a bar. He has four jobs to keep his wife and four kids the same ages as mine in boats and in their fancy homes. I called Jake and told him I was going to spend the night rather than drive all the way home. Angie passed out at about 1 a.m., and I went to bed in the guest room. At about 3 a.m., Steve appeared in my room and crawled into bed with me. I didn't discourage him; I liked having sex with a man, especially one who's a good friend.

Dear Jan,

Dawn broke when I finally realized that I don't ever, never want to be the only person that you love. If I were that one, and the only impossible one, I would be chained. I'd never be free. Nor could you. And it's inhuman, irrational nonsense to ask any person to love only one person. Love enhances existence only if it's almost universal—with special qualifications for certain people in your life.

When I told her what happened in Algonquin, she didn't seem jealous, as long as I was safe. She had Alex, she said, so why shouldn't I have a man when I wanted one?

Jan on May 8, 1974

At yesterday's conscious-raising session, we were asked how we felt about love and our past experiences with love. We both were so heady we could barely contain ourselves. We were sorry for those women who had nothing or only negative experiences with love. We had to be careful not to spill out our joy at what we've discovered, especially when the next question asked was, "Do you feel as though you can love another woman?" Our affirmations had to be subtle, of course, and we generated lots of laughs comparing the psychological or the physical aspects of "Can you love yourself?" For the question, "How much of your life is organized around love?" we both were prepared with a few poems so we could control our obsession. We wisely omitted our ecstatically blissful compositions that we'd written for each other.

After all these hectic times and relationships, I took a late-night TV break to enjoy a courageous comedian I relate to, Phyllis Diller and her raucous laughter. She's broken through the male-dominated stand-up comedy scene, and hits the mark now with most of my friends on topics we share: being married to Fang, housewives with moldy ironing stored in plastic bags in the refrigerator; "My kids grow out of them before they get ironed." and "Housework can't kill you – but why take a chance?"

Now, it seems that I've become a small city religious liberal who has been transformed into a minor-league feminist lesbian activist, an underpaid professional working woman and, I presume to my immediate administrators and a few others, an embarrassing social outcast. Yet Diller still speaks for me saying, "My 'consciousness' is fine; it's my pay that needs raising."

Bea and I spent the rest of the day together before going home to our families. Our yard work can wait. The winter's dead leaves can blow away. I've done enough of what I have to do. I have to pursue what I want to do. I asked myself once, "How can I get the response that I need?" I got it! It's real! I've felt the earth move.

Bea on May 16, 1974

This morning, we talked of violence in our rap group and later, we settled down in gentle afternoon time before Jan and I each headed for home. Perhaps because I've told most of my stories to the group and because I'm so happy being in love with Jan, I couldn't relate:

> How has violence intruded into your life? How do you feel about violence? This can be broken down into a range of topics: a. violence and heterosexual sex; b. violence as self-expression and purgation of oppression; c. violence as a political reality. This could also include such topics as self-defense, defense of a group under attack, terrorism, and violence as a way of keeping women, or any other despised group, in their place.

I know Jan's afraid of Alex, but it was Marie who told me about her husband's ultimate act of passive aggression. They co-exist as a family and argue about the kids and what he doesn't do when and what she wants to be done. One night in their basement family room while watching TV, they started bickering and it grew nasty. She didn't say if they'd been drinking. He sat there pretending to read the paper and Marie waved her arm, gesturing to make her point. Somehow she smashed the fragile glass of an antique kerosene lamp and realized that a shard had become embedded in her wrist and she almost fainted. She grabbed for a cloth, pleading for her husband to help. He sat as if nothing was wrong.

In shock, she made her way up the stairs, almost fainting at the top, where she stopped and called him for help again. Bloodstains smeared the walls and the stairs and he never responded. She finally made it to her neighbors who called the rescue squad and they took her to the ER.

When she returned home, he had left the house. The blood was still there and eventually, she had to be the one to clean it up.

I didn't want to deal with the subject because I feel so alive. The women considered how they could conceive of your own death? But Jan gets into all this and after a heart-wrenching plea for justice and world peace, she went on to wax positively about crossing over to the other side when she's in her nineties living on the Riviera, as in *The Red Shoes* movie, having her limousine smashed by a train while she's on her way to be with her lover.

Other questions were beyond us at this time.

What have been your past experiences with death? Why do male politics rest so heavily on death: war, the Jewish extermination, the Indians, and today, the Blacks? Men kill women; women rarely kill other women. Why do you think this happens?

Heavens, that was heavy stuff to talk about. Wars will stop when women have equal power to govern and save children from males' preoccupation with guns, weapons and war.

With pleasure, Jan and I found peace together after lunch.

CHAPTER 3

Jan on May 28, 1974

The Memorial Day weekend was great because we were creating our Door County vacation space for our friends as well as for us. We installed insulation and paneling on one half of our new barn's main floor, which would be our major living area. Now we added a small gas furnace and gas refrigerator with propane tanks on the outside back of the barn. I put up curtains with country patterns to make it more homelike. It was primitive, but it would improve as time progressed.

My mind was planning gatherings for everyone I cared about and my heart was filled with anticipation of bringing them here. If we could control the flies, we could even have visitors sleep in the loft. Our elders could sleep in the little trailer. I slept anywhere I wanted, including in the new hammock I bought for shade in the ridge's woods.

My mind was also planning my homecoming, and Bea and I met earlier than usual on Tuesday morning. Enough of all this restraint on our lovemaking. I was going to assert myself and when she came into the house, I locked the doors, took her by the hand, and climbed the stairs to celebrate our reunion. But rather than going into my studio, I took her into my bedroom. The sun sparkled on the lake in a cheerful pattern of springtime warmth. I had surprised Bea by coming into this inner sanctum of married monogamy, and in catching her off guard, she did not argue or resist.

We took off all our clothes and she slipped into my side of the bed and I into my husband's side. We held each other tenderly as any couple would, almost as on a honeymoon. Compared to the rough carpet on the floor, the crisp, clean linens that I had prepared and the soft mattress drew us together as if we were in a cocoon where our velvety, soft, and silky skins could meld into one sensual essence. Everything was right. Nothing was unnatural. We were attuned to each other with the deepest affection and emotional understanding that we need and have to offer each other.

"Because it feels good, that's why I savor touching your lips, sensing your skin for no other reason, for no hidden motive other than that it feels good to hold you, to feel you next to me," I whispered. "My body says yes to your tender moves. I'm rewarded by each subtle gesture, by our mouths moving quietly, exploring each other's skin."

However, we couldn't continue to relax after our gentle, unclothed loving. Being conscious of the sounds of any person who'd discover our vulnerable selves and with sensible logic, we grounded ourselves in reality and left our nest.

Though we were inexperienced at this aspect of making love, we had the savvy to change the sheets and pillowcases to remove our fragrances before we went downstairs. I made us a drink and lunch in the kitchen. I then opened the curtains that I had closed to keep Adele from seeing my companion follow me up the stairs. Of course, the mere act of closing those curtains could arouse her suspicions because I never drew them together.

After lunch, we took our second drink into the living room, where Bea sat in the armchair next to me curled up in the corner of the sofa. She started tuning my guitar that I never could learn to play, let alone get it in tune. "It's an inexpensive guitar; they never hold their tune," she explained.

We heard the back door open and for the first time in the history of my marriage, my husband came home from work in the middle of the day. I can't believe it. He must have sensed that something threatened his domain.

He was stunned to see Bea with me, alone together; we've always circled ourselves with friends and their children when he was around.

"Alex! Did you forget something? Can I fix you some lunch? Bea's trying to tune up my guitar so I can try to learn to play it. We're only having a drink. I suppose you don't want one during the middle of the day."

"No. Thanks." And he turned around and left the house.

We looked at each other, dismayed. "He could have killed the both of us if he found us earlier, me first," said Bea.

"I've been waiting for that volcano to explode." I trembled, "since I went back to work. I can still feel his heat."

"And I feel the warmth of our loving so completely," Bea responded with a gentle touch and a kiss.

To Bea,

You give me gladness as a gift—
A most precious offering, most heartily received,
most gratefully acknowledged, most joyous gladness,
sublime, supreme, superb gladness inside.

Jan on May 21, 1974

One Saturday, during cocktail hour, when the kids were out with their friends, Alex directed me to sit on the couch with him, "I want to talk."

That's different. We chatted about tennis, wallpaper, the plans for remodeling the kitchen, the new brochure I was preparing for church, and even about my work. I was really getting into this.

"But," as he shifted his body to look directly at me. "I'm concerned about how much time you spend with your women friends. There's Marge, of course, and Bea, Anne, and now your tennis partner, Sandy."

"They're all from church and have kids and are interested in religious education and we have a lot in common. Marge and Anne have been friends for years."

"And that Bea Lindberg! I've seen her hugging you a couple of times. And I think you're spending too much time drinking with Adele after supper."

"You know that we all hug when we see each other and say goodbye."

"She isn't like the rest. She hugs like she wants to hang on."

"And as for Adele, all you have to do is walk over and join us around her kitchen table. You have your fishing and hunting buddies and I'm sure you're close to your colleagues at work after all the hundreds of hours you spend with them in overtime and on business travel."

"Well, I look across into Adele's kitchen window and see you two talking so seriously and deeply, but it takes you away from home even though you're only next door, and I'd like to know what you're talking about."

"Are my friendships with wives of your teacher friends from the old days bothering you too? Like Amanda and Betty? And what about our high school friends, Lucy and Esther?"

"That's different because we see them mostly as couples. And it makes me angry that you'd rather spend time with the women when we go to parties than sticking with me and being my companion."

"Geez, Alex. You don't need me to stand at your elbow to support your social life. And when I don't, you sulk."

"It seems to me that you're extremely devoted to them and spend an abnormal amount of time with women—and I'm concerned about some lesbian overtones among your friends."

"Don't worry, Alex. We're having so much fun being newly converted feminists, and we loved laughing and rapping over our shared experiences.

"And at the man's expense, my expense! Newly converted feminists—striving to make us look stupid."

"That's not true. We don't want to put anyone down. Unfortunately, it's easy to do that on occasion. Women have gathered together and supported each other for eons in their tribes and circles and groups. We seem to empower and enlighten each other to be bolder and more self-confident. You don't seem to mind having a more responsive bed partner, do you? And some of us have jobs and that affirms us when the paycheck comes around. You don't mind having my extra money for our trips together, do you?"

He shifted his weight toward me. "Are you sure that everything is all right?' His gray blue eyes stared at me from under his bushy brows. "I can't help my sensing lesbian tendencies among your group of friends."

"Alex," I said quietly as I gently put my hand on his arm. "I can't speak for each of them, only myself. Don't worry. I have everything under control." I didn't think I lied because it was under control—from my point of view.

Without sighing to give myself away, I rose from the sofa and went to the kitchen with my heart pounding and peered into the refrigerator to plan another satisfying meal before I'd lose control with a smug smile. I decided on steak. Steak is what they'd like with a good salad and a baked potato with lots of butter and sour cream."

He was staring out at Lake Michigan when I came back to the room. "Alex, let's go whack a few tennis balls before supper. We'll leave a note for the kids to tell them that we're at the park."

I noticed while talking with him, that the more independent I'm becoming, the more facial hair he's growing: his moustache, eyebrows, sideburns, even his nose and ears. And he's getting grayer too, almost like the images of Moses holding the Ten Commandments.

Bea on June 10, 1974

We Unitarians around the world and for centuries have always revered nature and spent Sunday services in parks or camped together, often congregations suspend services for summer breaks.

Traditionally on one Sunday, we'd have a brief service and share a potluck picnic in a park. With all our activities, especially folk dancing, we adults and our kids have grown so close that we planned a weekend campout together at Sanders Park.

WOW! Maybe we could spend our first night together in the pop-up trailer that I'll rent.

Mother Nature didn't cooperate and Friday night's campout, which was to start after the folk dancing party, would start on Saturday morning. Undaunted, we asked Marge if we could picnic in her driveway after the party, where I was so full of joy and anticipation that I played the guitar and sang with everyone for hours.

After more talk and wine in Marge's kitchen, and after some devious alliances, we ended up with Jan's Jenny, Marge's Tim, and my Jill sleeping in the tent trailer with us—It's always wise for us to be with others in a group—and Anne and Marge slept together in Jan's VW campervan. As we each stumbled out into our assigned spaces, kids first, we listened to the raindrops falling on the canvas until our kids fell asleep. Jan and I, in pajamas, zipped our sleeping bags together—to keep each other warmer, we'd say if we were asked. But we didn't need to be warmer, nor did we sleep.

Quietly so as not to wake our beloved children, we nuzzled and kissed and stroked each other so quietly through the entire night, except for a brief nap, until I turned to wake and found her in my arms. The hidden joy overwhelmed us wrapped in loving embraces gently so we didn't rock the wheeled rig that brought us together for our first trembling night. We whispered words of love and happiness in each other's ears and stifled our elated exuberance like girls at their first sleepover. Near dawn, I realized the canvas flap on my side wasn't secure and we giggled quietly after I whispered, "A person could fall out of here," a line to use often as our secret code.

Marge fed our gang breakfast and we headed south to set up our camp with friends all together with Jan's next to my camper.

What a beautiful Saturday, eating, drinking, playing games. I provided a shoulder for Betty to cry on and guarded Jan while she slept in my camper until Alex and Matt claimed her, taking her back into their space and into the VW camper to sleep. Though damp, we uncovered some wood for a campfire circle with singing and stories. I was dead tired and slept almost unconsciously until a thunder crash woke me at 5 a.m. The dogs next to the park woke as well, only they didn't stop their whelping for hours after that.

It rained in spurts on Sunday morning but I made enough coffee and breakfast for Jan and her family while quietly singing my song for her, "Mother Earth."

MOTHER EARTH

> Mother Earth, Mother Earth.
> Nurture me for I love thee.
> Lake and hill, I can't get my fill
> of your sweet land,
> your sea and sand, your trees and sky,
> your mountains high.
> I love them all, your spring and fall,
> your warmth and snow.
> All these I know are mine,
> my Mother Earth.
> Mother Earth, Mother Earth.
> I in turn will nurture thee
> to keep you free for all
> to see for all to share
> preserve with care,
> my precious Mother Earth.
> My precious Mother Earth.
> My precious Mother Earth.

I knew Jan, sleeping next to her husband, would be awakened by my song for her. Sunday's outdoor church service was damp and friends bounced in and out of my trailer, swaggered barefoot in the rain and mud, and teenage girls washed their hair in the rain.

We each packed up our soggy shelters and drove home our separate ways.

Returning back home and surveying that scene, I reflected on the one highlight required to complete our weekend; to have Jan with me at home for a warm, cuddly, quiet, lazy, and loving Sunday afternoon nap, holding each other close to share by osmosis and to rest up from this crazy, mixed-up wonderful weekend we've had.

Jan on June 10, 1974

Dear Bea,

Something needed is missing to complete the crazy, mixed-up weekend we've had with the preparing and packing with anticipation, the disappointing weather and frustration with changes in plans, the creative problem-solving capitalizing on chance, the electric excitement matched in crackles of sleeping bag zippers, and the muted joy of our quiet togetherness with our offspring sleeping beside us as our family together in loving unity. After our tender awakening after so brief a nap, we quietly whispered and muffled our happy laughter within our sleeping bag.

We'll cherish the rigors of tenting forever, the attention you gave me, the nurturing you gave others, the grand group singing led by my lady, your hardy laughter creating good feelings, your responding with comfort to friends in need while I catered to my husband who wanted me too, this tangle of people all wrapped together under awnings in torrents of rain.

The scenes are symbolic of each needing the other, some desperately, some possessively, some mischievously, some helplessly while we two exchanged glances and our eyes talked silently, telling us of our priceless possession of loving each other amid all this chaos and my insides responding with chaos in kind.

With the rain and the dogs and my quiet acceptance of lying awake next to my husband, I waited for dawn and heard your voice singing "Mother Earth" between thunder and rain. I'll never forget the childlike abandon of jauntily striding together down the road to the privy with our half-rolled up jeans and our bare feet splashing and our arms crossed our shoulders as Mark Twain-type comrades, as partners, as buddies jovially celebrating our camaraderie while walking away from another behind us who watched as we swaggered along down the road.

Jan on January 21, 1973

When I became a part time reporter, I bounded past the business offices and bounced up the stairs to the newsroom, where friendly colleagues greeted me. I was armed with fresh enthusiasm to add my liberated insight into each new assignment.

As a homemaker, I dedicated time to listen to Studs Terkel on WMFT, Chicago's fine arts radio station. I wasn't aware of it, but Studs was teaching me how to interview people with humor and compassion and ask thoughtful questions at just the right time.

Each weekday I'd absorb his interviews from George McGovern and Martin Luther King, Jr., Mahalia Jackson to Carole Channing. I cried when eyewitnesses related details of the John and Robert Kennedy and King assassinations. It seemed as if those who inspired me, us, to believe in the future, to hope for a peaceful world, were picked off by a bullet, one after the other.

Terkel's interview touched another nerve by introducing me to feminism. What a revelation. I began to identify what was wrong with me and why I was unhappy. I don't remember the names of the women who spoke about Simone de Beauvoir's book, *The Second Sex*, but I immediately went to our library to check it out while I waited a week for my local bookstore order to arrive. The librarian told me that I couldn't take the book home because it was a reference book, so every day I read it in the library until I had the book I ordered of my own. I was liberating myself and for the first time, I found written information and affirmation on women loving women in de Beauvoir's Chapter 15, "The Lesbian."

Hearing Terkel's on-the-spot radio interviews during the 1968 Democratic Convention and the police and anti-Vietnam War protesters in Lincoln Park, Grant Park, and on Michigan Avenue made me rage. Then I watched it all on TV. These events contributed to my deepening social and political awareness.

And that damn Democratic Convention. As members of Another Mother for Peace with our church women and others, we were outraged at the War in Vietnam and then how Mayor Richard Daley's police waded into crowds of protesters, brutally spraying them with Mace, clubbing and battering them with nightsticks and dragging the bloody protesters, reporters, and bystanders caught in the milieu into paddy wagons.

Alex defended the police because of reports that some protestors took buckets of fecal matter and urine to roofs and threw the detritus on the crowds. That stupid act of a few was worse to him than the millions of military and civilians killed in Vietnam and Mayor Daley's police brutality. I turned my burning anger against Alex; it had been growing since he belittled McGovern at the start of his campaign.

These violent police and National Guard actions were seen across the world on TV between convention speeches, including Senator Abraham Ribicoff's condemning the "Gestapo tactics" of the Chicago police while Mayor Daley shouted vulgar reactions back at Ribicoff. These history-changing, disastrous political events unfolded among our families, in our homes on TV.

The most disastrous—the shocking assassinations of our three leaders—stomped on our hope for a better world: first President John Kennedy, then Martin Luther King, Jr., and then Robert Kennedy, killed only two and a half months ago on June 6 when he won California's primary.

I was a poll watcher on that election day in 1968. My eleven-year-old Matt walked around an inner-city neighborhood in the early evening dark, urging people to vote Democratic and nine-year-old Jenny babysat at our church so parents could help get out the vote. My husband had told us that he was going to vote for Nixon, and I stared him down as he crossed the school gym to the voting booth. After the polls closed that night at our late and silent supper together, Alex told us he had changed his mind and voted for his family.

Born in 1931 during the Great Depression, I've seen and learned a lot—so far.

WW II	1939-45
Cold War	1947-91
Korean War	1950-53
Vietnam 1954-75	
Hippie counter culture	1960s-70s
"Where Have the Flowers Gone"	1962
President John Kennedy sends military advisors to Vietnam	1963
President John Kennedy assassinated	1963
Malcolm X assassinated	1965
President Lyndon Johnson sends Marines to Vietnam	1965
Martin Luther King, Jr. assassinated	1968
Robert Kennedy assassinated	1968
Chicago police riot, Vietnam War protests at Democratic Convention	1968
US Air Force Bombs Cambodia	1969
Kent State shootings/UW-Madison's Sterling Hall bombing	1970
Pentagon Papers	1971
Watergate	1972-74
US Supreme Court legalizes abortion in Roe vs. Wade	1973

The entire world is in turmoil over Vietnam. We've bombed Cambodia to hit North Vietnam sanctuaries with massive attacks that hit peasants and turned them into ferocious fighters against us. CBS News reported that, "When the planes finished bombing, the insurgents are gone, but so, too is the village. We need to stop Nixon by working through our senators and congressmen to end funding of the war. Of course, Nixon and Kissinger insist that protesters and even our elected legislators who rebel against their Southeast Asian policies will kill government efforts to win the war or negotiate for peace. We're also accused of not supporting our troops. I say the best support is to bring them home.

CHAPTER 4

Bea on May 12, 1974

Marge will begin working in Lakeshore Med's personnel department. Of course, Jan's happy about having her friend working with her. That means that Marge will resign from the Religious Education director's job. She and the committee talked it over and they asked me to replace her. I told them I'd think about it. I may as well get paid for what I'm doing for free.

On Saturday, I went to Jan's to record my new song on her tape recorder. I could tell that Alex was angry that I was there. But we had a pleasant morning with the music. After talking over the RE job with Jan, I called Marge and accepted the job beginning in July.

Our worship committee did the Mother's Day church service and Jan actually sang a song she said her mother would sing and play over and over on her old piano, probably to brainwash her.

"M" is for the million things she gave me.
"O" means she's always growing old.
"T" is for the tears she shed to save me.
"H" is for her heart of purest gold.
"E" is for her eyes with love-light shining.
"R" is right and right she'll always be.

Put them all together, they spell Mother,
The word that means the world to me."

Then she shifted her mood and sang, "Sometimes I feel like a motherless child, a long way from home," and combined it with "Summertime and the livin' is easy…with mammy and pappy standing by." Knowing her life story, the medley of songs was totally appropriate. She has a lot of guts to sing with her untrained voice, a cappella too, but she's not intimidated and is comfortable with our congregation.

Bea on June 14, 1974

Jan came and we hitched up my Dollar Sign and launched her. I manned the helm to take her south of the harbor where I anchored offshore and lay a blanket on the cockpit floor where we could sunbathe in the nude. First, we slathered lotion all over each other and we laughed and played with our sleek selves as the boat gently rocked us like baby-lotioned toddlers in a crib. Of course, we made love as we toasted our oiled selves under the cool blue skies. Oh, the joy of sliding skin to skin.

I kept listening for any passing motors, Coast Guard or sailboats coming to check to see if its crew had abandoned the boat. We would have surprised any sailors who came aside and peered at two naked women in the cockpit on this merry afternoon. I felt so accomplished and strong to control the boat, the trailer, and the car so we could have this adventure that I'd planned for so long.

Jan on June 25, 1974

Alex and Matt took off on a fishing trip to Green Lake and Jenny was at Girl Scout Camp. It's time for me to come out to play.

That afternoon, while I was in the kitchen, lightning and thunder crashed into my daydreaming, and the idea of Alex and Matt fishing in a storm actually brought thoughts of Alex being lost in the lake. Of course, Matt would be saved. I quickly shook that out of my head, but I was surprised at how desperate I'd become to change my life. Yet if I did change, I still would have to work through my family's trauma, and what about Society with a capital "S" striking my dreams with lightning and thunder? Intolerance! I could use our big house to open a battered women's shelter so others would surround us and we could try to live our lives in secret. How absurd! How naive! How drastic!

While still alone in my home, I invited Bea to spend the evening with me. I'd planned this for a long time, but now it's June. So? A romantic rendezvous with a fire? In the summer? Why not?

Searching deep into a closet, I found my slippery-satin comforter, a favorite quilt from my youth, and built a cozy nest on the living room carpet in front of the fireplace. Opening the hearth's glass doors, I banked paper and tinder topped with smooth, white birch logs. Votive candles wait to be nudged under the paper at the most appropriate moment to ignite the stack of wood above them. Another stack of peaceful Delius and Satie recordings quietly accompanied the full moon rising on a darkening June night, sending sound waves and light rays through open windows. As Mother Nature blessed us, we gave each other gifts of love as the flames turned into embers.

She found her poem among our garments to gift me more and whispered, "Holding you. Loving you. I sing six guitar strings, all vibrating at once in perfect harmony echoing from you—both of us in tune with ecstasy. Love. Love is so deeply complete. Love with such range—filled with melody as we play our music."

Pulling home into the driveway from his favorite pub, our window-peeping next door neighbor George quietly stumbled back down my front porch steps after he looked through the corner of my huge front window. Shocked, he retreated and staggered passed the porch's overgrown arborvitae bushes and crept through the narrow pathway between our houses and two backyards. He missed tripping over garbage cans and household debris that couldn't find another place to be. What he saw may have even made him sober.

After entering his back door into his kitchen, he whispered audibly! "Lois! Jan and Bea are making out in front of the fireplace.

"What! George, are you sure? How can that be?"

"I saw them through the window!"

"What in the world made you do that!"

"Damn it, Lois! I just wanted to know why smoke was rising out of the chimney. Good thing I didn't walk in the back door and just say "Hi."

Jan on July 1, 1974

Continuing my lifelong commitment to my father and his business, I continue juggling my loves, my work, my family, and my father's need for me to decorate six 4th of July parade floats this year.

Bea came to watch me, she said, to learn how in case I needed her to help me. But she's off to the Unitarian Universalist church camp at Lake Geneva for a week and I won't be seeing her for a while. My focus now is to get these floats decorated for the parade. Since Alex and I were high school sweethearts, he's helped us— when he isn't working, and now Matt and Jenny make it three generations of float builders that my mom and dad started before 1930.

After the parade and work are done, I'll drive them to church camp to join their UU friends in the teens' dorm.

Bea on July 2, 1974

The worship sessions and all-day religious education workshops at the camp are good. I'll be able to replace Marge as the new RE director in style. Psychologist Rachael Sandler seems to have become our UU counselor with her intensive TA workshop offerings. Of course, the adults play, sing and dance at Club Cratty after evening vespers. Rachael, Marge, Richard, and I went to Cratty and brought a beer that we drank until 1 a.m. after most of the others coupled off and went to his or her or their cabins. This morning Marge and I decided our code word would be "Abstinence" all day, but I had two drinks at Cratty, wrote my letter to Jan, and went to bed.

Dear Jan,

Amidst all the hectic business and pleasure out here, I have you. I ate breakfast with your song this morning and I had you. In the Haunting House workshop yesterday, we were asked to build a house for some objects we considered most precious and/or symbolic. I didn't have the whistle you gave me to call for you, but I was wearing my ring with clasped hands. So, I built a house for that. Explaining later why I chose that, I told them it was like the words to the song, "Life began again the day you took my hand." And I had you in my mind, in my heart, in my soul.

Now I'm thinking you probably won't get this letter soon enough before Thursday, but that's all right because then, lovely day, I will have you.

Rachael gave me two powerful strokes, perhaps three. The first was at the workshop when she said, "You know, you are a very attractive woman." I'll live on that stroke for weeks and weeks. Then when we were at Club Cratty, she called me aside when I was dancing with scruffy old Oliver and said, "Be careful, you might wake the dead." I knew I danced well, but she saw it too. The third was when she told me I never missed a pickup on a remark involving double entendre. I thanked her, God damn it, for those strokes. She gives them out of no motive or reason. She just gives them—and that's why they were so powerful.

Jan on July 5, 1974

I hadn't been to the UU camp for years. This year Matt and Jenny wanted to join our church's youth group even if they'd miss two days. I convinced Alex that I wasn't needed to tear down the floats after the parade and that I wanted to stay at the camp too. Though I was exhausted from long hours building floats and the heat and the early morning start for the parade, we arrived at camp in our VW camper bus yesterday at 4 p.m. and surprised everyone, including my kids' friends who were with their teen peers at their dorm. Dancing at Club Cratty after supper brought out the teenager in me. I really pulled out the stops and even worked in a bit of The Twist.

After a small fireworks display, Bea and I disappeared into the curtained VW van set in its horizontal sleeping position with pillows and sleeping bags.

It was delightful to be alone together where we could relax, be open and completely trusting, yet never completely free from fear of being discovered. In our lovemaking, I finally surrendered my inhibition to her desire, her gift of ecstasy, our intimate sensation. I gave myself to her in the evolution of our sexual explorations. Yes, I surrendered but not without qualms about my husband's claims on me. This was it. By accepting this passionate gift from my lover, I no longer belonged to him. I had finally crossed over into another life. Bea and I bonded our physical selves; our pleasurable fantasies had become intimate realities.

In exchange, my body was so intense at my time of loving Bea to orgasm that I felt that one could swing an axe at me and never cut through my skin.

During early morning with muffled sounds and the van rocking in the dawn, some before-breakfast tennis players knocked on our VW and then ran laughing towards the courts.

Bea on July 5, 1974

Jan, perhaps I never realized how much you loved me. I knew how much I loved you, but I never could have believed the warm, open acceptance of your love. You were saying you loved me so completely that you would share me with anyone. That is—complete love, not possessive, not petty, but secure, complete loving acceptance of a being, a total human being.

Sometimes it seems we've said everything on the subject of love. How I love you and how you love me, and then—as always on a morning like yesterday we are brand new lovers making brand new love, yet spiced with the herbs of knowledge and the comfort of familiarity.

> Take me with you into the corridors of your body.
> Lead me down through passages of delight.
> Let me descend stairways as I shed each chain
> that binds me to convention—
> as I free myself from the tight bands
> of restrictive mental discipline.
> Lead me through and into and down
> so that I may become encompassed,
> encircled, entranced by your love.
> Take me to the place where I can give you
> everything I am—without reservation—
> without unnecessary reserve
> with the greatest tenderness and gentleness.
> Take me with you—Lead me—
> and I will take you with me and lead you
> through passages of the intimate, infinite me
> that reflects you and is you and yet is me.
> One and one makes one.
>
> Bea on July 6, 1974

Bea on July 7, 1974

Dear Jan,

I was exhausted and had to deal with the chaos of kids at home, but I'm feeling better. I went back to work today and felt better and more productive. I also began to organize the church school and the curriculum for the next year. I always feel better when I can accomplish something—the old American work ethic. We both have it programmed into us.

My sons were beautiful. I'm glad when we were talking on the phone that you heard the moment of their returning on furlough from the Army. It was nice to share that with you. God, they're so handsome and taller. Jim towers over me. He's taller than Josh now. They stuck around and we rapped the latest news for a couple of hours. Then they came back later after going to the movies with the girls. God, they're so beautifully healthy. My sons have become such good friends, too. It's funny. I was chuckling at the pictures that were flashing through my head of how I used to dress them alike when they were little because they were so close. Now, Uncle Sam dresses them alike and they're still close. Josh is really looking out for Jim, and I think Jim is appreciating it.

The steaks are done, my vodka and tonic is almost empty and it's time to eat. I think I'll take myself to see *A Woman Under the Influence* movie tonight.

I love you.

Bea

Chapter 5

Jan on July 10, 1974

I sit alone at midnight in this beanbag chair and feel surrounded by womb-like pressure and I smile. I watch TV and I laugh at the jokes that celebrate life and I remember how I live. I close my day with enough human emotion to span infinity as my body, my spirit—my whole self responds to the expanding aura of myself. I love you as I love myself, as I laugh, as I shudder and sense our magnifying spectrum—wide and bold, clear and vivid, pure color, pure focus, pure senses, pure absolute loving love.

You grab my heart and make me cry with joy, with depth from basic needs of wanting, of needing, and of holding on to love and having love hold onto me.

I love you beyond the love that merely satisfies—I love you above that narrow dimension. I love you beyond human needs as you fill my soul and challenge my insight and demand my patience to the extreme and reward me with the most loving soul spirit of tender eyes, of nurturing, of caring.

And I am lost in the loving—

I'm headlong to proving my universal human need to love, to live, to be me. (My mind is spinning. I must remember tomorrow where I've hidden these words.) I'm sitting. I'm staring. I'm writing with feelings. Though my brain has retired, my body remembers. Though my handwriting fails, my memory surrenders to this most beautiful day.

Jan on July 11, 1974

Matt and Jenny went out to be with their friends after supper, and my husband was reading the paper and watching TV.

I put my draft of my *Thank You for April* manuscript into a large envelope from one of my Lakeshore Medical Center public relations projects that was marked "Photos." My typed *April* document described in detail the advancing intimacies of Bea Lindberg's and my lovemaking starting April 1 to 18. If I were to have written more about the next day of my memoir, my celebration of our passion, I would have captured on paper how our sexual expertise, our intimacies, have advanced with more momentum.

"I want to shout out our love from the rooftops," I'd declared that afternoon.

"You'll get us in enough trouble with that writing of yours," Bea warned.

We two had shared the most soul-bonding afternoon at our church's Emerson House, the site of our two Transactional Analysis weekends last November and February, TA with Rachael Sandler that released long-held, lifetime restraints for us.

I was preparing to return to Emerson House after supper for a party for Bea and Marge, who was ending her tenure as the first salaried RE director for our UU church, and Bea was taking over the position. Bea followed in Marge's footsteps and Marge followed in mine, the last volunteer in that role.

Marge was to begin her new career as the employment manager at Lakeshore Medical Center and was hired by our friend Nick

Dixon who's tapped another intelligent Unitarian for his purposes—as he had recruited me.

I wanted to give Bea my Thank You for *April* manuscript. Knowing how damaging this document would be if something happened to me and if family members could find it, I wanted it in Bea's safe hands. Our inner secrets would remain safe with her.

In a rush, I put the envelope on the kitchen table because I remembered that before I left for the party, I had to go to the basement freezer to bring a chuck roast upstairs to defrost so I could make my special camping meal tomorrow to take on our trip.

That's when Alex passed through the kitchen, saw the envelope, picked it up to see what was inside, and during those minutes, he read these words:

Jan on April 1, 1974

"I miss you, Bea," I told her when I answered her phone call right after my husband left for work.

It was the truth and I never realized it so completely and honestly. I finally knew what she had been telling me was evident to her since November. Not only did I miss her, but I truly loved her—deeply and unconditionally." Life would never be the same—that is, if my jealous husband in his rage, didn't instantly kill me. I not only loved another person, but that person was a woman, and that person was Bea.

I never made it to the party and never made it to Door County. No one did because Alex called our guests and canceled this weekend at Woodridge. Of course, he didn't say why. I'd betrayed his trust and I was a lesbian. How does a husband explain this to others?

"How could you do this to me? What about Matt and Jenny? What kind of a woman are you, Jan?"

"I'm the same woman you married, the one you made to obey your rules and your expectations, and I can't help it that I've found great happiness in the last several months. I didn't want to hurt you, Alex. I meant only to fill the needs that you cannot."

"Crazy, misshapen, distorted needs, Jan. I've sensed something wrong. And you told me you had everything under control." He paused to take a breath through his clenched teeth. "You have everything in the world that any woman could want. Why? Why? What did I do wrong?"

"I'm not going to make a list for you. I don't want to hurt you any more than I already have. The kids aren't home, so we can think some of this through before we tell them. I don't want to hurt them either."

"You should have considered that a lot sooner."

"Alex. Rather than talk and shout and be mean to each other, I will offer you my journal to read, and you have 'April' in your possession. Let's take a breathing time and think all this through." He sat stunned with my half-finished "April" manuscript drooping from his hand as I went upstairs to my studio to get my hidden journal. I could barely breathe as my heart throbbed and my body ached with every step.

I called Emerson House from my studio phone and Anna Spence answered. I was crying when I told her I wouldn't be there. Then Bea and Marge knew something was seriously wrong and they decided that only Marge could confront the seething Armenian, and later she knocked on our door while Bea sat in the car. Alex wouldn't let Marge in.

I didn't know if I'd live through the night, but after many hours of sullen debate, I went to bed next to him, both of us exhausted from our confrontation. He demanded that I never see Bea again, then added, "Yes, you can see her once more to tell her what happened, but that's it!"

And we began the grinding, dreadful process of resolving or of losing what was between us as a couple—all three of us—Alex and me or Bea and me.

Jan at 7 a.m. on July 12, 1974

Matt & Jenny,

Dad's at work. I'm at Emerson House writing and thinking. We'll be busy most of today. I want him to go with me to see Sandler if I can get an appointment with her today.

I did something to hurt your dad's feelings very much and we have to work this out. I love him and I hope he loves me enough to understand and get over his hurt.

I'll do my best for us, and I'm sure your dad will too.

Love, Mom

Bea on July 12, 1974
July 11: D-Day! Discovery Day!

Jan and I shared such a happy afternoon and then the shit hit the fan in the evening. Alex found "April" and if he read only the first paragraph, he would know about us. God! Poor Jan. I asked Marge to check if she was all right. I would do it, but Alex would probably strangle me on the front porch. Bravely, Marge knocked on the door but was turned away. We came back to Emerson House and she helped me by listening to my terror and grief until 4:30 a.m., when we each drove home.

Jan called me at home when she woke at 6:30 and I flew out my door and drove to see her at our Emerson House at 7. We fell into each other, sobbing as if we had lost our children. As we settled down, wiping each other's eyes and reddened cheeks, our suffering only increased when we discussed our options.

"My husband, the patriarch, will not accept anything other than a virgin to grace his bed, which I was—exclusively his—and a trustworthy and "true" person by his own definition of the term. Then for me to actually allow another person to love me, to touch me."

"Yes—a woman. I don't know what Jake would do if he found out. And I don't even care. What I care about is you."

"He wants me to cut you out of my life, to never see you again."

"That's impossible. Does one of us have to leave the church, leave our families, to move to another state?"

"I'm so sorry I was careless with our manuscript. I wrote it for you. It was to be a powerful, intense secret that we were to have shared. I wanted it to live long after we may have forgotten the intensity of our feelings for each other."

"He'd find out sooner or later." Slowly I stood up to separate myself from her and to get a drink of water. I turned, looking at her from a distance. "Remember how you kept losing your car keys when you came to see me? Were those signals to be discovered!"

"God, I don't know. Why would I subconsciously do that? I love you so much. Bea, I can't give you up."

"Do you think he'll tell others about us? I haven't even started my RE job. I may have to resign."

"No. No. Don't do that. We're supposed to be a liberal and understanding congregation. Besides, I don't think Alex wants anyone to know that he may lose his wife to another woman."

"I sent Marge to be with you last night because I didn't want you to be alone. Then I was the one who wasn't alone because she stayed with me until 4:30 a.m. Jan, I told her everything because I wanted her to be around to catch you when you fell. I told her that she couldn't begin to understand the intensity of our relationship. She never will. How can anybody who has never felt it? I'm not attempting justification either. I suppose what we had, what we did, was wrong by society's standards, but I was never one to accept any standard."

We talked until noon and we were both desperately exhausted. Jan came close to me to begin to say goodbye, but I put up my hand to keep her distance. "Bea, I will never give you up! But maybe we should try not to see each other for—" Her voice cracked and her body bent as if she would be sick. "—two weeks? God! Even speaking that is painful."

My devastated heart pounded. I could hear it. But I continued to be the strong one. "Two weeks. Fourteen days. How many hours?"

Jan looked at me as she stepped away from me, closer to the door. "Alex and I are going to see Rachael for a crisis consultation tonight. I will do my best to defend us without getting hostile and setting myself up to lose my children." Her body looked as if it would collapse in pain, and she gasped for a breath. "Two weeks is a long time. I will say that we will try."

"All we can do is try. Yes. I love you. I must send you on your way to deal with what you must do." As if a magnetic force cracked between them, Jan backed away from me, turned and slowly, mournfully stumbled out the door to her car as I stepped to the window and watched her drive away.

Chapter 6

Jan on July 12, 1974

The deep and painful wounds that we inflicted on each other made a long, silent drive to Rachael Sandler's home where she led us down to her basement therapy room. Alex felt that his sound judgment and society's values would win me back. When I vowed that I would never give up Bea because of what she meant to me, Rachael said, "Oh. You want your cake and eat it too." I didn't answer but thought, "Why not!"

Alex looked defeated. I didn't dare antagonize him any further. "I'm a quiet man," he said, "who wants joy and happiness and I've worked hard to get it. I deserve it. I want it. I'll do whatever I have to do to make it happen. I'm now afraid I'm losing all my dreams and expectations. I am angry. You have betrayed me."

Rachael helped him process all that and she asked me what I would choose. "I'll try to be true to him and to the children, and I'll try to resume our life together as it was, but no one but Bea can understand my grief," I moaned. "As far as I know, my children have anticipated this, but they don't know what caused it," I rationalized.

We agreed to continue to see Rachael again and we returned home. We'll return to work in the morning. I'll stop folk dancing and play doubles tennis with Alex again and also in my women's league. It will help to burn off some of my hostility and anger, but will I have the strength?

Bea on July 15, 1974

I'm being tortured. My despair is so painful and I'm losing hope that Jan will come back to me. I guess I must take care of myself without her. What can I do? Become a hermit, lock myself in a hotel room, turn off the pain with alcohol, commit suicide, divorce my husband, do nothing and wait, or get better and begin to live again.

Emerson House to pack up my stuff and drafted a letter to the Church Board writing that I could not accept the RE director's position—and almost mailed it, but Marge and Jan talked to me on the phone and convinced me not to send it.

Then I threw myself into my work, called church members and booked Sunday school teachers as volunteers. One night I passed the time by stopping at Marge's. She was building her dulcimer from a kit and I started mine. We caroused until God knows when, playing the piano together and singing for hours.

On Thursday, I went to Betty McGregor's for our women's rap group reunion party. Jan was there, but we stayed on opposite ends of the room. Some tension was released when I went to their narrow little bathroom with cupboards reaching the tall ceiling. Unaware that Betty's cat was perched on top of the cabinet, I screamed when it jumped down and landed on me. It was a good thing I was already sitting on the toilet.

My sense of humor and of the absurd must help me get through all this. I'll focus on my kids again. They need me.

After I finished building my dulcimer, I spent the rest of the day drinking, writing, crying and driving.

God I missed you! But I'm not supposed to tell you.

The peak experiences we share have paled everything else in my life.

We are technicolor against a black and white background.

Think back, Jan. It wasn't long ago that you based your euphoria, your total emotional fulfillment on an unrequited love for Marge, when this was your only strength—your love with a capital L, a love that was all one-sided.

Now what have you lost? You have lost love with a capital L that never lessens, never wanes—no matter what the rules of the game, no matter how we must abstain from the merely physical, from the merely mundane.

When capitals are involved, who cares about lower cases?

Jan on July 18, 1974

Has it been a week—more like a month, more like a year since fate stepped in to stop this multi-dimensional view of life unrestrained, of love, of the future, a vision unencumbered by others' dimensions? Can life, can love, can the future be defined by a week that seems infinite, by love dutifully bound as weeks turn into months and months turn into years and years turn into lifetimes of finite limitations? Will my whole life turn into a pastime? Green leaves wet with rain cry for tomorrow's sunshine

Love belongs to those who share its meaning, who laugh with its joys, who cry with its sorrows, and who grow in love while reaching for the heights and depths of their dreams. I love you my love. You are the heights and depths of my total emotional fulfillment. You have given me everything I've ever dreamed of and everything I never dared to ask of anyone.

You may share your joy and happiness with others but you must not let them take it away.

Alex writes about Woodridge

Woodridge is
like no place
I've ever been

Like every place
I've always wanted to be.

Bea on July 22, 1974

Jan came back from Woodridge, their Door County land, last night. We had breakfast today at The Manor House under the new rules of the game and we talked until noon. We were shattered by those rules but we believed we could make it.

"I'm miserable, Bea. How are you?"

"My poems that I wrote last week will tell you, but I'm afraid to let you see them with the restrictions we've set for each other together."

"I know and I have poems too. But if you don't mind, I'll keep them hidden for a while.

"Hidden. Yes. You're such a great hider, right?"

"I'm so sorry. What can I do to undo my carelessness?"

"Nothing now. Jan, your reach for freedom happened to involve me. I'm strong enough to realize that. I even know, perhaps more than you do, that's part of what caused our relationship. But I also know, perhaps more than you do, that what we have and what developed because of our attempts at reaching for autonomy are stronger than either of us realized."

"I feel more like a servant now than I did before."

We each responded after long, uncomfortable moments, thinking and trying to be considerate and calm. "Well, in our attempt for an equal relationship—neither possessing the other, neither owning the other, we caught a comet by the tail."

I paused, thinking of that metaphor. "We found a marvelous, beautiful skyrocket life. It united us in a commitment we weren't prepared for. We may never be ready for it. I'm not stupid enough to believe that 'love conquers all,' or that 'love makes all things right,' but love, in our case, made what we had right. I talked to Marge about it. She said she probably could have pulled it off, meaning our relationship. I told her that anybody could have gotten away with it who didn't have to write everything down. God damn it. Jan," she whispered over the table, "you had to write it all down."

"Yes! I had to celebrate in words, precious words to keep later for others to celebrate. We both celebrate it with words, Yours, Bea, are especially poetic. Sometimes I think your prose is like Edna's poetry."

"Who's Edna?"

"Edna St. Vincent Millay!"

"Shit, Jan, more like some TV soap opera serial. This would be a great series. What the hell! No one else could have left husbands and family as much as we have—risking it all. And you, Jan, especially were flaunting our relationship because you felt that it must be right, that there couldn't be anything wrong with something that felt so right."

"You knew it too. We kept getting stronger with each precious day we shared. I don't know what will happen now."

"Hell! We're two adult women who've played the proper role of women for more than twenty years. We have each loved a man, borne his children and raised them well. We have been leaders in our communities, in Scouts, in church, in schools. In your volunteering, your newspaper reporting, and now public relations—in a hospital, no less! We've played the game exactly like it was supposed to be played. We've stuck with our husbands and devoted ourselves to our children, and then, at age 42, your 'Summer of 42,' as you call it, we suddenly took a chance for ourselves, suddenly took a crack at our own happiness down a different road…"

"Which may mark us forever. We may be labeled with any number of scary stereotypes—"

"—Because of a chemical reaction that burst between us. We may be called bisexuals but not, hardly, lesbians. Only because we dared to grasp life more than ordinary people. Because we dared an intimacy that is denied to most people, to almost every woman. We wanted it and found it on a million different levels."

"Bea. Do you want to see Rachael?"

"Hell no! I'm not crazy. I may be a non-conformist, something out of the ordinary, but that does not mean I need professional help.

I've always held the definition that sanity is equitable with complacent conformity, and hasn't it always been, but my non-conformity does not automatically imply abnormality."

"Rachael told me that you're not as open with her as I am."

"That's true. It's true because I don't trust anybody like you trust everybody. If I think I need her help, I'll make an appointment."

"I visualize Rachael with you, Bea, Alex and me in this little circle, trying to come to some understanding. At least we have each other and Marge and Rachael to talk to about this. He only has Rachael, unless he has a significant friend that he can trust to unload all this."

"Friends or not, no one will ever understand how I fought the sexual aspect of our intimacy. How it tore me to pieces again and again, and how I tried to break our relationship a dozen times. I know how you tried, too. It is all in your journal. We fought our chemistry—and ourselves fully knowing in the end, we would lose more by denying it than by accepting it. And even when we couldn't escape that part of our loving, I especially was torn apart during every encounter we had. But I was growing and learning a lot about myself—and about you, Jan, and about all women, too; that our capacity for loving is infinite, that what you and I shared was ultimate, especially, the multi-levels of love that we filled and understood: mother, daughter, wife, sister, spouse, lover, child and friend."

"You told me in one of your early letters, Bea, that I—me—'I longed to mother the shaky child that peers from behind the facade of all that strength—'"

"—and I too longed to be mothered by your tenderness and understanding."

"Jan! Marge's friend visited her last week and we three had an intimate letting-our-hair-down talk, and she said, after having endured the break-up of her marriage, that she had a man interested in her at work and it made her feel like a woman again. I know what she meant, having felt that as well, but I said it's too bad we need men to make us feel like a woman. And then I became inspired with the thought: I've never felt more like a woman, more total woman-like than I have in my relationship with you, Jan. That may seem strange, but it's totally true."

As we were ready to leave the restaurant and resume our grim, restricted lives, I told Jan, "I don't know what will happen. I know neither of us is happy apart from the other, but are we ready to take the step that would put us together?" Perhaps in the distant future? Our roles are written. We'll play it out, I know.

Bea on July 23, 1974

Lots of luck with the two-week trial. We never made it work. And now I'm nearer to her at Emerson House and the church. She came Tuesday to see me and brought me some raspberries. Then she came by again on Wednesday and Thursday, all under the rules, but God, the tension between us was unbearable,

Marge, Jan and I go out to lunch. Three times when Jan left, I hugged her and she me, but it was more than a hug and we both knew it. She came to see me every day! I knew neither of us could take much more, but she comes, and part of it is out of defiance to Alex.

I was afraid for her, and for me, too, so on the way home yesterday, I made a vow that I would never touch her again. She doesn't understand plain language. You have to write it in poetry! I told her my vow and berated her for making it so hard for us, for torturing both of us, and how I could no longer be caught in the vice between her and Alex. When I called her and told her, she wanted me to be the strong one and I am now. I am a surgeon doing what had to be done. It's the only rational thing to do.

When I hung up the phone, I felt it was over at last and somehow, I would get through my loss. I was calm and coldly rational. But she called back a few minutes later. She was crying.

"Damn you! Damn you! Damn you!" I swore. "You never let me go. You make it impossible for me to do the right thing for both of us."

"I feel as if we're back in March when I told you I couldn't do what you wanted me to do."

"Jan, listen to me. We must be rational! To see each other is too damn dangerous, especially for you because Alex knows about us. He could divorce you on those grounds and you wouldn't get a thing and he would get the kids, too. I could never live with that responsibility."

I knew Alex was there when I phoned her the first time, and he saw Jan burst into tears when I said goodbye and hung up on her. After her second call, she told me they had another fight about me and he left the house in anger. I finally convinced Jan that we could only talk over the phone, and we could do that as often as we needed to speak with each other.

I hadn't been off the phone for more than a few minutes when my husband turned on me. He has a marvelous facility for attacking a wounded animal. He goes after me when I'm down. I suppose I'm much too strong for him otherwise. It began about money, but it wasn't that and it spread out to all our issues. I told him calmly and finally that I would never depend on him for emotional support again—or ever sleep with him again. I felt divorced for a long time anyway. I told him that I would never let him diminish me again because I was a damn good woman!

I repeated my old line, "I am a writer, an artist and a musician."

He answered again, "I never wanted any of that. All I wanted was a wife and mother for my kids."

I almost laughed out loud. It's the same old story, isn't it? "I'm a damn classy broad," I told him. "How many women do you know who have written two novels or built a violin? And I'm a damned attractive woman, too!"

"I never denied that. I don't care about that!"

"I know, and that's the weird thing about it." I asked him what he wanted to do. I asked him if he wanted to throw me out. I told him that probably was the logical thing for him to do. He mumbled something and then I said, "But Hell! I won't go! I'll get the house and the kids and you'll still have to support them and me. You are the one who has to get out."

He doesn't know about Jan, although a long time ago in January, I had a long, impassioned talk with him because he had heard me say, "I love you" to Jan over the phone one night when I was upset. I told him I loved Jan, really loved her and she loved me, and I had a theory that it was because I was looking for a mother and so was she. He understood or seemed to. He would never understand the rest of it if he knew, but like Jan remarked, he probably could care less if he did.

Well, he said he would get out, and then we were interrupted by a mob of kids bursting through the door, two were actually mine. Picture this script. The two of us unemotionally, calmly holding the wreckage of a twenty-year marriage between us and in comes these kids. One proceeds to blow up this giant sausage of a balloon he brought with him and sails it around the room. My son Joel and Jake and I all begin batting it back and forth, with all of us laughing.

I didn't talk to Jake anymore last night. He went outside and talked to my other son and his girlfriend and I talked to the kids inside. I fell asleep in the chair, amazed to find myself there in the morning and came up to Lakeshore Bay about 7 a.m. I'm in no hurry to go home. He will be there; he's still on vacation.

How many times can the shit hit the fan? Now my marriage is finished.

So, decisions have been made. I talked to Jan this morning and she had just finished talking on the phone with Marge. Guess what Jan asked her? "How does one go about getting a divorce?" What a mess!

Bea on July 25, 1974

Dear Jan,

Truth has been floating around in my mind for months that we are two middle-aged, imaginative broads with children and we've been playing Transactional Analysis's "Let's Pretend!" We played dangerous games to make life interesting and we've damn near lost it all, like a dope addict who opts for death because of boredom. I understand us. We'd rather play dangerous games than be bored to death.

I made a vow. I'll never touch you again. Do you want that? Why do you make it so hard for us? Is it because of defiance? Every day this week, every day, what you're saying is that Alex can't order your emotions. You love me and I love you. By loving me, you're daring him to throw you out, and I'm the agent. I don't like that role. I don't know how to handle that.

How much can I take? How magnanimous can I be? You have everything! I'm an outsider! I'm nothing! Yet you think I can continue with that?

You overestimate me. You totally overestimate me. I can't continue with the role you have assigned me. I'm an outsider. I'm nothing. And being nothing, I will have to live with that.

> I never knew what love was until you.
> I never knew what caring was until you.
> I never knew what touching was until you.
> No one ever held me through the night until you.
> Or protected me, or was tender with me,
> or patient, or kind, or soft, or gentle until you.
> I never knew what love was until you.
> I never told anyone I loved them
> and meant it in a special way until you.
> No one ever told me they loved me
> and meant it until you.
> And having tasted nectar from the Gods,
> how can I ever settle for less?

Jan on July 27, 1974

Somewhere in the consulting process and on the way out of her door after our session, Rachael asked Alex and me how our sex life was going. We both nodded affirmatively or said okay. "That's a surprise," she said, hardly a helpful comment to maintain our sexual compatibility. Alex and I did all right. I was available and active in the process, and enjoyed it most of the time.

One night he loomed over me during penetration and said, "If only we could start all over. If we could get over this."

I lay on my back, hidden by his shadow, my mind imagining a long, narrow poster with the word "If" stretched on it from top to bottom in Bodoni Bold as long, skinny letters, and beneath that one word, "If " with two letters, I imagined tiny words in one line, "…is a very big word."

Jan on July 29, 1974

My mother's 71st birthday is today. When I called the County Hospital to find out her condition, the nurse reported that she was a bit unsettled. My stomach turned in reaction to the memory of the institution's acrid smells in the cafeteria visiting room, but the new housedresses and candy that I bring may help me keep her busy— and my mind off of my situation.

My mind's been playing tricks with my dreams again. This one came to me a week ago and I dared to share it with my Lakeshore Med's lunch group of nurses who sit together in the new cafeteria's meeting room.

Dream scenario: "Room 101"
"I had a dream last night that was the most horrible I've ever had."

My nurse friends at lunch in the meeting room of Lakeshore Med's cafeteria looked at me most tolerantly. So many of our statements start with "I," and it was my turn now to be heard.

"I was in an empty room, large like a gym, and in the middle of this room was a metal box shaped like a huge sardine can. Three officers in unisex jumpsuits guarded the box. Only their blank faces showed in the shadow of their hoods. I recognized no one.

"One of them came to me, took my hand and led me to the box's narrow end. A second bent down to grasp the handle on the metal trap door. The third added authority to the scene.

"My elbow felt his firm nudge leading me closer to the edge of the box. When its door opened, I was to step into the box and lie down in the shallow darkness until I was released. 'At least they weren't going to put me in a straight-jacket,' I thought as I stepped through the trap door into the box and started to kneel to the floor.

"The door started closing in tandem with my movements. Then I heard a sound—a swirl of movement, a rasping of steel teeth across metal, scurry, scurry scratching around the inside edges.

"There were rats in there and I'm supposed to lie down to be sealed up in that box! I stood straight up in the center of that trap door space and defiantly declared I would do no such thing.

"I woke up with an incredible pounding pulse, crawly, clammy damp skin, shirt and sheets. My trembling was so great I imagined the vibrations would wake the sleeping giant next to me."

Hardly a luncheon fork had moved among the hushed listeners.

"How big was the box?' one of them asked.

"How big!" I responded.

"Bigger than a bread box?"

"Yes. Actually, it was as big as a full-size box spring and mattress."

Bea and I played tennis and talked, took walks in parks and talked, met at the beach and talked, attended church services and meetings and talked, lunched together, etc. She was working through the details of getting her divorce and I would endure the arguments with Alex. She designed the prospectus for this year's Sunday school program. I finished our new church brochure and, of course, spent enough time at home and at Lakeshore to keep everyone reasonably happy, except for the two of us whose time together was never enough.

Bea on August 7, 1974

I wrote a new script. I found out what to say, sensible words, and proper comments. No one will know what it costs or how it hurts. But I couldn't exist much longer in the vast maw, in the crushing grip of such intense emotion. It was driving us both out of our very beings—irrationality, chaos, the madness that we both shared—a pact to stop for a time, to rest, to get square, to organize, to take stock, to grow up a little if we can—if we ever can reach a time to look our situation squarely in the eye without hurting one another.

Hard, grow hard. Wake up from the dream and look around and pray it's only a nightmare.

Chapter 7

The New York Times on August 8, 1974

"Nixon Resigns: He Urges a Time of 'Healing'
Ford Will Take Office Today
The 37th President Is First to Quit Post."

"Washington, Aug. 8—Richard Milhous Nixon, the 37th President of the United States, announced tonight that he had given up his long and arduous fight to remain in office and would resign, effective at noon tomorrow.

"At that hour, Gerald Rudolph Ford, whom Mr. Nixon nominated for Vice President last Oct. 12, will be sworn in as the 38th President, to serve out the 895 days remaining in Mr. Nixon's second term.

"Less than two years after his landslide re-election victory, Mr. Nixon, in a conciliatory address on national television, said that he was leaving not with a sense of bitterness but with a hope that his departure would start a "process of healing that is so desperately needed in America."

Jan on August 8, 1974

It's more bitter than sweet, finally, to taste the victory of Nixon's downfall and watch him using his grandiose gesture of extending his arms out with fingers making a "V" for victory—or vicious or vindictive as he and his family boarded the helicopter to extract him from the White House.

His wife, Pat, looked comatose as Nixon performed his self-induced impeachment speech. I feel so sorry for her and his family, but not as much as I feel for those American boys and Asian people killed and wounded in this tragedy of a pointless war—and their loved ones. Why can't we find alternatives to killing and maiming each other in the name of nations, religion and race?

Gerald Ford said in his swearing-in speech, "My fellow Americans, our long national nightmare is over." I hope so.

Dreams and nightmares reveal manifestations of the inner eye, my inner self, captured and enriched with my written details in my conscious memory and serve to remember my stories. Most others are often lost in the night.

> On the Woman's Condition
> Pencil-searching to hold
> down an idea before it flies
> —a nighttime thought.
> Rummaging through
> the bedside drawer,
> finding only a tampon.

Bea on August 12, 1974

Jan and I needed to see each other and share what we'd been through. Jan came to my house for coffee and because the kids were in and out, she drove her VW van to Plymouth Prairie, close to where we first spent hours taking our earliest moves toward total loving making, only five months before. Those five months seemed like two lifetimes ago—hers and mine.

A depression in the narrow road was flooded, so she turned onto a prairie lane to head for a shady, sheltered stand of trees. But we only drove as far as the nearest clump of bushes before she stopped the car on the rutty path, turned off the key, embraced and kissed me. I had neither strength nor desire to resist. We gave each other the refuge and an escape into the oneness that we had denied ourselves for so long.

From a distance, anyone looking across the acres of prairie could pick out her boxy beige and green van, but we imagined we were completely alone in the back of the van with the seat flattened and all the doors opened to let the breeze bless us in our loving. Even the large back door gaped open to the wind, blowing the wildflowers and prairie grasses that waved their blessings toward us.

Our senses were alive with each other's touch as we kissed freely, without inhibition on this warm August afternoon. Sweet sunshine, sensual sweat, kissing inside the creases of neck, belly button, inside elbows, inside knees, inside my lover as she lay with her hands on my ears, guiding me to her center in a release of exploding tension that left her helpless on her back, and me, incapacitated with my head resting on the seat, my face turned to gaze upon her with semi-spent lust and with love.

My vision cleared suddenly when I saw movement across the field. In the distance, a large, rusty barn-red truck with several men in the back was bounding toward our van. "Jesus, Jan. We have to get out of here. Who knows what will happen if those guys get to us."

"I can't move," she said, lifting her head slightly.

The truck grew closer and the guys called to us to get out of the way.

I didn't wait to argue. I climbed over her to pull the back door closed, pulled myself together while I told her to do so too, and lunged over the stick shift between the front seats into the driver's seat. Fortunately, she'd left the key in the ignition. It would be a miracle to try to find it in one of her pockets or even to try to find her pockets. The van started all right, but I was unfamiliar with shifting the damn thing. With a slight grind, it lurched forward. Jan flopped around in the back while I caromed her van over ruts and ridges to reach a paved road where we parked again in a hidden patch of rushes to catch our breaths and recover.

Thrills. Adventure. Passion. Imagination. Joy and laughter again.

My incident hunger is about satisfied.

Jan on August 14, 1974

Rachael Sandler determined that a man's point of view would be a valid counseling option for Alex, so she scheduled a meeting in a four-way deal with Bill and his wife, a married pair of therapists. It turned out to be a cruel encounter for both Alex and me. Perhaps we found some couple comfort in both being equally devastated by their confrontations.

> We used some "games" to get started as a five-year-old:
> 1. take away my toys and love you;
> 2. take away my music and love you;
> 3. take away my night-night blanket and love you.

I didn't understand and I rejected the metaphor and their game.

"I live in fear, not anger," I told them, sitting across from the two of us in a closed-in consult room with four folding chairs on a faded braided rug.

Here is where Alex felt safe enough to unload his hidden anger at me; I was not at his side during the graveside funeral of our infant son, who died over ten years ago. I was still hospitalized when they set the date for the funeral. Early after his death, I offered to talk through our grief together, but he chose, as usual, to be silent and withdrawn. I couldn't imagine how he could have been keeping that anger in his heart all that time. I was able to express my feelings in writing, and he didn't even respond to my written words that could have opened a healing dialogue between us.

Rachael surely must have filled the counseling couple in on our issue details, yet they pretended that they knew nothing about us to force me, us, to say the words "that dare not speak its name."

During the endless hour, the psychologists accused me of whining, which I hated when I was a kid. She was as hostile to me as he was, yet they never said the words "bisexual" or "lesbian," nor did Alex. We never addressed those issues. Never spoke those words. They attacked me and what they labeled as my "in-fighting," which reflected what Alex did to me. Their giving me a choice of having a loving relationship with my husband versus a sexual relationship with another made me feel like I'm a compulsive crotch grabber. Alex's seething attitude about my love and my secret sexual orientation was pushing me closer toward lesbianism rather than bisexuality.

It's radical surgery, ripping out your vital parts and setting them, no, dropping them on the floor in front of you. When the session was over, they didn't even help us pick them up and put them back.

"Is it worth it all? All this agony?" I asked Alex.

To make the best of "a night out," he chose to eat supper at the Bull Dog Inn, the restaurant where he crushed my dream of being a professional UU religious educator, where he hurt my spirit so badly years ago. Supper was miserable. I wanted to vomit.

But worse, we went to a trendy art movie house and watched Lenny, about Lenny Bruce's tragic and tormented life that included an erotic scene of Bruce watching his nude wife perform cunnilingus on another woman. Finally, *Lenny* endures censure by society and dies of a drug overdose in a gritty, ceramic-tiled public toilet.

Could it get worse? When the movie was over, we turned to leave and saw the counseling couple that had disemboweled us three hours ago sitting two rows behind us.

Alex said he was sad that I had to go through that cross-examination. "That's all right," I said. "You hurt too. But it was nothing new for me—except that they're strangers." We struggled over this three nights in a row and it's too heavy. The next night he still didn't hear what I was trying to say, so I gave him some of my poems.

"Why did you have these out?" he asked.

"Because I always have to defend myself. These poems are more timely. They describe my grief."

"I've read your journal and tried to understand."

Alex accidentally broke a glass during his next night's interrogation and commented, while he picked up the pieces, "It's better than a broken marriage." And he looked at me, "You know I'm not a violent person. I'm a loving person."

Tuesday night's bantering continued to be frustrating because he doesn't hear what I'm saying as I walk on a tight-rope to keep my children, home and career. His statements were prefaced by assumed threats: options toward divorce and his ultimatum. Like an inquisitor, he asked me the one question I would not answer, if only on principle: "Have you had sexual relations with Bea or any other person since July 11? Yes or no."

One night I woke and found myself pounding him on his big chest with both my fists. I'd been crying out in my dream, "You fall in love with someone and see how you grieve when you have to give her up." He lay there tolerating the blows, looking at me with the saddest eyes, waiting for me to come to reality in more ways than one.

Yes. He does know what it's like to grieve when you love someone and may have to give her up.

Jan on August 24, 1974

I should be what I am. I shall be me and I shall love. I do live honestly and with compassion. I help others live happily, too. I must be what I am.

I may think that I'm living honestly, but I'm only rationalizing to make honesty seem true. I can't tell anyone of my love but my most trusted friend. Even my husband may not want to reveal our situation. Bea doesn't think she is a lesbian because she's been married for over twenty years and has four children. I don't know what I am, yet so am I married and with two children and I may lose them if my husband takes action against me. I may lose my beautiful home too, but that's not the most valuable possession in my life as much is it is with some of my friends who are dependent on their mean and abusive, alcoholic husbands yet stay in their marriages to keep their homes secure.

I'm becoming public relations professional in a highly visible position, and I must hide my true self. I love my work. I love being the hospital's champion, telling its good news and working to diffuse any bad news. So far, nothing has been bad. Maybe it will be if I'm exposed as one who creates a negative image of my hospital and my bosses. Yet I trust them all to defend me.

I "risk the flame" and tell myself that it "burns me not," but my back is physically killing me. I could hardly finish the tennis season, but I reached the women's singles finals before I lost to a determined Armenian woman. It didn't help that Bea came to watch me play and left right before Alex and Matt appeared during the third set.

When I'm writing in my studio or working in my kitchen, I wear two heating pads, one on my spine and one on my stomach, and move around the house with two cords, which act like "the chain, which keeps me from the flame." Strange comparison. The best remedy so far was Bea slipping into the house to see me, kissing me some and giving me Xaveria's erotic book to read.

Bea on September 7, 1974

My marriage is crumbling around me, Jake and I have kept a truce but we hardly sleep together anymore. I was having my needs met with Jan, so I didn't care about him; yet I did care because his interest in me is important. Sex had been part of our marriage, but it didn't happen anymore. And then I realized, "I have someone who appreciates that. I have Jan. We are equal, intellectually equal, and she values me and my talents. I don't think he's bright enough to know what's going on anyway."

I'm ragged from lack of sleep. I hated being alone on Labor Day but I kept busy with my friends. On Sunday, I took Rachael and her two kids, Jan and Jenny, Marge and Tommy out for a boating day on The Dollar Sign. It was cold but I put the kids in our wet suits and we had a great adventure learning to water ski.

Alone on Monday, I wrote letters requesting credit cards. Jan had gone to the bank to get her credit card and the clerk said that she couldn't get one without her husband's permission. Was she steamed? When she told what happened at the supper table, Alex said, "I'll sign a permission form for you." Steamed again, she shook her head. "You don't get it, do you? I shouldn't need your permission!" Finally, the bank relented and I think she may be the first woman in town to have her own credit card without begging for her "owner's" benevolence.

As the new Religious Education director, I reorganized the whole church school into teaching quarters and had volunteers team-teaching in every grade, which made it more fun for them and for the kids. The teachers' experience lasted only a few months rather than the whole year and they shared responsibility with another adult for the class and the curriculum. I had to get a lot of people involved to accomplish that, but the adults came through.

I'll lead worship services for the whole church school after classes and before letting the kids loose to join their parents at church. I'll play guitar and lead their singing and involved them in some fun projects.

As in the past, I'll direct teenage activities and that includes Jan's kids. Mine aren't interested. I've chaperoned their Liberal Religious Youth parties and their overnights. Most of them are part of our folk dancing family, but it's still more teenage stuff that I have at home and it wears me out.

Because we both worked flexible hours, Jan and I took every opportunity to be together during the stolen hours of the day and night. Marge and more friends would invite me to their homes for supper and we'd often go to their homes after evening church committee meetings where we'd talk, especially Jan, Marge and me, and drink until 1 or 2 a.m., especially Jan, Marge and me. Then I'd have to drive home—frazzled!

On Friday, Jan and her van picked me up at Emerson House for a Holiday Inn breakfast near River Woods, and after, we took the unpaved forested road away from traffic, parked and made love in the van under the rustling leaves. Luckily we kept the doors closed, but the window curtains were open and I'm sure that the guy who walked and pushed his bike to get around the van had a good view of Jan's nude backside.

After the initial shock of hearing and then seeing him squeeze by, we laughed at our lusting and insatiable desire to please one another under continuing adverse conditions. Flooded with desire, we are able to close out the rest of the world—most of the time.

That night we went to Anna's for the folk dance party. She recently had a new floor covering installed and all the furniture was out of the living room, so Jan took advantage of being playful again and did somersaults across the dense new carpet with other younger people following her example. I guess when she's with me, with us, her back doesn't hurt. Or else she doesn't care if it does.

Jan on September 9, 1974

Alex and I cut back on our counseling, but that's left him with no one to talk to about me, about my needing someone other than him, about my stepping beyond acceptable social standards. He's emotionally alone, unable to tell someone that his wife loves another woman. Maybe he's told my father and his sister, but I don't know for sure. I actually wish that he would do something wrong. I fantasized that he would finally let loose his rage and hit me. I would crawl to get my camera and take my picture to prove his abuse as grounds for divorce. I would go to Lakeshore Med's ER and they would vouch for my abuse. Silly. I'd probably end up dead and what good would that do?

For a while, his power manifested itself in compatible sex. We'd always keep the radio on a one-hour delay so we could fall asleep to music or make love with some noise in the background. One night Alex was on top of me during sex and I felt something strange; I realized that his tears were falling on my body and the radio music was playing, "Raindrops keep falling on my head."

On occasion, I would find a poem from him.

> I would like to be your friend.
> Friend, lover, co-compassionate
> about the feelings we share.
> I would like to be your friend,
> Husband, father, cosigner.
> Is it possible to be all?

I want my children and I want Jenny to be at least 18 before I run away from home to be myself. She's 13 now. Can I hang on that long? Can Alex? I suppose he thinks I will recover from this madness and return to him again.

What would happen if Jenny or Matt found out? How would they feel about me? Whom might they tell? Or would they, too have this huge secret to hide from the world? Would they be teased because of me and rejected by their friends? Would it influence their sexual identity? Damn! It's hard enough to survive through the "growing-up-straight" process without worrying about being a homosexual like their mother.

Nixon may have wrecked the country with Vietnam, Watergate and his other dirty tricks, but Bea and I are involved in our own undercover espionage within our families, our jobs and our community.

Yet I love Bea unconditionally and I will not give her up. Our mutual religious values were the initial bond of our friendship, and later when she reappeared in our midst, she changed from a motherly matron with bangs on her forehead like Archie Bunker's wife to the adventurous Avenger, the slim Emma Peel with sensuous eyes and long hair, our spiritual harmony became secondary in the intriguing and fiery potential that flared between us—the joy of loving as an equal partner, loving her as I love myself. Together we elevated each other into physical, emotional and spiritual ecstasy.

Living with the reality of our dominant heterosexual culture, it's a miracle that we actually found each other. How did that happen when women loving women are invisible? Blindly we share our female experience. We hunger for our gratifying emotional and sexual love because we are so tuned on to each other. We provide each other with the deep levels of support that we both require and have to offer each other.

Bea on September 16, 1974

Trauma! While Jan was winning all sorts of PR awards in Green Bay, Alex surprised me at Emerson House. I was stunned when I saw him come close to me at my desk. Woes! During our hour conversation, I told him several times that I tried to break off our relationship but Jan always came back. "I love Jan enough to give her up and return her to her home and family and all that it meant."

Of course, he doesn't believe me and though he didn't tell me, I know that he thinks I'm the evil witch in black who seduced his wife away from him. "You know I could strangle you, but I won't."

Changing the subject, I asked Alex what would he do if he had Jan to himself?

"I would hold her down. Pin her to the ground."

"And what would you do then?"

"Talk to her."

"Haven't you learned yet that holding her down or holding her back is just what she doesn't want? And for damn sure, you've done enough talking."

My fear of violence was unfounded. We both love the same woman, but he's lost the emotional battle to me. His weapons are their children, home, security and perhaps someday maybe she'll feel sorry for him. Yet I'm vulnerable too. I'm afraid that she will return to him someday soon. She has too much to lose. I'll be empty and alone again.

Strange. When he stood up to leave, I stood too. I didn't want him to stare down at me with those steely gray eyes. He approached me and I realized, "This is it!" and prepared myself for a blow. I was shocked instead because we hugged. He turned, walked out the door in a stooped-shouldered manner and drove away.

I called Betty and we went to a bar and talked over a couple of beers.

Jan came to see me as soon as she could. She was surprised that Alex came to see me and that he'd actually hugged me. Jan's comforting me gave me a chance almost to match her multiple orgasmic feats on this togetherness afternoon before I was to leave for Chicago to be with my friend Hope. Hope. What a beautiful name. What a healing concept.

Bea on September 21, 1974

My college friend Hope and I had a grand Friday night and Saturday, just like old times. She took me to a Serbian restaurant in Chicago. I was dressed in tight black pants and a body shirt—and black boots, of course. We did some line dancing and when the band started a tango, this handsome, swarthy man moved close to me and asked me to dance. I'd never done the tango before, but he was so strong a leader, I felt I could do no wrong. I danced with him like Rita Hayworth would have danced. The crowd at the restaurant cheered us on and I could do no wrong. All aglow, I drove back on Sunday morning and straight to church school, which went well despite my lack of sleep.

Bea on September 27, 1974

Dear Rachael,

I'm supposed to ask you if you would be interested in running a workshop for the teens in our church, what kind do you think best, how many, and how much? Could you please give me any suggestions and details?

Jan's not been feeling well. I found her at Marge's. She had been crying. Alex is after her all the time. When she has to go home, she feels like she's going to throw up. God, it hurts. Heights and depths all the time, and not much you can do about it.

Then a couple of days later, she said she felt like she had maybe lost a battle, but won the war. Me, I've been shaky and nervous, in "sheer terror" since two weeks ago when Alex came to see me. I keep thinking I must do something! But I can't, or I won't is more like it.

Yesterday, she took me with her to visit her mother in the hospital. What an experience! I leaped to so much insight, empathy and love. I know another part of the reason she loves me. I knew it all along, anyway. I guess you might say that we are reparenting one another. It is too precious, too full of peak experience, of transcendence, of total satisfied needs. It is also filled with frustration and sadness when we can't be together. My relationship with Jan is all I have to satisfy my needs.

That Goddamn indifferent klutz I'm married to. I don't know how much longer I can take living in a house where we hardly speak to one another, let alone sleep in the damn Goddamn bed where I'm afraid to move for fear I might touch him. I never ever slept on more than about twenty-four inches of bed anyway. The couch would be much better if there wasn't so much damn traffic through the living room all day and night. Somebody ought to use me for a study on human overcrowding. I know scientists have fiddled around with rats and proved they experience definite changes. One change is I'm getting a damn backache from sleeping on that couch.

Did I tell you I've programmed myself out of a job at home? I hired my daughter to keep the house so she could support her new car. Jake's dad gave her a thousand dollars to buy it. He said the boys could earn theirs, but it's hard for a girl to just babysit money. Hah! It's hard for any women on just woman's money! My new system is working out fine, except that I had two opposing thoughts: O.K. Terrific. I don't have to do all that crummy junk anymore. Free. Free at last. The other, Christ, they don't need me at all anymore. None of them. Not a damn one of them. How about that for yin and yang?

I could walk out and everything would run smoothly and I wouldn't be missed one bit.

I'd better wind this up before it gets to be another novel.

Love. Bea

Jan on September 30, 1974

Bea came to Lakeshore to have lunch with me today. I took her through the cafeteria line and joined my favorite group at one of the big round tables. Then I gave her a quick tour of the hospital.

As the communications director, I'm to tell the public and the employees that their community hospital is a competent, caring place filled with competent, caring staff. I'm happy with this excellent job in the center of this hospital world where I write stories, photograph people and experience human interest events as varied as children needing stitches and tonsillectomies to Saturday night shooting victims and automobile accident cases entering with sirens blaring or elderly people being taken to nursing homes or dying quietly in the night.

My contacts with the staff are as broad. I communicate with employees at every level from the deaf-mute lady sewing garments in the basement laundry room to the egocentric neurosurgeon who likes to get his picture in the paper.

I was happy that Bea could join our hospital group for lunch and hear their chatter about the routine matters of their day: last night's TV programs, the weather, trips and conferences, government controls interfering with patient care, insurance problems, the nursing director frustrated at staffing enough trained persons to carry out physicians' orders and the patients' demands, and juggling everyone's expectations.

The more, the merrier and the more we learn from each other in our women's middle management power lunches. But it's becoming somewhat of a threat to the younger hospital assistant administrators who never sit with us like our chief administrator, Clark Young, does. He's ready and willing to walk in with his tray filled with food and learn about what's going on with his nursing team.

The group is like a magnet at this communal table as we blend the major events in our work and in our lives with trivia.

"My mother drives me crazy," said Donna Durand. the nursing director. "She was so worried about me when I left for the conference after that storm. Honestly! Where was she when I needed her in high school?"

"Well," she said, fingering her cigarette, "she treats me like a child. When she sews a skirt for me, she still leaves a three-inch hem in case I grow out of it."

Laughter circled the round table. They leaned back, celebrating this concise example of the mothering instinct.

I egged her on as the good mood swelled. "Tell Bea my favorite story, Donna."

"Oh, that one," she responded, taking the bait in the heat of her triumphant good humor.

"Well, we had orders from the surgeon to ambulate this woman patient after her operation," she said shifting her weight toward Bea. "Ambulate means ambulate! So, we went to her room and told her that we were going to do just that. 'But no,' she said. 'No. I can't walk.'

"We wouldn't take her No for an answer. We told her that everyone ambulates after surgery. The doctor wrote 'ambulate' on his orders and we'll help you ambulate. So, we stood at each side of her, raised her up and firmly but gently guided her to the toilet.

"While she sat there, the old lady shook her head in disbelief and said, 'I must tell my sister I walked. I walked!' and she started to cry.

"That's nothing, dear. Most everybody walks after surgery. It's good for you."

"'But,' she quivered. 'But, I haven't walked for fifteen years!'"

Bea on September 30, 1974

The DAY! I had a busy day back and forth between church and Emerson House and then had lunch with Jan at the hospital, plus a tour. She moves about that place and it seems that she knows everyone's name. I love watching her in action.

Sorry to say, when I drove home, I stepped into the kitchen and was shocked to see Jake helping Jill clean the refrigerator. "Jake! In over twenty years, you've never helped me do any cleaning around this house."

"Well, she needed help. You never did."

Jill started crying. "You gave me this job and I can't get anyone else to help me. The boys ignore me when I tell them what to do."

"You need to tell me that? I've been through all that for twenty years. At least your father's helping you. I couldn't get him to do that!"

Jill ran out of the kitchen, grabbed her purse and coat and ran over to her friends and stayed the night. "Now look at what you did!" Jake barked. "Why did you pick on her? And didn't we make an agreement never to argue in front of the kids? Have you come home drunk again? Well, at least it's in the afternoon, and not at two or three in the morning."

I looked at the hungry bunch waiting for supper. They seemed to be leering at me, faulting me for not taking care of them. They were all down on me and I packed a change of clothes and left for Emerson House.

But first, I stopped at my dad's apartment to tell him that I was leaving Jake so he would hear it from me first. He didn't say much and finally I asked if he would be able to help me with some money until I could figure out how to support myself even if Jake would have to give child support for Jill and Joel. My own father, Clarence Ducky Holmes, sat for a while thinking about what to say as I fidgeted and fumed at his indecision. Then he said to me, his only child, his daughter, "I'll have to talk with Jake before I can give you an answer."

Bea on October 5, 1974

When I opened Emerson House's front door this evening, I was surprised to find some New Age Agape group meeting there. Nora Carpenter, our trustworthy church friend who is also a therapist, could see how unsettled I was and took me into the kitchen where we could talk. Betty Willing joined us and invited me to come into the group where I soon found myself like fresh meat in the midst of being analyzed by all these people, mostly strangers, asking me personal questions about my parenting, my family, and my life! Enough! I went upstairs and started to settle in to sleep on the couch when Betty Willing came up and invited me to sleep at her house. And I did, on her floor covered by the sleeping bag I carried in the trunk of my car.

I went back home to see Jill and get her straightened out and met with the attorney father of one of the kids who hang around our house. I need to find out what my rights were. He told me to tell Jake that he had to leave. Surprisingly, he did, today. I moved back in and took over the housework again.

Fortunately, I'd updated and signed my teaching files so I could follow through when Betty McGregor told me about a teaching opening at Lakeshore Bay's Learning Place, the private school for children with learning disabilities. She told the school about my abilities, so I called them and made an appointment to be interviewed on October 9. When they asked for a reference letter, I asked Jan to write one and what a good job she did. Later I drove back and forth to church early and stayed late, then came home to cleaning, washing, etc.

Jan on October 8, 1974

Nothing's better to cheer a person about to get a divorce than travel and adventure, so I rounded up people who were free to take Bea for a day on the town in Chicago. Our friend Betty was the only one who could join us on such short notice. Because my lovely old VW van was too unreliable for such a trip, I traded Alex's red Mercury sedan for the day.

I drove directly to Chicago's Old Town and found a favorite Mexican restaurant where we ate a spicy lunch and drank Mexican beer to quench our thirst. We remembered Marge's son's beer can collection and decided to save the cans for him and tossed them in the car.

We searched through the Chicago Art Institute for one of Bea's and my favorite painters, Ivan Albrecht. His work is not the kind that cheers one, but his paintings, like the movie's final image in *The Picture of Dorian Gray*, give a dark, dystopian perspective that actually enhances Bea's mood because she appreciates his unique themes and artistic details.

At our next stop, I actually found a parking place on the street right across from the John Hancock Center, where we zoomed up 93 floors to the classy cocktail lounge for the spectacular view of Chicago and Lake Michigan—and a martini. Betty had two. Then we drove to Ricardo's on Rush and another parking space made it possible for me to stop and show them the three Ivan Albrecht paintings that grace the back of the bar. Of course, we had a drink there too.

It was suppertime and I headed up Halsted Street to Greek Town and the Parthenon. We parked in the crowded lot across the street and were greeted by handsome waiters (I think Betty pinched one.) who served us well as we ordered appetizer saganaki cheese with flaming brandy, moussaka, squid and gyros so we could share our dishes. Of course, we had to have a liter bottle of roditis wine. This meal took a while to eat and after chewing away on my squid, I lost myself, concentrating on consuming the tentacles in front of me, until I glanced up to see that my companions were gone. I was alone at the table. I always was a slow eater, but this was a surprise. Then I saw my two companions sitting at a table of eight businessmen who were watching the laughter and mischief that spilled out from our table and they sent out a signal for us to join them.

With my awkward naiveté, I grabbed my plate of food and glass of wine and joined my rowdy companions as we entertained the men with actually funny feminist stories, sad but clever details of Bea's planned divorce and those were highlighted by tidbits from Betty's old divorces.

Several rounds of ouzo topped off the evening when we finally realized that the waiters were standing in a row with white towels folded across their arms along the Grecian grape-viney wallpaper leading to the door, waiting for us to finish our party and leave.

I stood and followed my friends, not knowing what would come next. Our table had been cleared. Who picked up our bill? We didn't. Would these guys expect us to go with them after we left the restaurant? Would we end up in some hotel room getting gang raped for our share of the bill?

I was not prepared for this.

The men escorted us out the door, waved a friendly goodbye and turned to go their way, walking on the slanting city sidewalk into the shadows. We grabbed onto each other to swagger down the uneven curbing and across the street to our lonely car waiting in the dark, unattended, unpaved lot.

Betty's knee gave way, she said, staggering into Bea who fell, and on the way down, hit her forehead on the car's trailer hitch, getting a terrible whack and was actually unconscious for a few seconds. When Bea came to, she realized that Betty was on top of her shouting, "Bea! Are you all right? I'm sorry, Honey. Please be okay!" Bea's forehead was bleeding, but she somehow was instantly sober. She untangled herself from Betty and got up to look for me.

I didn't see a thing when I looked back for them after hearing their voices because the ouzo, squid, and all the tension finally hit me. I staggered to the driver's side in front of the car. God, I felt sick. I leaned on the front fender and I threw up whatever I could toward the space next to the barrier stopping us from falling on to the speeding cars on the expressway below.

"Where's Jan?" hollered Bea. "Oh, there she is! Goddamn it! She's sick!"

Betty suddenly went wacko and declared that we two were a couple and we should go home without her. She would manage on her own. "I'll walk home," and she staggered away from us into a dark corner. Bea let go of me, ran after Betty, grabbed her roughly by the coat, spun her around and aimed her fist right under Betty's nose. "You come with us now or I'll cold-cock you right here!" Betty sputtered and immediately obeyed.

Bea pushed Betty into the back seat and locked those doors. Then she helped me into the passenger seat. I was in no shape to drive us home. Bea had to drive those miles in Alex's car. We probably should have checked into a hotel room, but in the condition we were in, perhaps no one would give us a room.

Betty was raving about being a third wheel. Bea was bleeding down her forehead into her eye. I was so nauseated I could barely lift my head to direct Bea to get on the Interstate from Halsted Street.

Because it was past midnight, we made it out of downtown Chicago quickly and as we turned on the Eden's Expressway to go west, Betty announced, "I have to pee!" Where do you pee on the toll road when the rest stop thirty miles down the line?

Bea pulled over and stopped. I volunteered to help Betty as I staggered out into the fresh night air, holding Betty up as well as keeping her from running away from me. In the dark, we walked in tandem away from the car to the edge of the car lights and— Boing!—straight into a segment of the Interstate's miles of eight-foot-high chain link fencing topped with barbed wire. We were lucky not to be permanently imprinted by the chain-linked pattern that we bounced against.

Instead of peeing right beside the car, Betty said she would wait until we found a better place. When I dozed off again with Betty in the back seat, Betty grabbed Bea's breasts over Bea's shoulders from her seat in the back. "You should be with someone like me," rasped Betty, "someone who can give you the love you deserve!" Holding Kleenex to her bleeding forehead with one hand and steering the car with the other, Bea struggled with Betty's assault. "Ye Gods, Betty! Stop it!"

We continued riding through the night until Bea found a furrow along the Interstate fence where it was safe to park. I woke and helped Betty step out of the car and led her toward a grassy ditch in the dark hollow. "Go down there. No one will see you from the road."

I soon heard, "Shit, Jan! I'm up to my knees in the water here!"

"Well, add your own water so we can get home sometime before dawn."

Somewhat relieved now but extremely wet and muddy, Betty folded herself again into the back seat and quieted down some until we unloaded Betty at her house. "Shush! Don't wake up my husband and the girls," she noisily whispered through the finger poised at her pursed lips.

Then Bea drove to her home and thanked me for a memorable day as I stared at her blood-crusty forehead before she sent me to drive home. It was after three a.m. when I slipped up the stairs and into the bed next to my husband. I knew he was awake, boiling over with anger. "I'm relieved to know you are still alive," he steamed.

"I'm sorry," I apologized, quietly hoping to extinguish the flames. "I should have called you from a payphone." Obviously, I was busy and never thought about calling anyway, being grateful that we weren't raped, in a car accident, in jail—or dead. This was the wildest adventure I'd ever had in my entire life and I savored every detail, muffling my glee in my pillow next to his.

I ignored the morning's alarm and let him get up first to avoid any arguments before he left for work. When I got to work at my desk, my phone rang. Alex's furious voice seethed through gritted teeth hissing about the state of the car with wet mud and beer cans in the back and vomit on the front. I listened and said, "Well, at least we made it home." And after I quickly hung up, I burst out with naughty, rascally laughter.

Bea on October 9, 1974

Sheesh! My head looks terrible, all bruised and abraded, and my eye is black and blue. What will the principal think at my Learning Place teaching interview? Well, I didn't postpone it and when she took me on a tour of the school, one child asked me what happened to my face. "I fell down, Kid. Haven't you ever fallen down?"

I guess that can happen when you have a day that I call "Three Sailors on the Town."

Jan on October 24, 1974

Bea was hired as a teacher at Learning Place and loved the stimulating teaching techniques used in this small school with autonomy in the classroom to use her creative, innovative teaching. She was doing a fine job in the church school as well.

I was working harder at Lakeshore Med, doing an eight-hour job in six hours so that I could have two hours left over to see her each day after her teaching was done. We would continue to meet in my VW camping van, at church, at Emerson House, and at any and every place where we could comfort and talk with each other. Her life was even more turbulent than mine.

Bea not only made the church school function, but she also worked with Tim Bayfield and Andrea Patterson, the church secretary, to help with adult church activities and publications. Tim took the bus to Lakeshore Bay because he didn't like to or couldn't drive. His wealthy widowed mother, now deceased, was a Unitarian leader in Milwaukee. Tim would often ask Bea for a ride and they'd pick up Marge after work and enjoy cocktails at Tim's spacious home. He knew all the gossip and used top-shelf booze. Bea once gave him such a full-blown goodbye hug and a kiss on her way out the door that he fainted after he closed the door.

The Learning Place teachers had their "staffing" Friday night drinks at The Pump, and Bea became the life of the party with a whole new set of friends to entertain with her stories and communing with her colleagues about teaching in an under-funded school with improvised materials or none at all.

Of course, folk dancing and its parties were another option.

After committee meetings, parent meetings, church board meetings, UU supper clubs, and UU human sexuality classes, Bea would most often go to Marge's and talk and drink and smoke around her kitchen table. I often sat around that kitchen table to talk to myself.

In between, Bea would drive home, feed her kids, and if she didn't have somewhere else to go, she'd fall asleep. She put a lot of miles on her mother's old green Plymouth.

CHAPTER 8

Bea on November 12, 1974

Halloween! I brought a science set and art supplies from home to use in my classroom. Monday was my first official day of actual teaching and that's exciting. The kids were wound up for Halloween. Someone had a good idea to take them to the pumpkin farm, but it was so crowded and I was sure I'd lose one or two kids among the cornstalks and pumpkin piles. I wore my black dress and hat and became a witch.

Dearest Jan,

I'm overloaded with input. Details drive me out of my mind, but I will never forget you. You are in every pore of my skin, every cell in my body. I'm rushed, hassled and harried, but you're always with me to make me smile secretly—or broadly for all the world to see. Know that the love link we have is interlocked, intertwined as tightly as the double helix in the molecules in my cells.

Happy Halloween

Last Friday on the same day I started teaching, we had a Wapatuli party for my Jim, who's leaving at 6 p.m. for a three-year tour in Germany. Jake, the kids and I had a pizza supper together and then we took him to the bus. Josh will leave for Hawaii in a couple of weeks. Jan surprised me by coming late in the evening to be with me during this emotional time. Of course, I was crying and she was holding me in her arms, both of us sitting in the living room floor when Joel startled us by charging through the front door to find us. He said Hi and stepped over us on the way to his room.

Jan on November 14, 1974

I am 43 today and Bea has been regaling me with crystal-themed birthday presents and poems every day since November 4. I've never been so indulged. Besides finding time somehow to see each other every day, she hates to miss any opportunity to party—and to make love together.

> Love as infinite as space,
> as clear as bell jar air,
> as fresh
> as spring grass fragrance,
> as inspired
> as an idea waiting to be free,
> as bright
> as a champagne bubble
> reaching for the rim
> of a crystal goblet
> wanting to be touched
> and quaffed by happy lips,
> as warm as the waves
> of heat vibrating
> from fireplace flames—
> infinite, clear, fresh,
> inspired, bright,
> reaching, wanting, warm—
> there is no single symbol to capture
> the essence, the intense invisible
> power and magnitude of my love.

Bea on November 27, 1974

Jan works hard to get the jobs finished so she can have time off preparing her house for Thanksgiving. I don't have to do that this year. I'll take Jill and Joel out for dinner. But, surprise, Steve Murak called me on Monday and we made a dinner date for Wednesday. Why not? He and Angie aren't going to last much longer together. Dinner at the Holiday Inn on the harbor was pleasant, but I didn't expect it, nor did I argue when he told me he had a room reserved for us. We had a pleasant evening together.

Bea on December 26, 1974

Jim came home on the 18th and looked terrific in his uniform. I'm so proud of him. I drove to pick him up at the airport and we talked until 4 a.m.

His homecoming and our various church-related Christmas parties give me a warm glow, except when Alex is there. He stares at me all the time. Jan and I exchanged presents and we had a beautiful afternoon at Emerson House.

I cooked a Christmas Eve turkey, then SLAM, Jill and Joel refused to go to church with me, but Jim went. I was truly hurt until we did our traditional Candle Dance during the Hanukkah part of the service. On Christmas Day, the kids went to Jake's, and I went to Marge's mother's home for dinner. I ended up crying. Got tight but got through it all. This afternoon I met Jan at Old Main for a piece of pie and cup of coffee and we talked of Christmases when we were kids.

Bea on December 28, 1974

I'm subdued. I vowed abstinence this morning and had only two drinks all day.

Yesterday, Dick Shannon invited me to a sauna party with a brass quartet playing. I felt like being in the Jet Set, to live and live hard. Jan and Alex and the kids were invited, so she had to behave herself. They went into the sauna, but when Alex said he didn't want to go into Lake Michigan, Jan put on her shoes and a towel and scrambled down alone. She actually went into the water and experienced such a shock that she could have floated dead in the freezing water before she realized how stubborn and foolish she was to be alone in that condition. She made it up the hill and made the best of the rest of the party.

I went in the sauna twice and then went skinny-dipping with my hot body in Lake Michigan too, but with Jenny and Dick. Somewhere there, I was making out with the French horn player. Then I was smashed. I went off the road twice on the way home, but I made it. Hard depression! I will survive!

> I don't write too much, anymore, only when I have to—
> only when compulsion drives me.
> I like to internalize, to let the words walk
> around inside of me, to shake hands with one another—
> make new friends until they start to like one another
> and begin to sing and dance and annoy the neighbors—
> until they spill out onto the street of paper
> rowdy, and laughing, and human, and right.

Bea on January 1, 1975

God! What a Sunday! After church, I went home to find that my kids wouldn't be home for dinner so I went to see *Airport 75*. I went home again to check and still no one was there, so I decided to come to church for "Buddhist Meditation." Betty was there too, and we went to the Motor Inn to eat but they weren't serving food, so we had a drink. Then Betty wanted to look for our friend Emerett and she took me to a gay bar. Wow! Swish. We were the only women there except for the bartender and she looked like a man. I spent the whole time trying to communicate with a deaf mute in sign language. Then we went to the Silver Lantern and stumbled right into the arms of a gaggle of Russians. I found myself sharing a bar stool with a handsome "Frenchman" kissing me—almost strangled me, almost getting laid on the bar. He could speak no English and I suspect no French either. WILD! Betty and I managed to escape, though I don't know how. Sheesh!

On New Year's Eve, I was elegant in my black dress for a party at Emerson House. In addition to playing my guitar, I learned to sing and play "Auld Lang Syne" on my newly made dulcimer. Of course, I got high but stayed savvy and slept at Emerson House until 5:30 to sober up, finally getting home at 6 a.m.

> Rejection. It can be so subtle.
> It can compound itself. Easily.
> Suppose you write.
> Suppose you send it off to a publisher.
> Suppose you get rejections slips,
> Time and time again, over and over.
> Piss on it.

Suppose you're married. Suppose your husband says, "I'm too tired. I don't like the taste of stale wine. Get lost, sister. I don't want you."

Suppose you approach your father with the fact that you've just left your husband and ask him if you could borrow money if you need it. Not now, just in case you might need it. And suppose he says, "I don't know what to say. I don't want to get involved."

Suppose you sleep with some guy who is supposed to like you and he can't perform. Whose fault is that, eh? Rejection. Boy, is that subtle.

And suppose you're involved in a relationship that is beyond the realm of acceptance in society: a) that is courting capital rejection and b) that you both know it is impossible. Subtle. Subtle. God! What a set-up for subtlety.

Cheer up, kid. Lay off those organ tones of misery.
Golly. Don't be depressed. It bothers me.
You're not your usual self. How come?
Why aren't you joyful and laughing?
But be careful. Don't you dare have gallows laughter.
That's bad for your health.
Cheer up, Kid. Life is so fine in America.

"You make me so happy," she claims. "Alex only loves me. He is after me all the time. We screw at least four or five times a week. He cries because he loves me. God, it's awful! My Jenny loves me and hugs me. She's growing up. She's becoming a woman. Wow. Isn't it neat! Matt ran in a race today. He came in second. He's practically tops in the city for his grade level. He gave me a hug. He loves me. My father offered me his upstairs apartment any time I needed it. Isn't that great? I only won four first places, three seconds and one honorable mention. How come you're depressed—it bothers me. Don't you have gallows laughter now? Golly, you're a good sport."

Obviously, I'm not! And this is going to make you hurt and angry! You're going to say, "I can't help my good feelings. I can't help my successes." And you can't. Nor can I help the way I feel. I've written it all out and analyzed it. I wanted the bottom line. Will you ever see it?

Bottom line. Depression.

What's your problem, Kid? Why? What for? What can I do? What's my problem? Jesus. What do I have to be depressed about? My marriage of twenty, no, twenty-one years is gone. (I hardly count the last year because of its emptiness.) Kaput. Done in. Turned to ashes in my hands. Charred, crumpled, blackened, powdered and blown away. The motions are gone. The words are gone. The paper and essence are gone. There is only an empty space where that thing once was. A thing. An object. What? A marriage. A pairing, a partnership, and yet it's over?

Bottom line. Depression.

Hello there. I have a feeling that I know you. Gee. That's funny. I do too. Can we meet for a drink? Sure, why not? A girl has to live. How about us spending the night together? Sure, why the hell not?

Bottom line. Depression.

I want to hold your nude body. O.K. Go into the bedroom. Struggle off the clothes. The martinis pump and circulate the blood. Body to body. Hairy chest against soft skin. Sweat. Movement. Silence. Bodies moving. Emptiness. Straining for something. What? What is it? What are we doing? Who cares. Keep it up. No. It doesn't work. Or then maybe it does, sort of. Gee, that's fun. Swell. Golly, you're a good sport. Proves we're human, doesn't it? Just what we needed. Cheers.

Bottom line. Depression.

I love. I loveloveloveloveLOVE. Not accepted. Don't tell anybody. Ye gods! What if someone should find out? NOT ACCEPTED! We loveloveloveloveLOVE! Impossible situation. You cannot love. NOT ACCEPTED! Hide. Be devious. Bury it. Keep it hidden. God, good God. Want. Want. Want. But be careful. You may never really have. Have. Have. Have, but never, never really. The outsider. You'll always be the outsider. The space between the cracks to keep her from falling. The space between the cracks, but water washes out the lime. Life erodes. Wears away. Life loses its grip.

Bottom line. Depression.

Golly, You're a good sport. You understand my situation. Swell.

Bottom line. Depression.

What's your problem, Kid? Golly, you're a good sport!

Jan on January 9, 1975

Dear Rachael,

I feel so warm, so whole. I've survived disappointments and deadlines yet have created good programs and positive feelings at work. When I walk, my back may ache but my spirits are high. My work gives me a sense of being qualified and important. It's satisfying to acknowledge the good care that Lakeshore Med people do and I couldn't find a better career.

Our Christmas Eve program at church without a minister is truly based on faith in the spontaneous, creative trust of people to share and risk themselves with me. When the program ended, there was more hugging and warmth among us all than I've seen outside a TA weekend workshop.

Our friends reinforce each other in so many beautiful ways. It helps me to be strong at home when I have these resources elsewhere. Yet my body is suffering from the wish to run away and much of the holidays were spent in pain in my back and front torso.

Alex is still a shadow, and why shouldn't he be? He's working hard and travels a lot, but he's always done that. He's using his feelings to try to control mine, but he's always done that too. I'm different now, though and I'll not trade my good feelings for his. There's no war. We're not talking much but he's signed us up for that New Age group each Thursday in February on communicating our feelings. That might help him, but I'm still afraid to risk being truly honest with him because I'm not ready to have my children taken away from me in a custody battle that could also put us all in the local news.

He wrote me this note. I know he feels betrayed. It's a loss of his dream. I can't help that now. I have my own dreams, confused as they seem to be. I actually feel sorry for him sometimes. And I'm afraid of him too.

Notes from his memo pad
"from the desk of Alex Carnigian"

1. Marriage is a bond between two people who trust in each other no matter what.
2. I hurt because what once was a strong mutual bond has been crumbling into nothing.
3. You have broken my trust with your need for love beyond boundaries I can accept.
4. When each goes a separate way the bond is eroded until the marriage is broken.
5. I was wrong to think that basic security from wanting would fill our individual emptiness.
6. Why can't we work together to renew our weakened bond that once was our strength?
7. With mutual trust, cooperation in undertakings, entertainment, financial security, loyalty and understanding,
8. I love you but I can't do this thing alone. We must renew/continue—together.

Late one night, I explained to him that my major flaw is that I love too much, and if that's the case, I'll take love rather than his possessiveness, jealousy and hate. And I went peacefully to sleep.

My concerns about Bea continue to grow with her impending divorce and her frustrations with my trying to balance her with my family and work that is expanding in importance as new demands are made on me from all departments. I seem to be under constant tension, but most of it excites and inspires me. Discounting some of her fears, Bea told me she's not afraid of the New Year. Nor am I.

On January 2, I spent the whole day with Bea. We made omelets, drank white wine, perused old school yearbooks, listened to Helen Reddy's "I Am Woman" and other albums, discussed Erica Jong's *Fear of Flying* and enjoyed other delightful pleasures. That evening she and Marge went to the movies to see *Flash Gordon.*

Alex seemed happier when he came home from work and found me cooking supper, so we were able to be together in peace and harmony with the kids—and later as a couple.

Jenny was ill, so I stayed home with her and untrimmed the tree. Christmas is over. My New Year's resolution is to celebrate the cup more than half full and live one day at a time.

I finally found an osteopath for back treatments. He's near Bea's which allows me to see her at her home. Bea's treatments are much better than his; maybe both will help. After my last appointment, I was frayed, sore, empty-headed, exhausted and ready to snap. And I entered Bea's home and I felt safe. I sat on her sofa, my heart was calm, my mind at ease, my body warmed. When I tried to leave to resume my duties of my day, I stayed to be healed with love until I could move and be healthy again.

Jan on February 10, 1975

Bea needs more than wine and conversation to cheer her up after all the stress she deals with. We need to play on this gloomy winter's day close to Valentine's Day. We need to be free, for an hour at least, where we can rekindle the heat of our summer's gratification, remembering our abandonment to desire and pleasure—intense intimacy under adverse conditions. We've been too busy filling others' needs. Now's the time, I say, to take control and give each other joy.

At home, at hidden times, I've been reading Xaviera's *Erotica and Odette's Pleasures, The Secret Garden of Sexual Love between Women.* I can't imagine where Bea even found them to buy for me. At work, I could barely concentrate on my newsletter assignment, waiting for her call to pick me up after she could escape from her work and I could escape from mine.

I wanted to kiss her immediately in the hospital parking lot when I jumped into her car, but instead I put my hand so that no one could see her thigh as she drove the few blocks to Emerson House. Unlocking the door, I stopped her hand from turning on the lights and led her into the farthest corner of the kitchen—out of view. When we took off each other's coats, my eager energy pumped through me and I easily lifted her gently to sit on the counter in the corner. She wrapped her limbs tightly around me as she surrendered to me. I've never felt so headily aggressive or so totally accepted. Slowly unfastening zippers or buttons, we inhaled each other's essence and kissed hair, eyes, mouth, ears, the crevices at the collarbone, inside the elbow and cupped hands, tonguing, tasting, absorbing. The softness of her skin yielded to my hands and fingers exploring their lover's body and kneading salty sweat, yeasty fragrance, stimuli for our senses, mouths nipping and nibbling food for our souls.

Creatively we transformed ourselves into a world of our own, in a trance interrupted only by over-the-edge, altered-state orgasms—with lusty yet spiritual rapture.

Bea on February 10, 1975

In the kitchen–WOW!

CHAPTER 9

Bea on March 14, 1975

I'm divorced as of 10 a.m. today. Jan came with me and took the stand as my witness. Up until the court date, everything seemed okay but at the last minute, Jake hired his own lawyer so the settlement jazz was upsetting. We had a short but intense argument in the courthouse corridor right before the final hearing with the judge

I'm even shaking. But Josh came home the day before my divorce hearing. He's beautiful and so dear to me. Too bad he has to witness his sister and brother moving out on me to live with "Poor Pop." Josh's presence gives me some transition toward eventually coming home to an empty house.

Marge's been trying to get me into the dating circuit again and we went to the singles dance at some Catholic church. UGH! It took days to rid myself of the men's shaving lotion left on my cheek and clothes from dancing with them. Folk dancing with others in line and partying after, especially at Marge's house, is good enough for me right now.

<<<>>>

Bea on March 31, 1975

Important plans are unfolding. Jim called from his camp near Augusta, Georgia, and asked if I could drive his souped-up Chevie Duce with the Holly Hurst shifter to his Army post. Even if it's Easter weekend, Marge and Jan worked it out to go with me. Of course, Marge is considered to be our chaperone, but I don't think she is aware of this.

I said goodbye to Josh on Thursday morning as he went back to camp. I taught school and came home to take a nap. It started snowing about 3 p.m., so Jan and Marge left work early and we hit the highways with Marge tucked in the hatchback's small back seat next to all our luggage. The trunk was filled with the original tires that were replaced by Jim's preferred oversized wheels. Jan was in the front passenger seat and I had to drive because I was the only one who knew how to handle the Holley Hurst shifter and the 400 cc. engine. Besides, the roads became icy slick, the winds gusty and the visibility dense. I had to be the one to be responsible for our safety.

Jan took a turn to get us to Nashville, where we ate a southern breakfast. She drove while I shifted from the passenger seat. Marge would have driven more, but her feet couldn't reach the pedals unless we propped her forward with coats and all.

When we made our air reservations for the return trip home, we also arranged for two double beds in a room at Atlanta's Hyatt Regency on Peachtree Street. We drove up to our impressive hotel to let a valet help us unload. He asked for the key to park the car, and I warned him it was tricky to shift and touchy to drive. "I can handle this just fine, Madam," with an arrogant tone and looking down his nose at me. While we lined up to confirm our reservations, I felt a touch on my shoulder and turned to recognize the valet. "Could you please give me directions again on how to shift the car?" I went out with him, showed him what to do and flinched as the wheels spun black marks on the pavement and left a smoke trail while he wrestled the screeching car down the concrete spiral into the bowels of the parking garage.

We celebrated our accomplishment of getting to Atlanta with a round or two of drinks in our room, a shower and a nap with Jan next to me and Marge in the next bed. Jan had planned all the stops with dinner at the new Benihana's, where the oriental chef entertained with flying shrimp and steak fillets, then to the Atlanta Underground, but, Chicago girl that I am, I'm street savvy and saved the night by some quick clustering moves to scurry us onto a bus. That saved Marge's over-the-shoulder purse strap from being cut off by a straggly looking man with his hands in his pockets, probably holding a blade. Jan and Marge are so naive.

We went to the rotating top of our hotel for another drink before heading back to our room. Of course, the two of us couldn't sleep and when Marge was soundly snoring, we slipped out of our bed and went into the bathroom and contorted in many angles while quietly making love around the porcelain fixtures on a tile floor cushioned with layers of terrycloth towels.

In between lunch at the new Victoria Station's boxcars and dinner at Pittypat's Porch, including mint juleps, we saw the movie *Tommy*. Wow! We didn't know what we were getting into. I'll never forget the rock opera music of The Who, the irreverent themes, and the spectacular visual effects, especially when Ann Margaret as Mrs. Walker slithered herself along the huge, slippery chocolate tube pillows and writhed around the room singing, "Tommy, can you see me?" We three talked for hours about the movie's meanings and symbols. Jan identified with Tommy's "See me, feel me, touch me, heal me" and then the freedom he felt when he was released from the psychological traumas of his youth. We all could identify with those, except for Tina Turner's electrifying drug and snake scene— and the guy with the rubber fetish. Again! Wow!

We got up at 7 a.m. after another restless night for the two of us, and we picked up Jim at his post near Augusta. He was tolerant of being with the three of us as we squished into his car and drove about to see the city where the Augusta National Golf Tournament was in progress. We even got a bit sunburned.

That afternoon our flight home was quick and snappy. Marge's handsome young boyfriend Ron met us at the airport. We drove Jan home. When Charlie stopped by at Marge's and saw that she had Ron, Charlie came over and knocked on my door.

Bea on April 1, 1975

Dear Jan,

A year ago today, I told you I was so "damned in love with you I couldn't see straight." Curious fact! We both bought new glasses this year. I hated mine. They didn't look right. They didn't feel right. They hid my eye makeup. They made me dizzy. The bifocals were blurry. I found a million reasons not to wear them, but the idea struck me this morning. Perhaps I choose not to "see straight" again because I am so damned in love with you that I can't see straight and I like it and I want to stay that way without correction.

I love you.

Though I can't be with Jan as often as I want, I'm surrounded by people and parties. I played my guitar at Rachael's fabulous party to celebrate passing her Transactional Analysis clinical exams. I was a bit crocked and made it home at 3 a.m. I had a terrible hangover on Sunday but made it through church school. Then the Muraks came and we went to dinner and I took them to church and Emerson House to show them where I work.

I'm still going to classes, "staffing" with my teacher friends, going to Tim's for drinks, to Nina's for dinners, and to the church board and RE meetings. Somewhere in between, I went to see my Jill inducted into the National Honor Society.

Last night I went to Greek Feasts and made a date for tomorrow with a guy named Max.

There was a time when I would come home at most any hour to find teenagers moving about or sprawling on the floor watching TV, sleeping on the sofa, reading paperback novels and drinking soda or beer until I sent the friends home, made the kids turn off the lights and go to bed. It used to drive me nuts. Yet I enjoyed it too and was proud that mine was the home they all came to.

It's quiet now because everyone's gone. The house has the same furniture, same wall decorations, same books, but it's empty. The ghosts of the joys and frustrations haunt the place, but it's peaceful. Yes, peaceful. But after sharing each interest and hobby and activity with my kids and their friends, it's so lonely being alone. After twenty years of parenting them and providing for their needs, they leave me. I want them back. I need them and their friends, their noise and their aliveness, and I need them to need me again.

Some tell me to find a new male friend. New men aren't any better than the old one I divorced. The bodies are the same. The personalities are cold and selfish, the sweat and rutting movements, making sure they get theirs, meaningless shapes without feelings or commitment or openness or love.

It's so easy to go to the cabinet, pull out a brandy bottle and pour a double in a glass, take a deep drink, carry the glass and the bottle to the bedroom, take another, throw my clothes on the floor, swallow a third and final dose and fall naked into the unmade bed.

It will help me sleep.

Jan on May 29, 1975

For Bea's 45th birthday, she and Marge went to St. Louis for the weekend to visit Marge's friend Richard in his bleak apartment. When she's gone, I'm relieved that she is involved with friendly activities and that I can be with my family without worrying about her.

They brought me a gift from St. Louis, a small wall hanging with a perfect image of me at age three, standing with a tattered suitcase in one hand and a rag doll in the other saying, "I'd love to run away with you, but I'm not allowed to cross the street." Receiving it was somewhat painful because it was too appropriate, yet it gave me perfect insight into where I am now.

We continue to snatch time to be together. We play tennis, go to lunch, meet for minutes and go to the movies where we join the gang and I can take Jenny with us. We still go folk dancing when I can and when it's my turn to have a party at my house, Bea fends off the eye-to-eye glares from Alex.

I worry about her meeting all these guys. I hope nothing happens to her. She told me that I turned her into a sexual magnet, shooting phonemes into the atmosphere, a firefly that attracts the males to copulate. "You did it! You turned me on," she kidded me, and everyone is chasing me. If you hadn't pressed the switch, I probably would still be back in my little home with my family."

I reminded her when Sandler told her she was "a mass of seething sexuality" even before we fell in love.

Bea confided that she was relieved when she finally got her period. I hadn't even considered a potential pregnancy, and what a relief when she went to Family Planning, where they supplied her with prophylactic products and a thorough physical check-up in that department.

Marge keeps trying to "straighten" Bea and even drove her all the way to Evanston to a singles dance. Bea told me she had two polyester leisure suits panting over her. They and their aftershave made her feel as if she needed to take a bath. And Marge keeps passing Charlie over to Bea. And then there's Max, who takes her out and then, as Bea says, "The usual thing. Ho hum." But she also says that sex is good exercise.

I'm not jealous. How could I be? I'm also at home with Alex, living as a person according to acceptable standards as judged by others who don't know about my other life. And my husband, so far, has not disclosed my secret. Also, I'm still concerned about her stability, so her liaisons with others may help fill her needs when I may not.

Alex will be home more on weekends now that the ministerial search committee has finally found a new minister, a warm and flamboyant, guitar-playing young man to assume church leadership—a great change from the traditional, brain-centered UU minister—a change needed with our playful and loving congregation. The Rev. Doctor Tony Logan is right out of the seminary and a bachelor who has a lot of potential. After having our ministers come and go, one of the committee members asked how long he intended to stay with us and Tony answered, "As long as you'll have me."

He has a bodacious sense of humor and will motivate younger people to continue coming to church. He'll add a lot of energy to our congregation, and most of them tolerate the touchy-feely hand holding that he asked us to do at the end of his trial sermons before the congregation voted to accept him.

Alex spent days with that committee searching for the best minister. Our church wanted to live down its reputation of being "high risk" for a minister; we'd had trouble keeping one for long for various reasons. Once when I passed Alex while he talked on the phone to another search committee member, I heard him say, "Let's deal with that issue if and when it arises." I wonder what he meant by that? I didn't ask.

Bea on June 30, 1975

This June has gone so fast! I rented the trailer again for the year-end school picnic and for the church picnic. In fact, on Saturday morning, Marge and I and the Carnigians were the first ones there. Alex made an omelet for our little family, including me. Jan and I could hardly be together this time except to take a stroll in the woods and sing around the campfire. I copped out early.

The tension is getting to us. And Jan's ailments continue.

One day I felt so terrible I could hardly move. I called in sick with a sore throat and a temperature. Undaunted, Max came about 4 p.m. and eventually we checked in at the Holiday Inn. He bores me. The next afternoon Jan was able to break away and we had a loving afternoon together. Then Charlie called at 5:30 and we went to see my father, who was okay, to the Silver Lantern for drinks and we sang all the way home. Charlie left at midnight. No payoff. It's okay.

Of course, Jan had to build floats and do her Lakeshore Med's work. I came home and sawed off the top of the willow that broke in Sunday's storm. Then I slept and slept—right around the clock.

I went over to say goodbye to Jan, where she was decorating parade floats, went folk dancing later and crashed at home with a low-energy emotional level. Then yesterday, I arrived at UU summer camp at about 2:30. I stopped on the way and wrote two letters to Jan and mailed them. Camp started with the usual kick-off dance where singles mingled, then Club Cratty with Marge and Rachael and more. I staggered away to my room and passed out.

I'm not too well today, but I went to the "Option of Being Single" workshop and got angry when the leader paired us up. How ironic. Is there no option, even in a "being single" workshop?

Bea on July 1, 1975

I don't feel well this morning. Dizzy. I've been lying down for a couple of hours, so I'm a bit better now. Marge arrived last night and her entourage came to greet her: Tyler, Richard, Oliver and Tom. Terrific, eh? I started drinking early in the afternoon and then joined Marge in her attempt to get crocked. So, at about 7:30, I fell asleep and stayed that way 'til 7 this morning. I still felt plastered at breakfast. Marge made it to bed at about 2 or 2:30 after looking at the stars with Richard and doing the Club Cratty bit. After breakfast, at about 9:30, I had a terrible wave of dizziness and had to come back and lie down. Am I making any sense? What the hell is wrong with me anyway? God. Look at my handwriting.

Dear Jan,

Your special delivery letter arrived. I know, Babe, I know. It was quite a surprise to be searched for and found by the U.S. Postal Service.

Marge wants to make a pact to swear off booze for today. I told her not to involve me in her vows. She said she didn't intend we'd sign it in blood or anything else. She had a terrible hangover this morning but was her usual fun self: cursing, crabbing and complaining at breakfast, where we sat with Anna and Betty. We had a great time teasing her. If the sky would fall on her for swearing, Marge would be buried in clouds.

I still feel goofy. In spite of my refusal to make a pact with Marge, I've made my own pact with myself. My body can't take it. If I dry out some, perhaps my sleeping sickness and dizziness will go away. If not, I'm going to look for the tsetse fly that bit me.

I miss you, plain and simple. I keep thinking of our two nights here last year. But I'm going to try to feel better physically. Maybe it's only my period. My chemistry gets more extreme the older I get.

Take care, my love. Don't work too hard or get too tired, and please don't overstrain your healing back.

I'm going to lunch now.

All my love.

Jan on July 5, 1975

Dear Bea,

I survived the 4th again and swore never to do it again, but so what else is new? We had an extremely tense beginning starting at 5 a.m. Many final details loomed large as the minutes went by. Then on a critical turn heading to the parade's line of march, the huge trailer cut it too close and ripped the side framework and much of the paper on the float. It seemed like hours before we finally reached the line of march to make carpenter and paper repairs. I was working under the most intense pressure, pinning and stapling and patching like mad. Jenny was help but she kept saying, "five minutes to go— two minutes to—"

Then the soundman didn't show up to run the tapes on another float. I was all alone checking for the last details and anticipated having to run the damn machine or sing the damn theme song myself. I looked underneath the decorations to see if I could connect it. Yes, I did but I'd have to ride the entire line of the parade under this hot box with the machines and batteries. Just in time, a friend associated with the float volunteered to do it.

After the parade, we dismantled the batch and collapsed at 5 p.m. Then, like every 4th since we've lived on Lake Michigan's bluff, we entertained all the relatives and their friends for the fireworks.

I tried to call you at home two times before I left for Door County this morning, so I guess you stayed through to finish at Lake Geneva. All I can do is hope you're better while I'm away.

I'm taking note pad and my mother's typewriter with me. It's so peaceful here. I hate to jar the atmosphere with this clunker, but it's served me well typing stacks of term papers and articles, but most of all, hundreds of loving words to you. Among the books I'm bringing are Marge Piercy's *Small Changes* and Carolyn Heilbrun's *Toward a Recognition of Androgyny*. Heilbrun offers an exciting concept that depolarizes gender where we can choose our personal behaviors as individuals, modify a society that is dominated by the power of masculine aggression and eventually create a truly free human society.

I'll space the quiet times with some work around here. I'm too tired to try to paint our barn. Maybe I'll draw one in my journal.

See you Sunday when I get back. Take care of yourself until I return.

I love you.

Bea on July 5, 1975

I had a headache that got worse and I fell into a deep depression and cried and cried. Rachael, her daughter Mindy, and Marge stayed outside my cabin until Mindy came to me and led me out on the deck to sit with them. Otherwise sleep. Sleep. I felt terrible until I went on the boat trip and swam and sunned. Somehow I've endured this bad scene, especially when Jan will be off to Door County for a week.

Joy! When I got home, my dad and my boys, home on leave, came and stayed and we talked for hours. Then I snoozed and ate.

When they came back with their friends and stayed till 2 a.m., it was like old times.

Jan on July 13, 1975

(Stuck under Bea's door at 10:55 a.m. Sunday)
Dear Bea,

I've tried to reach you since Jenny came home from the church teens overnight at Emerson House. She said you left Emerson House at 2:30 a.m. and she didn't know why. I'm concerned that you may be sitting at home and not answering the phone. You were so low when I last saw you.

Please give me thirty minutes to get home and call me at any time to let me know you're all right.

Don't be angry. I'm worried about you.

The wait is long when words won't come
to capture time and what it means.
A day is long when chores undone
clutter the mind with lesser tasks.
A week is long when you're kept apart
from those you need to share each thought.

But months and years go quickly by
to blend those weeks and days and time—
You blink your eyes, it seems to me,
and another season begins to be,
a new beginning with those you love,
another year, another plan.

Time speeds by for those aware,
for those who cherish the minute's grace,
for those who know, for those who feel
the treasured tick of time unreels.
They sense in time life's point of view
as wiser eyes make images clear.

They sense the value of those they love
as each second spent makes life most dear.

Love—I love a lot of people.
Respect—I respect a few.
I love and I respect you.

Camping and campfires, liquor or not, Bea's and my emotions were always close to the surface. With our kids, we were on our best behavior, but we were never certain of what the atmosphere would be as far as our feelings were concerned.

Marge has been a good friend to us—and we to her. We can be open with her and she has endured our many outbursts of frustration, loss and injustices. Each of us, in turn, supports her feelings. Marge is now my sister and Bea is my lover, both dear friends and soul mates. We share everything. We help each other. She is Bea's best friend and their adventures are often wild and hilarious, sharing some of their escapades with a variety of males.

We drink a lot together and a lot alone. Martinis are important to help me get through the evenings at home. Alex never complains. He seemed to prefer having a tipsy wife at home than a happy one away from him.

Jan on August 10, 1975

King Arthur may have made merry with his valiant knights, exchanging battle stories while reveling at his round table. But on my precious Woodridge acres, I'm a loving Queen Jan among my jolly mothers and daughters eating hamburgers, baked beans and potato chips while revealing mischievous adventures at my rectangular picnic table in the barn.

My merry maidens were Bea and Jill; Anna with two of her three daughters; Betty with her two daughters; two Kramer girls and their friend; Marge's mother, Nina; and my Jenny and her friend Beth.

At first, some of them were squeamish about using the outhouse, but they discovered that leaving the door open helped as long as no big bugs flew in.

We toured Door County's beaches, parks, art galleries and shops. We bought a huge tin of freshly picked Michigan blueberries at our little corner store with the tavern across the road being the only other business near us. We drove to a little beach and swam in the warm, shallow water of Buckaroo Lake. Those of us who went in deep enough, took off our suits and tossed them in our rubber raft so we could skinny dip, dive and moon the sun with our bare, white buttocks.

With a harvest of food to prepare for hungry women and with Bea mastering the grill, some of them relaxed and stretched out under the sun. Beth was nibbling on grapes when she got the idea to plant one in Andrea's navel while she was snoozing on a blanket.

After supper, we went to the Fearful Fun spook house. The terrified Kramer girls grabbed Anna and pulled on her so hard that the buttons popped off Anna's blouse. The frightening monsters were kind enough to turn on all the lights to find them for her. Then we thought Andrea had gone into shock because she started jumping up and down, screaming that something was crawling inside her pants. We circled around her trying to help with sympathetic screaming from the girls. Her hysterics caused the grape that was embedded in her navel that afternoon to burst free and roll inside her pants, down her leg, off her trembling foot and on the ground.

On Sunday morning, I asked our farmer neighbor if we could hike down their cow path to the back of their property and we paraded helter-skelter around the cow pies, through the barb-wire gate into an isolated pasture. The friendly cows came to see what was going on without stomping anyone's toes or pushing us about. Like pirates, we found the farmer's treasure-filled dump with animal skulls, bones, old buckets and skillets, a loosely woven leather horse blanket used to shake off biting insects, and more delights from the country, including broken shards of pottery, flowers and grasses for bouquets. Betty's eight-year-old found a whole cow spine still connected somehow. She insisted on taking it back home. We told her she could have it, but she would have to carry it all the way back to our land. And she did, plodding up the path holding the bone structure on her back that was almost as long as she was tall. Betty was surprised by her daughter's persistence and suddenly acquired strength.

After more swimming, various members of our gang drove home, away in different cars, except for Anna, Bea and me. We took a nap, the three of us, had a late supper and talked and drank wine in the clean night air with cricket sounds responding to our voices softly yielding to the peaceful night. We slept in the trailer again with Anne in the space above the couch that converted to a semi-double bed. This time I was there with Bea rather than Marge, my unrequited love from the past, and the results were much more rewarding.

On Monday, Bea took us on a pilgrimage to Bailey's Harbor on Lake Michigan, where she and her family spent time camping while visiting Jake's father and then to the Green Bay side of Door County north of Sturgeon Bay, where her parents had built the log cabin that was still there. We looked about, but no one was home.

Not in any hurry to leave for home on Tuesday, we walked the Ridges' wild flower road, cleaned up the barn and cut the weeds around it. Deciding to take a nap before driving home, Anne slept in the trailer while Bea and I made love quietly and gingerly in the double hammock on the ridge of our woods, slowly and intensely, so as not to tip out and land on the rock slabs below.

CHAPTER 10

Bea on August 13, 1975

After our supremely healing and loving Door County experiences, I wasn't prepared for what happened at home. The doorbell rang at 2:30 a.m. and I panicked, believing something happened to one of my kids, so I jumped out of bed and ran to the door to be surprised by my dear friend's husband, John.

I met Jan for a coffee in Lakeshore Med's cafeteria this morning to tell her in low tones what happened to me.

"Bea, I'm so sorry you had such a terrible experience last night. I've been worried that something like this would happen to you. Weren't you afraid to see that drunk at your door?"

"My God, that's why I cried, and that's why he finally left me. I'd seen him and his wife a couple of weeks back. He told me that I looked like a lonely woman and he would come to help me out. That Goddamn son of a bitch! The only way they think they can 'help you out' is to stick you with their dick!"

"I know."

"Yes, you do. It's the same old machismo John Wayne 'I'm gonna kiss me a grizzly bear and lay me a pretty gal' routine, and we consent to it too. But I didn't this time! I have in the past, but I fought him off. It was absurd! I offered him a drink and I never should have. I should have turned him around and pushed him out the door. I'm learning—the hard way. I'm learning the rules.

"I even told him I was bisexual now and he said all I needed was a good screw. He said he knew I wanted it. And he would force me. I got scared and went to the bathroom to look for my diaphragm—and I couldn't find it."

"It's in your closet."

"And then I asked myself, what am I doing this for? I told him, 'No! And I mean No! I'm not giving in to this shit any longer.' I used to give in. I used to lie on my back and get it over. That's how Jake was—even on our first date, and I married him three months later. That's what they think women want. And I won't give into them anymore! You can't trust them. I'm alone at home. They say they admire you for your creativity, for your intelligence, for your talent, but all they want to do is push their prick up into you. So, I stopped looking for my diaphragm, changed out of my pjs and put regular clothes on, stepped into the living room—and there he stood with all of his clothes off! I told him to get dressed and get out. Well, he put his shorts on—and then I cried. I never should have let him in."

"Oh my God! How scary!"

"He's moving around my house without any clothes on. He and all the others see me as one big cunt. But I'm not. Even you make me feel that way too because of all the crap I've put up with."

"God! I hope not. How could I make you feel that way?"

"It's the crap in my head. It's taken me a long time to get beyond that with us. It's the crap in my head—and the stuff that's happened to me in my life. But I'm learning new rules. You can't trust a man. I'll never let a man in my home again unless someone else is here with me."

"They make you more isolated than ever. I'm so sorry."

"Thank you so much for letting me vent all this. I feel better now. Despite what I say about us, I do love you."

I put my hand on hers, but I quickly removed it when Randy King passed our table and stopped to say hello.

Bea on August 17, 1975

I worked back and forth between Learning Place conferences and church—straight through to the church board meeting, and at 9 p.m. I was to appear at Learning Place for an interview with the Personnel Committee.

The next morning, I answered the phone to find out I was rehired at $7,500 a year. Jan and I celebrated with a late afternoon champagne at the shoreline rocks, where we now meet to talk. Then Marge, Nina and I went out for a fish dinner, folk dancing, the Furry Fox for two drinks and to Marge's until 1 a.m.

Today I slept until 10 a.m. and worked for seven hours on the church school prospectus, except when Jan came with blueberries, tea and brandy for our colds. She told me again she's won all kinds of awards for her Lakeshore Med's publications and PR projects.

She also told me that she and Alex had signed up for a November Chicago Council on Foreign Relations ten-day trip to Russia for $1,200 a person.

Jan on September 25, 1975

Tony Logan became our new young minister and the church was filled with new energy. Now many of the adults, including Alex, Marge, Bea and me, can cut back on church responsibilities.

A few weeks ago, when Alex knew I'd be away in the evening, he invited Tony over for a talk. I left them, barely speculating on what they were discussing—church business, of course. If Alex does tell Tony about us, so what! Ministers are supposed to listen to people and be compassionate. Besides, Alex needs someone to release his frustration and angst about my not getting over my "illness and perversion." I'm guessing that he does have one intimate friend he can talk to, Diana Dixon. They spend time together on her porch when he takes a walk with the dog. And he never took the dog out of the backyard before this. Who knows what they share? Nick must be a hard man for a husband. It must be killing

Alex that he no longer owns me, that my work is expanding as I advance in my field, and that I live my life beyond his control, though I try to consider my family and its needs.

Ironically and in spite of counseling and an unsuccessful New Agey couples group that climaxed with an exercise in how to give each other a foot massage, we seldom have an intimate conversation because it usually ends in an argument.

Last night we talked quite honestly with each other, and when we went to bed, I didn't want to have sex, and I didn't give in. I wanted to love him without being responsible for loving him. Does that make sense? So, he turned his back to me—and I to him as I started to create a list in my head that kept me awake. I got up and went to my studio, wrote my thoughts down and gave it to him in the morning. I encouraged him to do the same.

"The I Want List"

- I want you to take the initiative in expressing your feelings and activities.
- I want to stop laboring over our relationship.
- I want you to take the initiative to help me maintain the house.
- I want you to stop casting a cloud over my free time.
- I want you to grant me the time to write my feelings and thoughts without hovering over me.
- I want to go to bed when I want to go to bed unless you say specifically or lovingly that you want to make love to me.
- I want to hear you laugh out loud.
- I want to stop guessing about what you want.
- I want you to have more individual friendships.
- I want you to tell me before Saturday morning when you're going to work or going fishing, etc., on weekends.
- I want you to make the bed when you're the last one out.
- I want you to stop staring at me.
- When it's time to go home from a couple's party, I want you to say so.

Alex returned my list.

> I love you. I don't want to lose you.
> I don't want to end our marriage.
> I don't want to hurt our children.
> I trust you not to destroy all this,
> But all this has negatives—
> Let us continue free from fear
> Of love lost, of marriage broken,
> Of children hurt, of losing each other.
> Let us continue with mutual trust and love.
> Loneliness in marriage is a two-headed monster—
> How sad to endure. How joyous to conquer!

What is it about travel and relationships? It seems to me that our mutual love of travel is some sort of carrot on the stick to keep us together. I consented to go to Russia when Alex suggested it. It was an offer I couldn't refuse. St. Petersburg! Moscow! I never anticipated that I'd get to go there. So, we made another commitment to travel while our commitment to each other seemed to be running off the track.

Bea on October 9, 1975

I can't believe it! The two of us together! In Europe! I think Jan had this dream since she first read about Vita Sackville West's escape with her lover Violet from that *Portrait of a Marriage* bio that somehow justified our love as married women with children. That intellectual English Bloomsbury group, including Jan's heroine Virginia Woolf, challenged traditional sexual standards, including homosexuality. No. I think Vita may be her heroine.

We each paid $377 for a Chicago Foreign Relations Council charter flight for three weeks, leaving next July 8. We have to plan for additional money for all our other expenses because we will be traveling on our own. Europe! We start in London and return home from Zurich on July 29.

I've barely traveled except for Door County and the World's Fair in Montreal, towing a tiny trailer to camp with my grumpy husband and four kids.

The money that I have now after selling my house will help pay for my trip. I've spent months with rummage sales and settling family affairs to sell the house for a half share of my insignificant divorce settlement. I've found a one-bedroom, small but sunny second floor apartment just two blocks from Marge's house and closer to Jan.

Jan and I spent many a night drinking vodka and wine around Marge's kitchen table when Jan was free of her own agenda. Then while Jan took care of Alex, we took care of our own needs by finding guys out and about. What a trio!

Bea on October 25, 1975

Jan helped clean my new apartment with my new furniture while our gang of teenagers unloaded my few remaining personal possessions. What a job! I sold my home with six people living there for sixteen years, and now I'm down to three tiny rooms and a bath.

I'm so proud of my choices of new bookcases, coffee and end tables and especially my new mattress set just for myself—and anyone I invite to share my apartment with me.

I gave Jan the key.

CHAPTER 11

Jan on November 28, 1975

Alex and I flew out of O'Hare for our Chicago Foreign Relations Council's twelve-hour chartered flight over the North Atlantic to tour Leningrad and then Moscow. For once we traveled with a carefully directed ten-day tour so we Americans wouldn't get into trouble. When we left our kids at home with Alex's sister and niece, I overheard him say when he gave her the keys to the safety deposit box, "If anything happens to me, empty this box immediately."

Though I had enough to contend with issues at home, because of this trip I'd glance at an occasional TV news item about the Union of Soviet Socialist Republics——the USSR. As in the spring of '56 to the fall of '58 when we lived in Frankfurt, Germany, I tried to focus on our lives and tried not to worry about issues I could do nothing about—though Alex was assigned to a Signal Corp decoding center and we lived in the midst of The Cold War.

Before WW II ended in 1945, President Franklin Roosevelt, Prime Minister Winston Churchill and General Secretary Joseph Stalin and their advisors wrangled about dividing the war-devastated Europe and their enemy: bombed-out Germany and Berlin. The Western Bloc was led by the US and our capitalist-identified allies;

the Eastern Bloc, led by Communist Soviet Union and Slavic countries caught behind the Soviet Union's Iron Curtain.

Living in Frankfurt, Germany during the 1956 Hungarian revolution was scary when our Western forces, posted on the edge of The Iron Curtain, were trigger-ready to fight back against Eastern Communists forces who were killing Hungarians attempting a coup or escaping to freedom.

I wrote to my dad then, "It's been tense with the outbreak of the Hungarian revolution against Russia's occupation. Hundreds of Russian tanks went into Budapest to crush Hungary's attempt to withdraw from the Soviet Union."

I identified with the emotional level of the potential for war because of my teaching American teenagers of Army families.

"I feel for our Army kids at our high school here, most of all those living at the dorm, students who wait and wonder each day if their dads would be sent to that border and what would happen to them. We adults dreaded any threats of confrontation, afraid that another war would begin. An estimated 30,000 Hungarians were killed. Almost as many Hungarians left all behind to cross the borders of free countries in the West into safety.

"After the Hungarian revolutionary leader was captured and executed, Russian forces restored order and the Soviet-sponsored Hungarian Communist puppet's power was re-established. Fearing another World War, each day seemed dreadfully long, but unlike the four years of WW II, the two weeks of the conflict passed.

"Both the Russians and our government have nuclear weapons. This year our Country's first airborne explosion of a hydrogen bomb nearly wiped a Pacific atoll off the map. How could we help Hungary without someone on one side or another push a button to start another terrible war?

"Besides, troubles in the Near East are simmering at the same time. Colonies are declaring independence from their European rulers. France lost Algeria and Great Britain's circles of influence keeps shrinking, including England's control of The Suez Canal with Egypt's new ruler, pro-Communist Gamal Abdel Nasser.

"But Dad, we three couples friends, all non-regular Army, talk about what had and could be happening around us. Alex spends long hours in the top-secret decoding section and keeps quiet about that. On this day, however, we celebrated Thanksgiving together with a new sense of gratitude. The USSR in Hungary is better than another terrible war, especially when we're in the midst of it."

Then in 1957, the U.S. and our space scientists were humbled after the Soviet Union successfully launched the Earth's first artificial satellite, Sputnik, into orbit.

And in 1958, Alex and I joined other American 'tourists' to cross Russia's sector of East Germany on a U.S. military train to reach the fabulous "capitalist" sectors of West Berlin administered by France, England and the U.S. West Berlin 'glowed' in contrast to its sad counterpart, East Berlin, controlled by Soviet forces.

Ironically, a simple decision in our lives about college in 1952 eventually landed us in Frankfurt. Sophomore Alex chose to go with me, a junior, to UW-Madison. He could have stayed home his sophomore year to save money at our nearby UW-college extension campus. I wondered then if Alex wanted to be in Madison so I wouldn't drink and party and find another guy. Did he even know about the Reserve Officer Training Corps-ROTC? He must have known that, when he doubled up on ROTC classes in Madison, he'd be a second lieutenant when he graduated. It critically affected our lives.

This was during the Korean War, when several high school friends were drafted as privates. No matter what your rank, getting the dreadful assignment to Korea was a destiny we tolerated since that war started in 1950. I'll always remember that day living as a married couple near Fort Monmouth in Long Branch, New Jersey. I was making supper in our little apartment when 2nd Lieutenant Alex leaped up the stairway and gave me a bear hug with the ecstatic news that he was to be assigned to decode messages in the I.G. Farben Building in Frankfurt, Germany.

Europe! Europe! Europe! And I'd come and live with him in Frankfurt and enjoy the best of everything! Yah!

What a privilege we were granted.

I'm surprised now at this time in our lives to be with citizen Alex in Leningrad, the Venice of the North on the Baltic Sea with its rivers and canals, museums and massive regal palaces created in 1700 by Russian Czar Peter the Great.

Our hotel in Leningrad, the cosmopolitan city once named St. Petersburg, is the best, said the tour director who, like the Soviet government, wanted us to come away with a positive impression of the city whose name was changed for the 1920s Socialist leader Vladimir Lenin. Except for a scampering roach or two or three when we turned the lights on in our hotel room bath closet, our group was treated to the best of well-presented food and a pleasant variety of entertainment at several posh restaurants. Bottles of wine and vodka waiting to be consumed were placed within easy reach on our banquet tables for frequent toasts to our good fortune.

Of course, it turns dark quickly, like at their 3 p.m. on these cloudy, damp November days; however, the sun shined at the best times to appreciate Leningrad's Baroque architecture with pastel-colored palaces turned into museums brightening most of its stately buildings, helping to warm the northernmost major city in Europe.

The vast Palace Square, edged by square-rigger-sized banners of Lenin's face draped across the front of buildings, made me feel as significant as a gnat. The ornate State Museum of Russian Art with treasures of the past and Communists' politically correct works of art went on long hallways. Because of Arthur Frommer's guidebook book directions, we found the remote space where Modern and Impressionist paintings hung, and we saw those precious masterpieces in that out-of-the-way corner.

The government was spending its money rebuilding and redecorating its museums and palaces destroyed by WW II. I enjoyed hearing the hushed myths of Catherine the Great, probably created by her enemies, but she did live a long and successful life in a dozen or so monogamous relationships. At her dazzling palace estates, skilled workers were recapturing her era by scrupulously adding gold leaf to walls and ceilings and expensive decor inside the restored palaces that were mere fire-scarred skeletons of walls and floors after the Nazis destroyed their lavishly appointed headquarters when they retreated.

Watching from front mezzanine seats in Leningrad's Kirov jewel box theater for a sold-out performance, ballerinas floated weightlessly while male dancers flew across the stage to catch them. Too bad we were close enough to see their frayed costumes and seedy sets in comparison to the building's white and gilded décor, brilliantly colored decorations and our white chairs upholstered in plush red velvet.

Twenty years ago, when we went to the Frankfurt Opera House to see a spectacular *Aida*, Alex counted about 180 people on the stage plus camels and one elephant. I was too busy being enthralled then with the *Aida* to even think of counting anything.

Compare this to Frankfurt in the mid-50s? Frankfurt's city street lights were brighter and traffic buzzed about; new bank buildings seemed to rise above the Main River, shoppers lined the main streets, and American jazz and movies entertained many. (Can you imagine Gary Cooper in *High Noon* saying, "Vas ist los in diesem gasthaus?") Twenty years ago, some rubble and debris from bombings and burning still existed in Frankfurt and the European places we traveled, but Western Europe's war reconstruction made cities seem new while renewing the old. The U.S. Marshall Plan started in 1948 to rebuild war-torn Europe, but Russia's Joseph Stalin refused Marshall Plan benefits for East Germany, East Berlin and Communist-controlled countries behind the Iron Curtain.

One night Alex jumped out of bed in the dark. "Wake up! We're going to miss the bus," and he started shaving while I rushed about to find my clothes. I bumped into him in the small room and when I turned around, I discovered him calmly facing me with half his face still covered with shaving cream. "I just looked again and it's OK. We won't be late. My watch was upside down when I checked the time. We can go back to sleep. It's dark enough for sure."

Of course, it's a perfect time and place to lie awake remembering your life during World War II.

Dream scenario: WW II images emerge

V-E Day. Standing alone, watching from the sidewalk, I'm pressing my thirteen-year-old body against a storefront, protecting myself, keeping out of the way as almost every young adult in town celebrated the Victory in Europe by dancing in the streets, guys kissing the girls and tossing many in Central Square's garden pools.

Images of war bombarded me: indelible, horrific sights in movie newsreels, magazines and newspapers: Pearl Harbor and Bataan, Africa and Europe: Hitler in Nuremberg, thousands saluting him, igniting hate, inciting violence; Mussolini hanging by his heels, stabbed and bloody; most of Europe in ruins; concentration camp survivors staring with deathly hollowed eyes; bodies stacked on carts, shocking piles of human remains. The atomic bomb destroyed Hiroshima, then Nagasaki. Japan surrendered in August 1945. Unconditional surrender.

And my dad away for almost three years in the Navy Seabees in the South Pacific. And me at home with my fragile mom when I wasn't sent to a camp somewhere, off to friends, finally to a foster home.

Jan on December 12, 1975

Strapped into seats on a chartered Russian Aeroflot passenger plane for a noisy and cold forever flight south to Moscow, we felt blessed and deeply grateful when we landed.

When we weren't touring, we'd mill near and about Red Square. When we peered into the multi-colored onion-domed St. Basil's

Cathedral that stood alone from the red and grey brick buildings on the Square, I imagined being ruled in the 1500s by the czars and Ivan the Terrible. I was sure to have been a peasant scratching out a cold and desperate survival with only hope and faith to keep me warm. But what faith would I have? Perhaps merely to live long enough to see another spring.

I recalled my mother's Russian friend Rose Roberts whose Hebrew faith did not protect her father and uncles from being decapitated in pogroms after they were found hiding behind kitchen cabinets in their homes. Rose said they could identify them only by their shoes. Her mother arranged for Rose, then 16, and her three younger brothers to join Rose's married sister who lived in Lakeshore Bay. After that pogrom, Rose's mother grabbed the reins of their horse-driven buggy for a wild ride to reach the train, but when her mother raced to return to their town, the horse reared, the buggy overturned, and Rose's mother was hurled to the ground and died.

Rose and her younger brothers crossed many boundaries and boarded a ship to land on Ellis Island. She was seasick, "And a kind man gave me a lemon and that was all I ate on the boat, for how many days I don't know," she told me in her remaining Russian accent. They stayed on Ellis Island for more days. Her youngest brother tested positive for TB and she was told she had to return with him to Russia. They had no place to return to; her father and her mother were dead. But, her sister's husband was a printer at the *Bay View Times* and its publisher used his influence to bring Rose and her brothers to Lakeshore Bay to start a new life here. My mother was Rose's sponsor when Rose became an American citizen. And Rose took me in when my mother was "having a spell" and couldn't deal with me.

Another chill enveloped me on the dark Red Square in November; people stopped and stood at attention after making way for four black limousines with miniature Communist flags fluttering from each vehicle. The entourage slid smoothly over the cobblestones on the Square, slicing slickly through opening Kremlin gates that quickly enclosed them behind its fortress walls.

One evening, a young man who spoke English approached us, wanting to test his English, he said. We offered to take him for coffee but he declined. Looking over his shoulders and before he left, he accepted my book of Edna St. Vincent Millay's poems, tucked it in his inside coat pocket, shook our hands, thanked us and quickly darted off. A couple from our group joined us and we went into a nearby bar. When I went into the women's room, I witnessed two attractive young Russian women, one crying and the other comforting her while sharing some serious kissing. That made me smile.

The huge and famous GUM department store facing Red Square and across from Lenin's Mausoleum provided shelter as we roamed its wrought iron, ornamental walkways on each of its three floors. The gray skies added light but not warmth through its glass roof. In fact, the lights from GUM glowing out above the building illuminated the Square and the sky above it.

"God, Alex. Check the vending machine!"

We leaned on the railing and watched a short line of customers waiting a turn for a soft drink from the drab green metal case on the main floor below us. A man took a glass that was upside down on the vented shelf below the spigot. He turned the glass over, put it under the spigot, inserted his coin and waited while the glass filled with a lemonade-colored beverage. He drank it and returned the glass upside down again on the same spot, and the persons following in line took the same glass to repeat the process.

One morning, our tour director rounded us all up early to stand in an ominous long column of four people wide that took over three hours to reach our goal: Lenin's tomb. Our group chatted and made more noise than the somber Russians there to pay homage, but we hushed up watching the changing of the guard. I could visualize newsreel pictures of Soviet tanks, guns and thousands of Red Army troops marching on that Square, showing the world their Communist power.

Finally, but quickly we filed past Lenin's illuminated corpse, or a likeness thereof, lying in state in a large glass crypt since 1924. When we entered from the darkened corridor into the lighted vault, it would seem as if Lenin could have come alive as our eyes conditioned themselves to the brightness that surrounded his body. It happened so fast, so quietly; we couldn't stop to get a good look at the Russian leader, and we tumbled out onto the Red Square pavement into the cold grey day. I wasn't going to stand in line again for a second glance. Once outside, we walked past the gravesite of honored Communist leaders and one American, John Reed, a radical journalist who got involved with the Communist revolution.

Shivers would twist up my spine as we toured inside the Kremlin walls for hours.

I reacted similarly when Alex and I were on a U.S. Army approved tour of East Berlin in 1958. We saw historic images from the end of WW II with the bloody Red Army's battles to bring down Adolph Hitler and Fascist Germany and claim victory in Europe before any of the other Ally countries. Of course, the body count was enormous: the massive Allied air and Russian artillery bombing of the city; the aggressively advancing Red Army troops fighting against young German boys and elderly armed Germans who died defending Berlin; battered and starving Berlin citizens. Angry Red Army troops seeking revenge robbed, murdered and raped en masse for weeks despite official warnings of death penalties if the assaulters were captured and tried.

Our tour bus stopped at a vast cemetery with rows upon rows of marble containers as large as dumpsters containing unnamed dead bodies; how many are only estimates? Urns holding the soil of the six heroic cities that resisted the Nazis stood in places of honor. Surprisingly, wedding parties of joyful people crowded about to have photographers take photos of happy bridal parties showing respect for soldiers and non-combatants who'd been killed in that war.

When we went down into an artistically designed Metro station as clean and beautiful as an art museum, one of our group lit up her cigarette. The guide's frozen voice said, "We do not smoke in our Metro." The woman immediately dropped the cigarette and twisted it out with her foot. "We do not litter in our Metro," the guide said with disdain, and the humbled American tourist bent over, picked up the remains and put them in her pocket.

As in Leningrad, we had tickets to see Moscow's Bolshoi Ballet opera spectacle with "a cast of thousands" plus flaming buildings on the stage as the climax. Bolshoi means "big," and with over 2,000 seats, almost every performance is a sell-out. As in Leningrad's theater, part of the spectacle comes during intermission when couples parade arm-in-arm around the lobby and refreshment area. Here the upstairs area for the promenade seemed as long as a football field and the entire audience went up escalators to eat fancy chocolate desserts and drink champagne when they weren't strolling about in an oval parade showing off their best attire with their lover or spouse.

A bell rang at the end of intermission and we were almost demolished on the down escalator when those at the bottom could no longer move through the crowd to their seats and those at the top kept squeezing on. This hazard duplicated itself in the aisles when the performance was almost over. People started leaving to avoid the rush, causing an even bigger rush to get out of the auditorium.

The ten-day Russian trip was better for us than three weeks in Greece because we were on a tour with others, made friends and learned so much, yet the undercurrents of our personal relationship were with us all the time. At the many meals we shared, members of our group encouraged us to join them. One wife said that she could tell that we were a perfect couple because we would laugh so much together, enjoy each other and make others laugh with us. It was laughter filled with vodka, tension and endurance because of the many months of turmoil behind us and the bleak anticipation of the future.

Our chartered plane was hours late, stranding us with our travel companions in an airport lounge. Conveniently, several of us bought bottles of vodka before we entered the holding area and rather than wait for hours and carry them home, we opened the bottles and passed capfuls of vodka around our increasingly cheerful and congenial circle of fellow travelers, those Americans from Chicago.

We were happy to be home again with Jenny and Matt after our Russian adventure, but soon Alex found the right time to challenge me. He knew I'd planned to spend three weeks with Bea in Europe in July. I'd not told him, thinking it would be months before I needed to face up about that. However, he knew about my plans even before Russia after he found my canceled check among my personal papers in an envelope with a return address of the Chicago International Travel Council.

He keeps thinking I'll recover from my compulsion to be with Bea.

I keep hoping and dreaming that somehow this incredible three-way calamity will be resolved safely and sanely.

Dream scenario: "The Customs Man"

Travel has always been a top priority. And I've had my chances. I've traveled all over the U.S. and most of Europe with him. Before him, my parents and I, at five, drove west to California for six weeks. When I was ten, my dad and I took a train trip to Washington, New York City and Niagara Falls. Later I drove to Mount Rushmore with college friends and then as an adult woman Marge and I drove Adelle to Boston and New York.

On this night, in this dream, I found myself traveling without him. How did that happen? He's afraid I'll have a good time without him. Maybe like *Fear of Flying's* Erica Jong, I'll even allow myself to have a sexual liaison with some stranger. Maybe he's afraid I won't come back.

He's so protective, so virtuous, so straight. I know he's trustworthy, loyal, almost immaculately conceived. He's good and pure and true. But somehow, I'm traveling without him. Oh yes.

There she is and that explains it all. I'm traveling with my daughter, the chaperone.

We landed somewhere from a cruise ship in a shelter-type space as if we survived a hurricane. Are we hostages? It's filled with many people like me, trying to complete the details required by the government to disembark for home. My daughter was the only person I knew and she constantly disappeared—to avoid doing her share of the arrangements, I wondered.

It was a mess.

Baggage contents tumbled out by inspectors had to be rearranged in proper order. Some people were still sleeping in their berths. Others gathered up linens for the steward to collect.

We must prepare for the Customs Man.

I was doing my best to fulfill the requirements, but I was behind, feeling frustrated within a frenzy. Gotta get ready for the Customs Man, or he won't let you get off. Be prepared. Get your possessions ready for inspections. But remember—most importantly—you must leave the cabin before he comes because the Customs Man must not be seen. He does not allow anyone to observe him on his inspection rounds.

Where do we go when he comes?

Just hurry!

Here he comes!

Everyone's disappeared. My daughter—and where is my son? But I'm still in my underwear, sorting my baggage. What do I do? Get dressed or finish my packing? What about my daughter's things?

Suddenly I saw movement through the doorway and when I turned my head, I saw the man inspecting the open suitcases.

He stood silently staring down at people's possessions; a spectral sight, a pure white albino man wrapped from foot to head in porous gauze tied in a knot at the crown of his white hair.

I couldn't move for the wonder of it; like an albino deer, vulnerable and rare, yet he holds the power to determine my fate.

All was still. He did not move within this suspended time while I watched and anticipated our possible encounter. What would happen to me if he caught me looking at him? Now I know why he doesn't want to be seen. Not only is he vulnerable to nature's plagues, but he who passes judgment on others must hide his imperfection.

The sight stunned me. Finally, when I inhaled, he turned his salmon stare into my eyes looking directly into his. Then he turned and walked away.

CHAPTER 12

Jan on December 9, 1975

My infrequent office partner Randy King was on break from college and he and I chatted again about life's meanings and responsibilities.

"Your parents must be proud of you."

"Could be. Yes. I've been lucky, and popular, I guess, always, with almost everyone."

"It must help to be so good-looking with your dark hair so properly trimmed. Ever thought of a moustache?

"Tried that once but I thought I looked too menacing and I'd frighten the ladies away."

"Ah yes. You don't want to do that. And there are plenty of "ladies" to choose from in a hospital setting, that's for sure."

"But I stay out of any serious conversations, except maybe for you. I don't want to talk about how I feel. When you invited me to come to the TA weekend last year, I watched others work on their personal problems. You worked on frustrations with your marriage, I remember. Your sexy friend Bea was so shaky and cried a lot. Marge was pragmatic, sardonic, and her mother was sweet, trying to find something wrong with herself to work on, to correct. I passed when it was my turn.

"I could understand why you wouldn't want to risk yourself, especially when you're a budding young executive who might have to be hiring or—" I proposed as a joke, "—firing any of us."

"That won't happen because of me. I like Unitarians. You do neat things together, with your family and with your church. Unlike you liberals, my father was extremely strict. He wanted me to be an athlete, but I couldn't compete with the bigger kids and didn't like to get knocked around in team sports. So, I took up music—piano and guitar. My mother liked that. The kids would tease me. They'd whistle at me. But I'd made them like me by playing in a band. Everyone picked up that the music was cool and then I was cool."

"You are cool. This is interesting. It's quiet today; the phone's not even ringing. We can talk some more."

"Well, the girls started liking me for as long as I can remember, except for my sister, of course. But my best friend was Barry. I liked to be with Barry most of all. We could talk about everything and horse around and wrestle in the leaves and shoot baskets together."

"It's good to have a friend who shares your memories of those days."

"But Barry shot himself late one night after we went to a football game and walked home together."

"Oh, how awful for everyone, especially you when you'd just been with him."

"No one talked about why he did it but I thought a lot about it. I still do."

 What a shock."

"Yes. I guess so. Later I considered going to the seminary and that goal became even a higher priority when I could possibly get drafted and sent to Vietnam. Instead of going to seminary, I tried out the idea of being a hospital administrator."

"That makes sense for all concerned. You have compassion that's rare in business. Hospital administration will be a good match for you."

"I'm happy that you're interested in me as a person, and that we share this office when I'm not at school. You have an intelligent, liberal point of view. You're well-read on hot subjects like open marriage, active in anti-war activities with Another Mother for Peace, a Unitarian, a feminist, and a faithful wife. You see most issues from similar values as mine. I like talking with you. I trust you, Jan."

CHAPTER 13

Jan on January 29, 1976

Under the guidance of Anna Spence, Bea, Marge and I joined her to begin our first Intensive Journal Workshop experience under Ira Progoff with three hundred other people in an auditorium at the University of Chicago campus. The huge size of the crowd was not what I expected nor had experienced before, yet I had my three "sisters" who shared their journals with me openly, deeply and with trust. All this energy focused on Ira Progoff sitting alone on the stage speaking softly, encouraging us to listen to our souls and write down what we hear. All of us would write after he spoke, together yet individually. Sometimes I would hear someone crying.

I worked hard this weekend trying to settle my chaos through the journal experience, to capture the grief, anger and sadness process of my relationship with Alex. Now it's here, written down in a safe place under the guidance of a skilled and innovative mentor who devised this communication mode to help us to reach our deepest feelings.

I wrote this before my workshop trip and left it on Matt and Jenny's beds when I left for Chicago in the afternoon.

Dear Matt and Jenny, too,
Happy Birthday, Matt,

You and Jenny have become such beautiful people, and that's the greatest gift mother could have, a goal achieved, on HER birthday. In the past year, I feel we've become better friends. We talk more, laugh more, and understand each other more. You both are so mature for your years and responsible and fun to be with. You are creative and intelligent. What more could a mother want?

Happy Birthday, dear Matt, and we will celebrate your birthday when I get home on Sunday evening.

Love,
Mom

Jan on January 30, 1976
At Ira Progroff's Intensive Journal Workshop

Your Journal is registered with and is part of The Personal Growth and Creativity Program of Dialogue House Associates, Inc. 80 East 11th Street, New York, N.Y. 10003

After Progoff teaches, we were to follow his instructions and write our thoughts in one of several divisions and colored sections he has organized for our personal ring binder. His books are available to guide us when we continue our journal writing on our own.

I wrote: My hands are static, yet they tingle like a sleeping muscle coming back to awakening. I am neutral, maybe like a sponge, waiting for the process to begin.

Period Log:
Present period of our life;
Inner quality of my being

I write: I am tired of turbulence after more than four years of loving people and feeling responsible for them in the expectation that someone would love me and feel responsible for me. I wanted to be accepted. I needed to be nurtured and in my wants and needs, I accepted and nurtured many others, selfishly because I wanted it back so badly.

At this point, I have survived emotional turbulence: trauma—from intense love and possible loss of that love, from genuine caring for responsibility and risking the loss of all I am responsible for and from needing people and yet wanting to be free.

Crossroads:

Waking up on a May morning in 1972 and giving myself permission to love others beyond my family.

Working at my newspaper reporting career and getting raves from strangers who didn't really matter. My husband's opinion did, but he was silent.

Boredom with Alex.

Knowing I can be a good professional writer.

Loving, really loving others; euphoric though unrequited love.

Struggling, ever struggling with my need to love another person—a woman? Studying, researching, trying to find my true sexual nature.

Being held back by Marge, who was afraid of me and my love.

Joyful still because I didn't even know what I needed.

Overcome by fear of the potential risk as Bea insisted that I become my true self.

Finally giving in to my love and my nature, my true needs to love a sensitive, soft, creative woman who was also assertive, brash, fun and sometimes frightening in her demands and expectations. Boredom now! Never.

Working and striving in my new career at Lakeshore Medical Center, writing my first journals, having a tumultuous love affair and thriving on my bisexuality. Keeping everybody, especially me— satisfied. Coping with continued anger at home. Being shattered when my husband confronts me about my lover's existence. Fearing for the loss of my children and even my life. Fighting to be me and to know me. Enduring endless hours of grief. Talking. Group therapy. Family counseling. Anger.

Jan on January 31, 1976

I woke up at 7 a.m. on Saturday hearing my first mantra from the night before, "The water flows around me," and I understood that the imagery extension of my first process meditation could be my journey to meet death, my preconceived script of dying at age 93, hit by a train at Monte Carlo while riding in a Mercedes Benz on my way to meet my lover—or I'm with my lover. I feel no fear in the mantra; no fear in the revelation.

After our first dialogue writing exercise, Progroff asked the group to share feelings about their writing, and I eagerly raised my hand. I was the first one asked to speak, and then he surprised me by asking me to read my writing out loud to the group! I took a deep breath and I did it, thinking, "What the hell! I came here to work through my problems and I'll work through it. And who knows who I am here in Chicago." I was as shocked at what I had written and I may have shocked others in the reading. The room, filled with hundreds of strangers, including many nuns and priests who come to Progoff because they can express their innermost thoughts without being compromised, was weighted with quietness as I took a deep breath and began reading.

Intensive Dialogue with Alex

Stepping Stones: Brief focusing statement: where relationship is at this time.

Alex Carnigian is my husband who loves me in his own way and who has suffered terrible hurts because of my needs for independence, creativity and sexuality. He is "good for me" in established ways and he is bad for me as a whole, a growing person.

Alex, you smother me. In your goodness and your expectations for me, you smother me. I know I have taxed you beyond your limits, yet you expand just enough to keep me from bursting the balloon or the bag or the bell jar that closes around me.

List Alex's stepping stones:

1.	I was born in my house on January 27, 1931.
2.	I watched my father's anger at my older siblings as I stayed quietly at my mother's knee.
3.	My father died on my twelfth birthday.
4.	I couldn't cry.
5.	I was a good boy and did what was expected of me.
6.	I went to an Armenian church school for several hours a week.
7.	I had an unfortunate homosexual experience in my early teens. An Armenian boy I knew touched me and it made me feel dirty.
8.	I fell in love with an extrovertive, noisy, brash, creative, confusing girl. She could help me expand my personality.
9.	I was good in high school grades, athletics, and friendships.
10.	I married her and have two beautiful children.
11.	I work extremely hard and am successful.
12.	I am now afraid I am losing all my dreams and expectations.
13.	I am angry.

Alex: I am a quiet, intense man who wants joy and happiness and has worked hard to get it. I deserve it. I want it. I'll do whatever I have to do to make it happen.

Jan: You work at it so hard and it doesn't guarantee anything. You work so hard at keeping me in that "happiness" expectation of yours that you take the joy out of the happiness.

A: I'm good for you and you want to get away from me. You're crazy. You're going to lose everything you have. You make me so angry that I'm seething and wanting to cry out or explode or shake you until you see what you're doing to me and to yourself. You're ruining our marriage. You're the most important person in my life and you're killing me.

J: I'm tired of being responsible for completing all your expectations. I've taken care of you for thirty years and I can't be responsible for your happiness any longer, especially when I've been unhappy about having my needs and dreams and expectations thwarted.

A: You're so unhappy. Fuck you, Jan. You've got everything you want. We've adjusted our lives to fill your schedule. You've got it made. What more do you want?

J: I want to fulfill my responsibilities to my family in joy and acceptance of me as an equal person, and I want to be free to be creative and spontaneous and loving without your restrictions, your shoulds and oughts.

A: Your loving—Yes, you love people all right. You love. I hate what you do when you love. What are Matt and Jenny going to do when they find out how you love? Are you going to tell them, "Fuck you, too?"

J: I have never said that to you or anyone else.

A: But that's what you do—Fuck you, Alex!

J: It always comes down to this, doesn't it? All the good, all the beauty, all the caring and work and hours and years of dedication to the children, to our family—your family especially, change the focus of your vision of me now as one huge cunt. It's so sick, this vision of yours. It's so distorted and out of perspective. And when you're erect and want to use me for sex, you say you love me—yet when your penis touches my cunt, it tells me you hate me. You're violated by touching me, you're blaming me for emasculating you—and you become emasculated. And again, I'm tired of being responsible for you at the cost of my personal needs—and I won't feel responsible for your total self again.

Progroff thanked me and then told me to write down my feelings after reading aloud to the group.

(I'm trembling. My God! What did I say out loud? I want to vomit my lunch. I'm shaking all over. The bitter taste at the back of my throat tastes like semen, which I've never really tasted. Mayonnaise is creamy and choking, gag. Tears flood my glasses. My shoulders ache. My ears pound at hearing the fierce echoes of my angry voice. I feel the vibrations from each person in the room. What are they thinking? What are my friends thinking? Are they embarrassed by me? I am told to write these feelings, and yet I can hardly grasp the pen—I'm calmer now—deep breath, a coolness reaches me through my back and comforts me. Yet the choking feeling is an arid, metallic taste deep in my throat. I'm numb.)

Dialogue Dimension: Personal Sections—Dialogue with Society

Progoff explained the connections to historical unities, those with an inner importance of tradition as in marriage, a family that has a life of its own and social and political roots.

1. Being a Unitarian and a church school leader
2. Being a citizen of the world
3. Being a citizen of the United States of America
4. Montessori

5. Another Mother for Peace
6. Women's Liberation
7. Communicator for Lakeshore Medical Center
8. Lake Michigan viewpoint
9. Self-made woman
10. Armenian ethic

List steps and phases of how this flows through life experiences:

Women's liberation:
1. Photo of me as a five-year-old curly-headed Shirley Temple-style tough kid wearing coveralls standing on Hill Street.
2. Watching my mother's strength and will to survive by earning money with boarders, ironing, and initiating our float business. She was one of two women on the first Goodwill committees with all "those important men." Watching her assert herself with tough carpenters and laughing with them too, after the fuss was over. My father was the quiet one by comparison. Mother seemed to be the dynamic family member.
3. She could use every tool. She wore slacks and hired a tailor to sew a pants suit for her. Her movie heroines were strong and assertive: Katherine Hepburn, and Bette Davis. I applied for my Social Security number when I was eleven and then I worked at the zoo and baseball games hawking peanuts and popcorn and Crackerjack. I was responsible for helping put those floats in the parade or to stay at the shop when customers come or to answer the phone.

Later in our university double guest room accommodations, which were Frank Lloyd Wright-like and quite inspiring, Bea and I were bubbling over with affection and respect for each other and for our two friends. When we had gone to visit with Marge and Anna in their room, Anna offered advice as to how I could live a happier life with Alex. When she learned to overlook her husband's faults, he changed and became more responsible in their relationship. While she offered all these tips for a happier marriage, Marge just sat and looked at us.

When Bea and I returned to our room, we said we should no longer be dishonest to our dear friend Anna and we agreed to tell Anna about our love. Returning to their room, our nerves made us giddy and we spilled out to her that she didn't need to give Jan more advice about living with Alex because we two loved each other and that was what was important. She seemed a bit confused, but tenderly accepting. Marge lit another cigarette, thinking we would have another lengthy discussion, but we told Anna that we wanted to be true to her because we knew she would continue loving us. And then we quickly popped out of their room and into ours.

Anna was the first of our friends now to know, other than Marge. It was so good to tell someone who cared about us that we loved each other. I would so have loved to shout our love from the rooftops but it was so dangerous to let others know. Still, despite the danger, more and more people may have had their suspicions confirmed about our feelings for each other.

Depth Dimension: Symbolic Contact—Twilight Imagery Log

Meditation image: I see a spiraling tire of energy gyrating toward me, rotating to a center axis that I enter. I see an eye, smoking red shoulders, and a strong torso. The eye opens and I enter its center blackness. I'm in a room organizing character sketches on bulletin boards, characters are there in transparent forms and shapes, illusions. I am inside the spiraling gyroscope now and its ribs are spinning around me as I walk quietly in the whirling tunnel toward the red light in the spiral's eye.

Depth Dimension: Symbolic Contact—
Inner Wisdom Dialogue

Progoff explained Wisdom and expressions of and/or persons who represent wisdom. I listed:

Siddhartha by Herman Hesse
Bea
Marge
Fran
Maslow
Carson McCullers
Edna St. Vincent Millay
Simone de Beauvoir
Emerson: Divinity school address on Self-Reliance
Whitman: Oneself I sing, a separate single song,
    Yet utter the word, "En Masse."

Dialogue with Walt Whitman

Jan: You have touched me with your words, Walt Whitman, though I haven't read many. They are sources of strength and inspiration that I find when I need them.

"Oneself I sing, a separate single song, Yet utter the word, 'En Masse.'"

I worked and taught under those words as I tried to share the American literary soul to 17-year-olds. The words were on my bulletin board at the Frankfurt American High School in Germany in 1958. They gave me the strength to be myself and the determination to live for a greater good beyond that self.

Walt Whitman: If you cannot be your own person, you have nothing to give to others or to the greater entity. I was subjected to indignity and social punishment because I cared for men. I loved mankind and individuals. I dressed the soldiers' wounds during the Civil War and I gave myself to their needs. The agony of my soul is in the words I used to capture this grief. But those words were subject to neglect, to stifling, to oblivion because readers and publishers read them through homophobic eyes.

J: I really didn't know about them until your words jumped off the textbook pages to find me. In 1967 or 8, when I was especially lonely, I discovered the words to the Beatles' "Eleanor Rigby" song. "All the lonely people, where do they all come from? All the lonely people, where do they all belong?"

I began working on a church school worship service about loneliness. It was winter. March is a bad month for housebound people like I used to be. I looked through my hymnbook for responsive readings and I found your words. This is how I remember them:

"Whoever you are, you are he or she for whom the universe was made. You are the sun and the moon and the stars. You are the center. You are important. You are worthy. You are good."

Your words gave me strength as a single, separate person. The impact of words on others was revealed again to me, and I so much desire to have the skill and time to create inspiring words to share with other human beings.

WW: Why don't you do it? You can, you know.

J: I'm afraid of what it will cost me in family, in reputation, in security. You lost your family love because of your honest revelations of yourself and you were an outcast and very much alone. You lived a long life.

Were you glad you did what you did?

WW: My life is even longer now because of what I did. I am an identity to lost and lonely people. I am an inspiration to others. I am a voice of the heart of America and a voice from the soul of all people. If I were lonely and alone when I lived, if I were subject to neglect and abuse by those whose rules were rigid and narrow, I would have been more than compensated in being able to be close to people like you now.

Jan on February 9, 1976

I came home to a quiet reception. O.K. I needed peacefulness. In the morning, I talked with Alex, Matt and Jenny, showed them my Journal and said it was vitally important to me to be able to express my innermost feelings in it and could do so only if I knew only my eyes would read it. Both Matt and Jenny understood and said so. Alex was silent.

Alex has been especially non-communicative. I vow I'll never speak with him if I have to ask another question to make conversation. He's threatened and jealous again: of my friends, of Bea, of me and my accomplishments, and now—of my journal. I came home from work and resolved to drink only one martini, maybe two small ones. But by the time supper made it to the table, I was into my third large one, plus one glass of wine.

Jenny is watching us. Alex is assuming the maternal role, trying to compensate and, perhaps, competing, so when he kicks me out, she'll stay with him. These games make me sick.

Work was intense, productive and rewarding.

My hand hurts from all this journal writing.

I'm washing clothes and trying to think how I can write something positive about crusty, dirty socks.

Jan on March 26, 1976

I'm almost working full-time as Lakeshore Med's publications editor. When I started this part-time job, I was only to do a little four-page printed quarterly newsletter with photos that I'd take to be mailed to community leaders, board members, volunteers and employees. I learned a lot about designing and writing to fit the space.

The job grew when I started writing a bi-weekly newsletter for employees that would be distributed from a box near the time punch card racks. I never missed a newsletter deadline. Administrative secretaries would help type a finished copy in columns after Randy and/or other relevant executives reviewed and approved the material. Then I'd stick the articles in two columns on stationery-sized paper and jog down the hall and use the copy machine to duplicate enough to circulate. The newsletter was well read: I seldom found leftover copies in its distribution box.

The job and responsibilities have expanded. They trusted me to do my first annual report, I fend off the media unless it was a good story; then I could be aggressive in promoting it. I'm affirmed in doing this excellent work in a stimulating, rewarding profession.

But it seems that my hospital is in trouble. The union is negotiating a new contract but nothing's being settled. Lakeshore needs to expand and provide more parking spaces. The newly built hospital competition, St. Agnes, is now on acres for parking, single rooms and close to expanding new neighborhoods. Lakeshore Med has a view of Lake Michigan. Its neighbors are afraid my hospital wants to demolish its heritage neighborhood with its historic old school to the west or demolish houses to the east and north.

During this entire time, Randy King and I share an office with other administrative interns who come and go, but we stay on. For a while, he went back to school to get his master's degree. But for many months, we've become close friends and confidantes without my revealing the intimate details of my relationship with Bea. Marge is also involved with me at work and we share every lunch, work chatter and major problems. It's clear to everyone that we are best friends as close as sisters and I'm surrounded by positive and happy people who appreciate me. And I'm thriving as the champion of first-class Lakeshore Medical Center's staff, employees and the patients they serve.

CHAPTER 14

Anna Spencer on April 2, 1976

My son Alan introduced me to Ira Progroff's Intensive Journal Workshops and I took his suggestion and went to my first one with Jan, Marge and Bea last February in Chicago. I've been writing fanatically in my journal ever since, crying over my pages in my bedroom, remembering painful memories of the loss of my mother and the sexual abuse by my father who told me I was the eldest daughter and therefore was to take my mother's place. I'm suffering now with the present, my husband, my concerns about my growing-to-adulthood children, and my internal pain.

My second Intensive Journal Workshop with Ira Progroff is in this contemplative, monastic setting at St. Francis Seminary. Jan is here too. Her Alex and Jenny drove up to Door County together. She and I drove here in separate cars and are pretty much on our own. We have separate, single, humble rooms quite apart from each other and surrounded primarily by friendly and peaceful Catholic nuns and priests who can release their emotional qualms on the secret pages of their journals.

What a privilege to be here with this master, just as I have followed the teaching of Krishnamurti and have been in his inspiring presence.

Jan and I did walk together on a warm afternoon before chapel service. She remembers me as a teenager that she admired, and she remembers my being so serious all the time. I remember her beautiful mother and wonderful father who made me feel so worthy. When they came into our tavern, they treated my Italian family as if we were equal to theirs. So friendly, so accepting.

Now it's my turn to be accepting of Jan and Bea and their relationship. Of course, I love them both, but I guess I'm too naive to understand—but accepting, of course. Jan was able to speak openly to me about their situation.

"Jan, you are the most authentic person I know."

"Dearest Anna. How can you say that when it was only last month that Bea and I told you our secret that we are lovers? We've been hiding that from you and the world for two years."

"Yes, but you did tell me—and I trust you, love, and respect you as I always have. I only wish I could experience the deep love that you two must have for each other."

"And I love you, Anna. You are truly the most wonderful person."

Jan on April 3, 1976
Workshop Dialogue with Alex

Jan: Alex, I am authentic with everyone else. Why am I not authentic with you?

Alex: Yes. Why aren't you when I'm the one who really loves you and married you and provided for you?

J: You also set up a role for me and you've forced me to follow it until I could do no more. So, you're stuck with a robot that completes your expectation of me and I will play that role until the time runs out, whenever that may be.

A: Great. And what am I supposed to do then?

J: Frankly, my dear, "I don't give a damn!" But yes, I really do. I would like you to fall in love with someone else where you can start over and be happy. I would like to be your friend then and share your authentic feelings and joys. We've never talked about those feelings, you know.

Workshop Dialogue with Bea

Jan: Bea, I've just had a mantra meditation that I'd like to explore with you. It was a flash of imagery where we were standing before your apartment door. Big and white, the door was open toward us and we didn't know who or how or why it got that way. It was daylight. No emotional feeling was identifiable. I was the first to discover the open door; you followed me.

Bea: I always let you go first. You decide. You go first.

J: You say that, but you influence decisions in other ways, and if I make the wrong one, then you won't have to feel responsible. That makes me feel the responsibility of maintaining our relationship. Sometimes it can be a burden, but I need you and I do what I must to have your love, so I assume that responsibility.

B: You are the one who has to call the shots. I am not able to call you at will or to see you at home or be with you when I like. It's up to you to decide. You know when you have to go back, what you have to face. I can't tell you what to do.

J: What do you want me to do?

B: You won't like this, but I want you to live with me. I want to love you every day. I want to wake up with you and feel you shudder when I kiss you. I want you now—emotionally—yet intellectually I say no. But I'm changing.

J: I know and I want to do all this too, yet I can't desert my children. I won't. I won't leave Jenny as I was left.

B: You can't compare Jenny's life to yours.

J: I could have told people that my mother's not around because she's crazy. That's a lot easier than Jenny could say—that her mother's not around because she's a lesbian.

B: That's truly sad. Crazy is more acceptable than love.

J: Do you think we'll cross through that door together? Will I take you by the hand and pull? Will you push? Will we open it wider and walk through it together?

B: I want to now. I am so lonely.

J: I'm afraid you won't last long enough to wait for me to make the decision. But if you can wait, I know we will go together. And we can be happy. I'm really dreaming about a home for us—some quiet place where we can enjoy more a life together but where we can create beauty and poetry and songs and the widest of a spectrum of experiences and adventure. But I am afraid you can't wait and in your brashness and anger and impatience, you toss me up and down your emotional ladder. And that makes me more afraid to join my life with yours. It's a vicious circle in every way. Can't you celebrate what we have together instead of suffering over what is missing?

B: Jan. I'm jealous of you, your family, your home, your job, your respectability. You have it all and I have nothing. I'd like to trade places with you for only one day. Then you'd see how lonely it is for me.

J: Why don't you trade that loneliness for solitude? Why don't you paint or write? Use the time for something besides getting wiped out on alcohol!

B: You drink as much as I do. So does Marge. We're all alcoholics together.

J: At the risk of sounding phony, I think I can live without booze. I don't consume it like you do to drown your empty hours. I consume it to deaden my time away from you or from my work.

B: Do you think if we lived together, we would drink ourselves to death?

J: That thought has crossed my mind. It is a concern. Honestly, I love you, but I don't want to risk my children's love to move in with an alcoholic, yet I feel that if I do live with you we, together, will drink less because we will be happier.

B: I can't guarantee that.

J: Happiness cannot be guaranteed.

Jan on April 4, 1976

During a guided meditation led by Progoff, a fly was buzzing within the framework of a windowpane trying to reach for the light, the sun. It made a lot of noise and then rested for a second on the windowpane molding. I was dizzy when I closed my eyes and my heart was heavy. The open window welcomed pollen from the budding trees and I took an allergy pill before I opened my mind to record my impression at this quiet time.

All you need to do, Jan, is fly over the barrier. Just fly over the edge—risk it and be free.

I then found peace.

Jan's dialogue with Edna St. Vincent Millay (1892-1950)

Jan: Two books that I once bought at an estate sale "fell off" my bookshelves one day in the midst of my first journal writings. They were yours, Edna St. Vincent Millay. They were yours, and I sensed I'd discovered myself in them. I couldn't believe my eyes and my heart when I read your poems.

Your religious pantheism rang in my heart. I too would and do "spread the grass apart to put my finger on your (the earth's) heart."

Your openness to all experiences which "lay like a sword" between you and your husband. I share that.

Your tender love of a woman touched me where I live because I share that too. And your raging anger at the loss of that woman through death made me see the value of loving each day before a similar tragedy in my life would occur.

You too found a "night sister" who saved you from drowning. "What man would come out from a warm cottage on such a cold and dreary night to rescue me."

And you too took up causes, defending the underdog and opening yourself to public criticism.

Edna St. Vincent Millay: I am happy my words live on to touch others like you. I was childless, so hearing your appreciation and your connections helped me appreciate some immortality.

J: I was comforted by the fact that you've experienced many of the same traumas I have and survived. Yet your joyful self has always been shaded by anticipation of dread or loss, or grief. Were you ever happy?

ESVM: I think I reached contentment in later years living with my husband. But the euphoria of my youth is only a memory. One cannot sustain that forever, you know.

J: Your husband stayed with you through your lovers and the turmoil of those loves. He devoted his life to you and nurtured your creative spirit. Did you truly love him?

ESVM: My love for him was like loving a kind parent. I was devoted to him for enduring me and my emotional jaunts into peaks and valleys of experience. I never had a passion for him, though, except when I had it for others at the same time. Then I could embrace the world with love and passion.

J: How did you feel about loving women? You only hint about that. I would like to know more about that—for my own sake.

ESVM: Creativity is a fragile thing. Like the ego, it can easily be broken. I found a friend to share and to risk creating with and it was the ultimate sharing of my soul that gave me power to go on. I have faulted myself, and others have too, for using my love and lovers as creative sources, but what I found was so universally beautiful and meaningful that I was driven to tell the world. The tragedy comes, however, that you either burn yourself out or others do it for you. You need a resting place, a loving place to rebuild yourself—a safe harbor. My husband gave me physical safety and peace, but my friend gave me renewal and joy.

J: What did you give to them?

ESVM: Don't make me feel guilty. I hope I returned the exhilaration of life and love and beauty, but maybe I was a leech, too, sucking their spirits from them. I desperately hope not. How can my creativity hurt others?

J: I wish I knew how to avoid this for myself. I am afraid it will. Creativity will either hurt my lover and/or my family or it will kill me.

ESVM: I hope you find peace.

J: Thank you.

ESVM: No! May you find turmoil to generate the creativity that is in you to do the things and say the words that you must say. Peace will come long enough when you die.

J: My skin feels the soft breeze from the blue gray sky
of the open window. I love you, Bea.
I feel your breath in waves upon my face,
so soft, so even, just as I am breathing now,
peaceful and quiet pulses in rhythm,
close and warm, at rest.
The weight of days and weeks are leaving me.
Now I feel my throat choke with anticipation
of what may happen.
A white streak appears across my horizon.

Jan on April 5, 1976

Starting this beautiful Progoff day laughing with nuns at breakfast and waiting for more inner experience.

Everything will be all right. It's time to start a new life. The open door awaits me. I am me. I am strong. I am good. I am whole. I am me.

Love brings joyful turmoil followed by deep peace. Love brings stormy turbulence followed by quiet calm. The contrast is life. Life is love. Love is life.

I have had romantic love for two women. One spring morning in 1972, I awoke and realized that I was in love with Marge Manley and I overcame the fear and plunged in to explore the depths of this new feeling. My body leapt out of bed and I sensed that not only was a feeling ten feet tall, but I was weightless as if my feet were not even touching the ground.

Even after she dismissed my intense emotions to that of close friendship, my perceptions expanded because of what I experienced inside of me. It made my skin stretch, and my arms reached out to grasp fully all that was good and warm and soft and accepting—to embrace, to spin life around in my arms, to dance with the incredible inner joy of my transcending self.

Everything seemed larger, brighter, clearer, grander. The smallest things stood waiting to be observed. My eyes were opened and my senses expanded to the entire experience of life.

Connections with Stepping Stones

Bea Lindberg was to join others who saw my joy, but she returned that love in kind. It is so rich to be loved back. I sense others' curious smiles of acceptance and curiosity. They want to know my secret. They want to have what I have.

When I say, "Love people," they do not perceive it. They do not understand love. Each has a reference that clouds the word and the feeling. They may be jealous of my joyful nature because it doesn't originate from them, because my joy expands my life with others, because it fractures the secure foundation of a shaky structure. Others may be jealous because they want to have the same spirit and when it won't enter them, because of obstructions and barriers, those people get depressed instead.

Another may want to keep my love exclusively, to cut the bloom to keep for himself—only to let the love that I had for him die now in the vase in an empty room.

Others may be confused. My children can't understand my euphoric nature and are afraid I won't contain myself within their frame of reference. If they could only understand and accept the concept that love grows and multiplies at each loving encounter.

There are no limits. In an expansive environment, there are no boundaries, no shortages. But if love has to struggle to be, it may shrivel up and die in the frustrated waste of its energy.

Since love has entered my life, I have been pushed and pulled by incredible emotional turmoil. The strong, positive euphoric, creative flying creature that I was, and hopefully can be again, has been blasted in full flight with feathers flying.

My glass's frames glide like wings of my plane, their gyroscope pressure weighs upon my ears. Eyes closed, I move through space, the flying creature that I am. Flying creature? I'm not sure. My wings strain for flight yet snake me through close, tunnel coils of air, empty, cold, damp and dark. Uncertain of my form and goal, flying creature, am I a bat?

Startled and seeking for light, I sail up through a transom wedge of whiteness in a shadowed hall, blinded by the ceramic shine of a bare-bulbed bathroom's glossy glare. Flying creature, where am I?

Within this space, two fixtures stand side by side, one a used urinal, and one a disconnected toilet filled beyond the rim with flowers. My children enter with a basket. Fly down now to meet their needs! Tiny people, they wait naked at the rim of a vast tub and slip on the cold, hard slope to slide without control towards the whirlpool drain.

A voice resounds, "Every child needs help!"

The flying creature that I was turns to face the voice and sees a giant's radiant nose that glows amid an archaic beard and burning eyes, their staring melts other flaming features. A cannon shell-cased headpiece now evolves from the urinal image to become a chessman's bishop with an iron mesh mask protecting all but the bishop's eyes burning with electric shock waves from their source.

"Flying creature, fused by heat. Break that spell!"

And break I did with power enough to shatter the heavy monument that now lies hollow on the floor. Nothing's inside; no one is hurt!

Fearful imaginings take flight and free my soul to sing its song as my swinging strength beats on a gong and I bang bat, bong in celebration, striking a tumultuous noise so loud it can also crack the earth.

CHAPTER 15

Jan on April 7, 1976

I was a senior at Roosevelt High when Ray Schuster was a skinny little sophomore with black curly hair. Later he graduated from law school to join his parents' firm. With Dan Becker, the Local 100—Hospital Employees Union's chief negotiator in Milwaukee, Schuster offered to represent the Lakeshore Med's bargaining unit in their negotiations with the hospital.

Schuster is a powerful man with a mixed reputation. His tactics and those of his friend Jack Porter, executive director of the Lakeshore Bay Teachers Association, have been either fanatically followed or adamantly criticized. In addition to being the chief negotiator for Lakeshore Med's service employees, he is the legal advisor for the teacher's union and he represents policemen, firefighters, municipal workers and the boilermakers at a major foundry who's CEO is also the chairman of Lakeshore Medical Center's Board of Directors.

Randy and Marge are two members of Lakeshore Med's negotiating team of five. I don't think Marge says much during the meetings and concentrates on taking notes.

From Lakeshore Med's minutes of negotiations on April 7, Schuster claimed that because of the insignificant number of employees, the hospital was not able to maintain a standard of cleanliness and was at the point of being "filthy."

In a dramatic gesture, he threw a container of dead cockroaches on the bargaining table to emphasize the lack of a proper staff, claiming that those insects were found in the surgical units. Though everyone recoiled, most realized that those cockroaches could have come from anywhere. Schuster said that he did not want to put anyone on the spot, but there was discontent in every department.

Jan on April 24, 1976

Hospital proposals and union counter proposals are being presented without progress. In fact, meetings have been postponed because Schuster fails to appear. A federal mediator wanted to start its fact-finding but Schuster refused to comply and was neither in his office nor attending other negotiations. Hospital management is frustrated by outrageous charges made by Schuster and by legal restraints and untested laws affecting hospital strikes. Communication problems were often centered on what not to say because of the uncertainties of Section 8/G of the Taft-Hartley Act.

Bay View Times on April 30, 1976

"Lakeshore Medical Center and representatives of the Hospital Employee Local 100 have scheduled a negotiation session for 10 a.m., Saturday.

"The union's existing two-year contract expires at midnight tonight. Local 100 represents about 250 service and maintenance employees, including personnel in laundry, kitchen, housekeeping, stockroom and nurse aides, ward clerks and orderlies, and central service sterilizing personnel…No strike date has been set…Sources indicate that the union is still demanding more than a 100 percent increase in wages over a three-year period…Ray Schuster, the union's chief negotiator, has said, 'We've taken the position that the minimum wage at Lakeshore Medical Center should be $4.50 because we want to start bringing these rates up to where people can live on them."

"Bart Biggs, Local 100 chief steward, Friday said no strike vote has been taken."

WLBN Radio transcription dated May 18, 1976

"Employees of Lakeshore Medical Center staged an extended coffee break to hear some remarks from their labor attorney Ray Schuster this afternoon. The wildcat strike was about fifteen percent of their membership, further breaching relations between both groups. All reported back to work and no other difficulties were reported.

"A letter from the union to the hospital indicates formally that the union intends to strike on the 24th of May. Earlier, they had indicated it would be on Tuesday, May 11, but the hospital had questioned the legality of the notification of a strike. Negotiations are scheduled to resume in that labor dispute Tuesday before a federal mediator. Nick Dixon, executive vice president of Lakeshore Medical Center said, "We're willing to sit down and continue negotiations.

"Personnel Director Andrew Anderson: 'We have just been informed that there are two telegrams at the office that indicate that all bets are off and he (Schuster) intends to strike whenever he chooses. We are still hopeful that a Federal mediation conciliation service meeting scheduled for 3 p.m. on Tuesday will pave the way toward a successful negotiation for a three-year agreement. In the meantime, the management of the hospital will continue to work to the end of continuing excellent patient care and uninterrupted employment.'

"AFL-CIO Local 100 attorney Ray Schuster told media that the union will meet Tuesday, but the walkout could occur anytime and Schuster told why.

"Schuster: 'We informed the hospital that we will go to the negotiation session on Tuesday and if progress ceases, that we will definitely walk out Tuesday. The reasons are that they have physically threatened the shop steward and told him to get protection when he walks in the community. They are also intimidating other employees and are stocking tremendous amounts of materials in violation of the law. They have unilaterally changed the contract. They are operating as predators and the union can no longer allow that to happen.'"

Jan on May 22, 1976

Today five Central Service employees engaged in a sit-down strike for approximately one hour. These employees are responsible for the sterilization and wrapping of medical equipment and supplies used in surgery, in the delivery rooms, and in "positive culture" results when tests on equipment from the steam sterilizer show the existence of bacteria in a load of sterilized materials. Corrective measures are taken when positive cultures are discovered.

During the week of May 17, an abnormally high number of positive cultures were recorded. The supervisor also discovered that the ink cartridge on one sterilizer was put in backward. She discovered the next day that the cartridge on the same sterilizer was bent.

The supervisor prepared a letter and read it to his staff, expressing his concern about possible tampering with equipment. After he left, five employees engaged in the sit-down action. During this hour, employees did not supply orders, answer the phone, or sterilize equipment.

Helen Vanik, my neighbor across the street from the back of our house—and a union steward, was one of the leaders in the sit-down strike.

On TV news programs out of Milwaukee, Schuster was quoted as saying, "We need more people to keep the place clean. We have cockroaches and millipedes because the place is filthy. There are not enough people to keep it clean. One of our demands is that they hire more people.

The next segment shows Personnel Director and the hospital's chief negotiator Andrew Anderson answering the reporter's questions saying, "Several months ago, we had some problems, but we've since hired a new exterminator and we think we have the problem licked." Ugh! Why did he say that? His only knowledge of this came from a casual joke made during a coffee break with other hospital managers months ago.

When we heard his response, I set up Randy to explain to the reporter that all public buildings need pest control and that the change in exterminators was not because of cockroaches but because "the company did not perform according to our standards, and we fired him."

The TV men took no time to analyze this and did not edit out Anderson's statement. They chose to televise Schuster's reckless tactics.

How can you prove your institution is sanitary? No one seemed interested in this. I distributed disclaimers from a State nursing inspector who had been at the hospital two weeks before. But Schuster's inflammatory slurs made the headlines.

Lakeshore Labor Weekly, a powerful weekly union tabloid that began publishing during Lakeshore Bay's turbulent labor conflicts in the 1920s and 30s when our city was labeled "Little Moscow," isn't held to the objectivity that *Bay View Times* reporters are pledged to maintain. Its inflammatory headlines and sarcastic bias created more fuel to heat up not only both sides of the hospital conflict, but other unions: the teachers, firefighters, municipal workers, and police against the needs of the community: patients, doctors, employers, other hospitals and nursing homes in the state, the neighbors and the residents of Lakeshore Bay.

Fifteen or more department managers and the volunteer director met late this Saturday afternoon as in a war room, checking each department manager's plan of offense and/or defense against the inevitable strike of the laundry, kitchen, housekeeping, stockroom, nurse aides, ward clerks, orderlies, and surgical sterilizing staffs.

They described who will do those jobs and how and which functions have the highest priorities.

Coming around the table full circle, our esteemed CEO Clark Young turned to me, sitting right behind his shoulder, and, as if I were the hospital's cheerleader, he asked me what I would do? Of course, I've been informing the media of our facts and have been tracking all of their coverage, administrative and union communications, and posting them on the bulletin board and I would continue to do that.

I figured the strike would last only five days or a week at best. Unlike the others reporting around the boardroom table, I stood up to verbally salute their efforts, and with a rousing speech to rally all our forces, I promised, without conferring with Randy, now my boss, that I would print a daily newsletter on what is truthfully happening and on the progress of the strike.

The meeting ended and we're ready to take on whatever needed to be done. Those of us inside the hospital were inspired and united.

Jan on May 24, 1976

I've been striving to keep my family happy, responding to the media and co-workers on Lakeshore Bay's pending strike, and keeping Bea confident that I'll be available for her too. My workload is chaotic and I can arrange to be with her for only an hour or two. I would accomplish a day's work in six hours so we could be together until I had to return home to make supper and spend time with my family.

Alex hates my total commitment to the hospital and demands my time in empty togetherness. He's especially angry that I won't take off to go to Door County with Var and Sona for a week. Go! I'm happy to be free of his disapproving drain on my energy. My priority time away from work needs to be spent in peace. How can he forget those years when he worked eighty to one-hundred hours a week and left me home alone with Matt and Jenny when they were toddlers—and I was pregnant as well? He, of all people, should understand how important it is to be a part of such an important mission, a crusade where I'm working ten to sixteen hours almost every day and staying close to home.

They want me home but they can't stand my doing anything else but care for them. It's the same dumb program going around again and again. Except that I feel closer to my stronger self than before. I know that after this strike is finished, I can and will be the best PR director any hospital can have. And I'll continue to love people, even with the fear of being hurt again. I will be more wary, but what I will be primarily wary of is feeling responsible for those who expect me to make them feel good. They must be responsible for that.

Bea's birthday was close to home and I took her to the trendiest country roadhouse in the area, The Auctioneer's Inn. Antique auctioneer and collector Col. Helen Docker decorated her century-old wooden saloon with all her treasures, among them a framed *Bay View Times* article when I wrote about her years ago. That was the least of her décor that included a year-round Christmas tree.

Our reservation was at 9 p.m., but we arrived a bit early and drank from huge martini glasses in a most romantic setting on a sofa in front of the toasty fireplace. We placed our order and when we got to our table we saw all the couples, women and men enjoying themselves in this classy rendezvous.

We ate with little conversation—two women celebrating a birthday on a Saturday night. I think that Bea's mind clicked into her anxiety about us. Where is she without a man and why isn't she drinking wine and eating steak and lobster with a man instead of a woman? And why must she feel like a lesbian? Or whatever else goes on in her mind. Within the difference of one course in the meal, she turned into a surprisingly cruel dinner partner. She became snappy and irritable until I insisted that she stop this meanness. My stomach retched and I almost threw up. But I didn't lose control. I paid for the expensive, joyless meal and drove in silence for the half hour drive in the dark night to her apartment.

This morning, without explanation for last night's stunning eruption, she told me all the details of our church school program and how it was "a stupendous success." Somehow, without explanation, we were supposed to be okay again. She went to church school and I spent several hours at work. Early that afternoon, we met at her apartment and fell asleep with healing embraces to ease our stresses from the world beyond us.

Jan on May 25, 1976

At the 3:30 p.m. shift change in time for the evening TV news, pickets assembled with makeshift signs to march in front of my hospital—and the Milwaukee TV cameras. The entire day was as chaotic as this 3:30 scene with newspapers and radio stations calling me with their repeated queries, our meetings, and my name being paged repeatedly on the hospital's intercom.

At about 5 p.m., the picketers quieted down; the camera had disappeared for the day and I started writing my first daily newsletter. I called it "May 25" in a 78-point bold Helvetica press-down type that I could change to a new date every day of the strike. Its sub-title is in 16-point Helvetica: "employee/patient information." Randy King would be my chief contact to approve my copy before I typed it on an electric typewriter that appeared in my office.

I'd taken notes from Saturday's meeting, my resource for my first newsletter. I finished at about 10:30 p.m. and hand-carried the issue, still warm from the copy machine, to my time clock locations and nursing stations around the hospital. Administrators, nursing supervisors, and department heads circled through the hospital and when I handed them my first printed news bulletin, they seemed especially appreciative about having some communication that would keep them informed. In addition to questions answered and an information center phone number, my report included a paragraph on how each department would be maintained and who would be involved. Dietitians would join with food service supervisors to fill daily menus and special diets. School of Nursing faculty and students have completed their school year and will add their skills to nursing needs. Pinkerton guards are on duty. Non-patient care employees will cover various areas determined by a personnel pool. Auxiliary and Red Coat volunteers will continue to support and serve the hospital. Retired nurses began preparing sterile surgical supplies. Other employees joined the volunteers to help. Doctors' wives are cleaning rooms—even scrubbing the toilets.

In a finishing note, I requested calls to my office with news items, exceptional employee and volunteer contributions and patient comments.

With our city's history of labor conflict that I remember from my youth and from my parents' involvement in helping to promote unions and their causes, I never considered crossing a picket line.

After working fourteen hours, I left Lakeshore through the double row of pickets and pressed on toward home where I tried to rest, but my mind was too stirred up to sleep.

Is integrity valid only on one side or another? What cost does one pay for fear and intimidation? How does one stand up for what is right? Does it take strength to say no? Does it hurt to say yes? What forces push against each individual in a group? Does the group say yea and where does one say nay? Who will listen when power or crowds jeer? How could this all have been avoided? There are no easy answers.

In other newsletters, I wrote:

"'Make me proud,' was written in smudged letters on a picketer's sign. Anyone reading this would know that no one could make another proud. That picketer is already proud, and rightfully so, after twenty-plus years of dedicated service, of new babies born, or of patients nurtured here in the heartbeat of the hospital. Somehow 'making me,' doesn't do it. Somehow 'making me' can't be done.

"People working, people striving, people doing what is right, what is needed, what is going to bring us together again will make us all proud."

CHAPTER 16

"Strike! They did it."

"They followed that charismatic man, the Pied Piper who promised them dignity with money. The man who piped his tune and led them down the path was like the naive children of Hamlin when the town leaders wouldn't pay him what he asked. How could he promise dignity and money? How could he risk their security and goals? How could they follow and leave behind them the job they needed, the future they worked for, and the patients they cared for? There was due process. There were laws. Perhaps too many laws to understand. There were sides, drawn in twos at first, then in threes. Intrigue. Complications. Litigations. Injunctions. Attorneys talking. Understanding? It's all legalese."

May 26, 1976

The strikers received a letter from their Local 100 President Dan Becker yesterday telling them that the hospital's offer is the "best non-profit hospital contract in Local 100." He warned them not to continue the strike and asked them to vote on the enclosed secret ballot and mail it in the enclosed envelope to the office of federal mediators in Milwaukee.

Then Becker took off on a two-week vacation to England.

The letter reached the hospital through one of our union sympathizers, and we are all overjoyed by the news and expect the strike to be settled soon. I scurried to every bulletin board posting the letter with high hopes of a reasonable and quick conclusion to this tense situation. It proved it was an open breach between the official union and Schuster with the hospital in the middle. Our hope for a settlement faded by the end of the day when we heard that the strikers disenfranchised themselves from the union and turned their ballots over to Schuster and Biggs in a mass meeting where all the members' ballots were collected.

Becker's letter made news and my newsletters have become unofficial media releases. Photographers and reporters come to affirm the good work that continues at the hospital. Our hospital census is high. Two doctors volunteered to be O.R. scrub nurses if needed.

May 27, 1976

I'm careful not to antagonize the strikers while I'm crediting our employees and volunteers, but sometimes I quote my sources to show how volatile the situation is. One striker helped an out-patient out of a car to enter the hospital and that was mentioned, but our switchboard operator reported that they've received abusive calls "... nothing significant and probably due to the letter sent to employees from the 100 Union president."

I try when I can to use the humor that the staff brings to me rather than hostility. We all need some tension release.

"Chaplains Arthur Boulton and Tom James were delivering linens and sorting laundry. 'Why not?' said Tom. 'Cleanliness is next to Godliness.'"

May 28, 1976

"Harassment of those entering the hospital is increasing, but it isn't preventing people from getting in; it's making them more determined to do so. Meanwhile, free transportation for PM and night shift employees who need it will be arranged by calling the hospital's Hot Line number 4588. Supervisors will be at the entrances to meet you.

"And we should be getting better cooperation from the police now."

May 29, 1976

Picket line harassment continues and our confidence in the police and rescue squad members is cause for great concern. Schuster represents both of their unions. Would police protect those who cross the picket lines? Would the rescue squads cross picket lines to get patients to the ER?

Nighttime activities are increasing with violence always an oppressive possibility. Schuster also represents members of the boilermakers union, who were also on strike from the company managed by our Lakeshore Med's Board of Directors president. They join the night picketers when the shift changes at 11 p.m. Many picketers are rowdy and intoxicated.

Settlements are blocked. Injunctions, restraining orders and unfair labor charges continue. The assignment now is to sustain the morale of non-striking employees who work extremely long hours doing many tasks, volunteers who ignore harassment to help the hospital in every way, and patients and their visitors who are part of our united effort to endure and to win this struggle.

May 31, 1976

"On this Memorial Day, let us take time to remember the traditions we are sustaining with our commitment to this hospital and its patients. One hundred years ago this September, the cornerstone of Lakeshore Bay's first hospital building was laid here, and for even more than those one hundred years, dedicated people, as founders and volunteers and as loyal and selfless employees, have provided patient care for the people of Lakeshore Bay. No one has been turned away from this community hospital that cares for people and their needs, whatever those needs may be…"

An Auxiliary volunteer was running from her car to the front entrance when a picketer shouted, "Don't be afraid. We won't hurt you."

"I'm not afraid of you. But I'm late for work."

"…Dr. Bob Stewart volunteered to help in any way. He said that in the labor movement, 'scab' is a degrading word, perhaps the worse label labor can use on people who oppose them. However, in medicine, a scab is Nature's way of protecting a wound. A scab helps to heal wounds. And I'll be a scab if I'm needed to help heal these wounds at Lakeshore."

June 1, 1976
"Union Wage Increases Show on Thursday's Paychecks"

"The hospital decided that union members who have worked since Sunday, May 23, will see an increase in Thursday's paycheck, a 12% raise or no less than 35 cents an hour. Union members who resigned from the union and returned to work will not have to pay the group health insurance premiums to cover them for June, a savings of $30.66 for Single coverage and $80.60 for Family, though they must still have $14.50 deducted for his or her portion of the Family plan.

"Note:" reads the newsletter, "This is a monthly payment. The rumor that this is a once-in-a-year payment is false. The hospital pays these amounts for each employee every month as part of Lakeshore Med's benefits program."

This is a brief example of how careful I have to be in interviewing, writing, and checking all these details. I hope I don't goof up on anything.

Randy made arrangements for me to have access to administrative secretaries so they can type the newsletters when they're here. That takes some pressure off of me.

I've been quoted almost every day in *Bay View Times*, but I work hard to get others to speak to the media in case they ask questions I can't answer because I don't know what's going on behind closed doors. And I have to remain calm and happy to set an example.

June 2, 1976

Another day and it still goes on. There's no one representing the bargaining unit members to settle the strike. Schuster phoned Randy and said there was no reason to meet if Lakeshore wasn't going to give them what they wanted.

Dan Becker, the union's president won't return from England until June 7th. The federal mediator must decide when future meetings will be held. Meanwhile, I wrote about the background of all this and warned that striking employees' lapse in insurance coverage will be costly for them.

I found out that the strikers wait for my newsletter to be distributed so they can get copies to learn what's going on.

June 3, 1976

"Rumors, Distorted Misinformation Abound"

"Rumors, conflicting stories, confusion and misinformation keep people off balance, keep them busy reacting to corrections and hinder people from making intelligent decisions. Perhaps the best thing to do if anyone has questions concerning union matters would be to call the Local 100 representative at 453-4998 to double-check on the Schuster/Biggs group's answers."

Even some positive media stories brought stress to the workers and I had to placate and correct misunderstandings without antagonizing the media.

June 4, 1976

As with battle fatigue and shell shock, I moved about as if wounded while returning home to shower, change clothes and go back to work. Yet I was in no condition to produce a complicated explanation of Schuster/Biggs vs. Lakeshore Med vs. the Union. I reached into my office file and printed a "Wally Remembers" column printed four years ago in my Lakeshore Medical Center's Centennial News.

"These 50-year-old memories of Wally's seem especially appropriate now," I wrote. "In one story, he reflected, 'We were a big family in them days. The nurses worked twelve hours a day, but they all seemed to enjoy themselves.'

"In many ways," I summarized, "we are growing into a big family again that is determined to work together toward the important goal of sustaining the quality of patient care that all expect from Lakeshore. Who knows? Perhaps in thirty years, some hospital reporter will interview you about those good old days when times were tough but, to quote Wally, 'They all seemed to enjoy themselves in them days.'"

June 6, 1976

I'd written and approved articles for use in case I was ill or wasn't able to complete my double-sided letter-sized newsletter. On this Saturday and before I could leave my office and return to our UU family picnic at Forest Park on Saturday, I printed quotes from doctors and patient comment cards and started writing for the June 6 newsletter.

"A day or two as Lakeshore Med's newsletter editor"

"The phone rings from a TV station. The newsman asks for confirmation about charges made by Ray Schuster that Lakeshore Medical is not changing patients' linens to conserve the laundry. Sometimes you can't hide the shock you feel at hearing such a gigantic lie. 'OK. Okay,' the reporter said. 'We were just checking.'"

My article proceeds with four other charges and how we refuted them with media coming to film clean linen, floors and food service areas. Sometimes editors would delete our disclaimers and show only the animated Schuster and his scandalous claims. I would accompany all media in the hospital at all times. The security and switchboard operators were alert to page me when they suspected visitors were reporters. Often I would ask for media escort assistance from administrators or nursing supervisors.

"Are you willing to deny…'" repeated one accusing reporter who assumed that we had details we were trying to hide. TV with thirty-second segments would frustrate us, but the press usually took time and space to print details. Reporters got the facts to edit out rumors. We were tested under pressure many times and our hospital and its employees were proven to be a strong team of individuals working together with special and varied skills. This makes the days in the life of a hospital publications director proud days indeed."

CHAPTER 17

June 6, 1976

Bea set up her rented pop-up camper at Forest Park on Friday for our annual church weekend picnic, the Learning Place Olympics and overnights. She had gone with her teacher friends for Friday night "staffing" at their favorite pub, then on to the park to sit around the campfire, talk, drink and play the guitar with UU friends and families. She told me that noisy motorcycle riders kept circling the park, yet she wiped out alone in the trailer for a long sleep.

I joined the group with my family after work on Saturday. We were to sleep in the VW camper after eating supper and singing around the campfire.

Bea played games, even baseball, with the church school kids and teens who would be there on Saturday. She took a long nap through supper but she joined us before dark on a cloudless evening with our campfire sparks flying upward to meet the stars glowing brighter as the night sky became dark indigo. Family groups and teenagers kept coming and going throughout the evening. Three guys were playing guitars and she joined in for two more hours of music and song.

She couldn't hear the nipping and snipping banter that was going on between Marge, Pete, Alex and me. But she could see Alex staring at her while she improvised harmony and attracted attention with her bold melodies. The bottles of wine circled round and round and some of us drank as if to prove we could out-drink them all. Of course, we didn't have to drive to find a bed; all we needed to do was find our partner.

Nick and Diana Dixon, Marge and I seemed to be taking an R&R from our strike battles. I knew I had to go to work again the next day to write and print another newsletter.

Alex grew more sullen, especially after Marge and Pete started teasing him. He doesn't tolerate teasing and was ready to explode. Finally, Bea left the circle. She told me later that she threw up and went to bed. Quantities of that homemade wine to quench your singing thirst will get you every time. Marge and Tommy planned to sleep in Bea's camper, but Bea didn't wait for them.

Alex finished the last drops of wine, threw his empty paper cup into the bonfire, unfolded himself from his camp chair and purposefully stepped toward our van. I supposed he expected me to follow him, but I sat, still chatting with Pete who was getting overbearing with his fuzzy face leaning closer to mine. What did he expect from me? His wife finally fetched him away.

Marge and Diana Dixon followed Alex to see if he was all right as he stood by the van, his hand holding the frame of the side-view mirror. When they approached him, he turned to discover that it wasn't a compliant wife coming to join him, but two of her cronies. Perhaps he believed I was going to join Bea instead of him. Diana gave him a goodnight hug, which he returned, as is his bland hugging custom, and then Marge offered some comfort. When he wrapped his arms around her, he hugged numbly, then his muscles tensed and he squeezed her so hard she was bug-eyed and for so long that she almost fainted. He called her names between his clenched teeth. Diana had to tell him to let go while a surprised Marge tried to break away before he let her go. Both women scattered and then he fell into the van.

Later, Marge came to tell me that she had found a great option for a sleeping companion. She wouldn't be in Bea's tent and not to worry if I couldn't find her. She also told me what Alex had done. I decided to get a sleeping bag and pillow from Bea's camper where she was zonked out, and I stayed in a safe place in the midst of everyone, alone, except for the diehards still drinking and talking around the campfire. I slept on a plastic-webbed lounge chair close to the campfire's fading coals.

When I awoke at dawn, my first sight was Matt holding up a large lake trout that he had caught after running to Lake Michigan and back with his fishing pole. My champion long-distance runner. My champion fisherman who seems to be able to catch fish in a water bucket. He cleaned and cooked it over the refueled campfire grill and shared the fish with all who were awake for breakfast.

Before that, however, Marge and Bea shared one of the most intimate experiences, according to Marge, that she's ever done with another person—and she's done quite a few. She and Bea shared one of the park's remote two-holer outhouses plus a cigarette or two and had a profound conversation about marriage.

I'd written and approved articles for use in case I was ill or wasn't able to complete, given other obligations.

June 7, 1976

I've been lucky to find a Toyota "sports car" posted for sale on the employee bulletin board. I bought it and it's great—except that it's brown; but I remembered years ago in New York City when I saw two brown limos, one waiting for Bobby Kennedy and guests outside a Broadway play that Alex and I were attending, and the second on the Plaza Hotel corner where I was sure I had a glimpse of Lauren Bacall in the back seat. Black? Who needs a black limo? Why not be different, more subdued when you have everything else in the world? Brown is good enough for me.

The other problem is that it has a starter control that doesn't work unless you buckle your seatbelt. Many mornings I'd get into the car, and buckle up, but it wouldn't start until I got out, reattached the seatbelt to itself and, like a humble geisha girl, I'd put my hands together in supplication and bow, praying that it would grant me the privilege of starting so I could drive to my destinations.

My son has now acquired the VW camper bus. I guess it's his turn to take advantage of its many uses.

June 7, 1976

The Wisconsin Hospital Association's weekly newsletter mistakenly gave me a promotion by giving me the title of "public relations director." I'll take it. I reproduced WHA's letterhead and a news item on the front page of my newsletter, and on the second page, I listed the cast of characters in the "internal battle for control over Lakeshore Medical Center unit of Local 100."

The list of Local 100 officials lists six names: Gene Conet from Chicago who labels the Lakeshore Med's union as a "splinter group" that includes Ray Schuster as chief negotiator and attorney plus twelve striking employees including Bart Biggs and Helen Vanik. In listing each person's starting date, I realized that Biggs and Vanik's starting dates were the same: September 23, 1974.

"These factions must resolve their issues before Lakeshore Med's negotiating team, led by chief negotiator Joe Meed, can begin the negotiating process again and resolve this strike."

Tomorrow, I'll write about Joe Meed, a legal counselor and a specialist in hospital labor relations law. He was conscientious and patient and would take the time to answer my questions so I wouldn't print something that could hurt our cause.

I describe, "…the other members of our Lakeshore Med's team include Anderson, a veteran personnel director involved in Lakeshore Med's labor relations since 1969.

"Marge Manley, the newest member of the committee, with her employment management skills, is adding to her Master of Science degree by taking courses in labor and management.

"Randy King is in his third session of negotiations with Local 100. His undergraduate major was in personnel management.

"Frank Rossi is the plant operations administrator responsible for more union members than any other department and has worked and supervised in several of the labor categories. While in charge of Lakeshore Med's laundry, he maintained the longest department record of no turnovers, which lasted for six years. He speaks English, Italian and Spanish and understands other languages that help him relate to employees. He has much labor relations experience both here and in Miami and this will be his second collective bargaining session at Lakeshore Medical Center."

CHAPTER 18

June 10, 1976

For days when nothing significant happened, the newsletters had to be written. Many readers started collecting sets and when they'd return from a day off, they'd ask for back issues. While waiting for news to break, I searched everywhere for story information. I also learned more about the capacities of the 9200 Xerox machine and I started reproducing my photos in the newsletter. I'd worked hard to establish a good relationship with a photo-developing service so I could get my films reproduced as soon as I brought them into their studio.

Though grainy, the computer images also gave me the dramatic use of space to make my daily publication look like a small but authentic newspaper—and it helped fill the page without my writing copy.

While still waiting for the strike's resolution, I used June 9th's newsletter to describe governmental agencies involved, and then I defined about twenty terms used in union-management conflicts: arbitration, featherbedding, check-off, boycott, and the difference between job action, wildcat, sympathy, jurisdictional, general strikes, etc.

Today's issue featured a story with artwork from the brochure on the "new Super 15 Space-saving Combination Folder Crossfolder" laundry equipment. That has special meaning because all but four laundry employees were on the picket line.

June 12, 1976

In our today's newsletter, I report that three women in white uniforms carrying yellow plastic bags picked up picket litter after working their eight-hour night shift. Auxiliary volunteers are so anxious to help that one not only left her keys in the car, locking herself out in hurrying to get to Lakeshore by eight a.m. but when a security guard helped her get the car door open at 2 p.m., they discovered that she had also left the motor running.

On a late-night drive home from the airport, I asked Alex to drive by the hospital to see if everything was O.K. Incidents and harassment had started again with minor vandalism at the front entrance. The moon was full.

"As my husband and I passed the hospital," I wrote, "The troublemakers must have gone home or else they're meeting somewhere. Sometimes their leader brings them a jug of Muscatel and they have a late-night picnic. He likes the 11 p.m. shift change in the dark. His friends from other unions come to join him.

"A carnival sight awaited us when we stopped near the hospital's front door—except that this carnival wasn't much fun. Red and white lights from police cars were spinning across faces clustered in angry formations. Lights circling around were like kaleidoscopes flashing into darkened hospital rooms where patients were to be sleeping, bouncing off windows of the neighboring houses, being absorbed into the bright lights of Lakeshore Med's front entrance where three Lakeshore Med's supervisors were standing quite calmly in the middle of the milling, noisy strikers, guards and police. A baby in a stroller was a ludicrous sight that appeared when one of the strikers moved and revealed her infant on wheels in the midst of this disturbing scene.

"The catalyst person who stimulates this hostility almost every time he appears on the scene to call 'his people' to march with him was across the street angrily shaking his steel-shavings head of hair while he spoke loudly to three policemen. The incident has passed now, just some pushing and shoving. Eyewitnesses were making their reports. The crowd was dispersing. The strikers were pacing. They picked up their signs and went back to their posts. Police cars reversed gears and turned off the spotlights after sending the investigators off for the night.

"I returned to our car and my husband drove us home where it was quiet and peaceful, safe and secure, and I wondered how many patients were distressed by all this. How many staff members must submit to harassment to care for them? What would I do if I were a mother taking my sick child to the hospital? Both of my children were born at Lakeshore. How would I feel if I had to make my way through that gauntlet of picketers while in labor and ready to deliver my baby? How would I feel after getting a call from a nurse telling me that a loved one was dying and I should come to be here? How would I feel walking through that charade on my way to face reality? How many people look to this hospital each hour for help, for care, for safety?

"Through all these wonderings, I knew that despite these unnecessary minutes of irresponsible acts by a few, there are hours and days and years to a century, generations from the past until today, of competent, determined, and skillful people who are there, inside, and waiting to take care of us."

June 14, 1976

Director of Nursing Donna Durand and I were interviewed about the strike on the local radio station on Sunday. Our moderator was Harvey Harrison, another Lakeshore Med employee, so I didn't think being on a live radio talk show in Lakeshore Bay would be all that stressful.

Of course, media was always around, but the most opinionated words appeared in the *Lakeshore Labor Weekly* on the hospital, the teachers' union, and labor unrest throughout the city.

I sometimes finished my newsletter with some poetry I'd find like "What is a hospital," that had a great impact on readers. Before that, I'd discounted poetry's value in this context. I wrote some free verse to describe my take on the conflict, but I was advised not to use them because they could be described as too inflammatory. I tossed the poems into a filler file for future use.

The fear of violence grew on both sides of the picket lines. Telephone threats were made to those who wanted to return to work. Al Hart, a former chief steward, received the most threats and he actually was admitted to Lakeshore as a possible stroke victim. I printed the letter from this courageous maintenance man who came back to work and wrote his opinions in *Bay View Times* Letters to the Editors page. Of course, there are many strikers' letters, "Workers underpaid" and "Hospital Anti-union" and more that are written with such skill and professional vocabulary that it's almost automatic to think that some of their letters may have been written by legal experts and sympathetic teachers who were advocating, via Schuster, to go on strike as well.

June 15, 1976
"Union Factions Outlast Each Other for Power"

"The length of this strike of Lakeshore Med's service employees is based as much on intrigue as endurance.

"The intrigue is so complex between union professionals of Local 100 and the "splinter group" of Schuster/Biggs that even the Local's state president said, after he returned from a two-week vacation in Europe, that the situation at Lakeshore is 'the most unusual negotiation I've ever been in.'

"The ballots Becker mailed to strikers, the reportedly seventy-some that were returned will be counted tomorrow at 10 a.m. in the union office in Milwaukee. The ballots have been sitting there, the objects of controversy and uncertainty since May 28. When they are finally opened tomorrow, they will be merely advisory.

"And no one can predict what the union will do after the votes are taken and the results are made known.

"The endurance we need calls for strength and unity, patience, and understanding as the strike continues. The hospital and its employees, the community and all health care institutions in the state wait while the union factions struggle to determine who will lead those unpaid picketers out of this strike and toward a fair and equitable settlement with Lakeshore Med waiting for the bargaining team."

The newsletter also reported an increased census in intensive care and pediatrics units and the start of eighty candy-striped Volunteers.

Al Hart gave me permission to print his patient comment card. "During my recent stay at Lakeshore Med, I can't describe the wonderful care I had. My doctor asked me if I would prefer either Lakeshore or St. Agnes, as the strike was still on. I said to him that I belonged in Lakeshore. This is my hospital, my place of work, practically my whole life. I had top-notch treatment and I never had my back rubbed so many times. I thought I was some VIP. People are wonderful there and helped me to get well much quicker."

June 16, 1976
"Advisory Lakeshore Med vote favors terms"

"Federal mediators in Milwaukee today opened secret ballots on a controversial settlement offer to striking members of Lakeshore Medical Center Service Employees Local 100.

"By a margin of 64 to 4, union members who mailed in their ballots favored accepting the hospital's last offer. But the results of the balloting are advisory and apparently will have little effect on the strike by 250 union members, which began May 24…

"This morning, the remaining ballots were opened and counted by three mediators…No members of the local bargaining unit were on hand.

"Becker said the balloting margin indicated acceptance of the hospital's last offer, although they were few in number.

"It's a shame," he added, "that so many ballots were confiscated. Maybe Schuster has caused the people to lose four weeks of pay."

June 16, 1976
"Lakeshore Med Gets Bomb Threat"

"A bomb threat was telephoned to Lakeshore Medical Center early this morning, prompting a room-by-room and floor-by-floor search of the building."

That's the lead of today's headline story for my newsletter. A caller phoned the 3-MICU orthopedic nursing station, which indicated inside information on telephone numbers. She said, "Get out of Lakeshore before the bomb goes off."

It was decided not to evacuate patients; especially the thirty-four in orthopedic beds, as many patients were practically immovable in their circle electric beds, casts, or in traction. Patient areas were searched first, quietly but thoroughly, then the service areas were explored. Nothing was found during the search while patients slept quietly through the night.

Nick Dixon was proud of the staff. "They were super. There was no panic. The police and firemen did their jobs efficiently. Everyone was cool."

Mrs. Towney, who took the call, responded, "You were cool on the outside, but it's hard to describe how I felt on the inside. I was concerned about the patients. You know, the night staff is closer than other shifts. But I don't know how we'll be able to overcome hard feelings (toward the strikers) after this. It hurts us to see our people out there on the picket line."

"Tires Slashed Before Midnight"

Lakeshore Medical Center's attorney Robert Barrett met with Nick Dixon to observe the 11 p.m. harassment and witness these activities that violate the court injunction controlling picketing activities. At 11:15, Barrett and Frank Rossi went outside and startled three people who ran away from Nick Hart's car. When the two men went to the car, they could hear the air hissing from the punctured set of tires. They looked around and found that Randy King and Barrett's tires had been punctured too.

"Strikers Informed of Food Stamps, Where to Borrow Money"

Reports from strikers attending the meeting held at the Labor Center Tuesday at 9 a.m. revealed details offered on how to apply for federal food stamps and where to borrow money. A representative from a loan office was also there offering strikers $50 cash for a 50-cent deposit. No mention was made by the source about interest rates or payment requirements.

Jan on June 17, 1976

After printing the news about the vote count and a bill of rights for union members, I waxed eloquently.

"The 11 P.M. Circus Scene"

The ringmaster appeared again last night to crack his whip, and the players in this shadowy circus began their acts once more. Incidents, though more minor than Wednesday's bomb scare, happen frequently and threats to maintain law and order are constant. Hospital guards have resisted being goaded into action as tempers get raw under pressure. Employees are undaunted by name-calling and harassment. Patients are enduring the noise.

Sonya Anderson, P.M. assistant director of nursing, said the patients are living with the noise and they don't seem upset even though the street noise goes on for hours. "I can't see how they can get any sleep with all the shouting—unless they're stone deaf." It gets especially noisy in the intensive care wing where picketers congregate between the buildings and the noise rises to patient windows. The patients generally don't complain, however. "Actually, they and the visitors are admiring what we do inside," she added.

At the main entrance, the switchboard operators view the circus pranksters through the giant windows as big as an outdoor movie screen. What they see, according to Rita Follette, is Ray Schuster with various companions "who are not always our people," she said in her slightly British accent, "knocking on the window, laughing and pointing at those on the inside, teasing others and monkeying around to attract attention."

She explained, "In the evenings, when he's inclined to come down here, once he sees people in my lobby, often people who come down to watch him at his antics, then he starts attracting attention to himself. I turn away. I think you should walk away and not let him have an audience. If more people would do that, he would stop. There's nothing he can do. I will not be intimidated by him."

But the ringmaster's circus players are intimidated as he literally gets them into a tipsy line of disorganized and confused marchers and "Hup, two, three, fours" them around the building, commanding them to join him in the militant chorus, rabble-rousing the rank and file of his people who follow him around the extravaganza ring in the night."

Chaplain Arthur Boulton's writes to the editor

"Your work on the daily bulletins, Jan, has been excellent, but to me, there was a special beauty in your June 12 issue—beautiful descriptions, especially of the "catalyst person." I have been pondering that soul from the insights of my discipline—how fragile he is, his need to alter the conscious states of already fragile people before he can persuade them to be his people. I could sense in your descriptive powers the mystery that nighttime evokes when so much is shadowy, clandestine, poorly delineated, the rodent-like activity of those who feel strong only when the light of day and the light of conscious awareness have been safely and duly dimmed. We must see all of this in perspective, especially the catalyst's fragility—such an exercise in futility he has attempted—how desperately fragile he really is."

Shalom,
Arthur Boulton

<<<>>>

Bea on June 14, 1976

After finding Round Lake yesterday, I'm beginning to heal after dinner by swimming, morning worship and skipping UU school to go to the new Great American Theme Park with a couple of others who had the idea to "skip school."

Being human is the most difficult and religious aspect of our undertakings because being human requires that you accept the fragility and sacredness of human life.

"Alone again, naturally…." The song I heard on the radio comes back to me as I waded into the lake—the temperature is just right. I swam. I felt the healing waters and floated weightless in womb-like comfort. Comfort me, Mother Earth. It smelled good. A gentle breeze touched and caressed me. I looked up and was suddenly struck. The clouds were absolutely delightful, billowing tightly, and I talked to them and laughed out loud. "I ate you last night—or the symbol of you, you cauliflower clouds, but nothing like your perfection. You and God-like in your being, more perfect than your earthly symbol that I ate. I could worship you—and I ate you last night." A pleasant joy spread through my body, a revelation, an "aha" experience. I suddenly realized something I must share with people, Jan especially, to make them understand. I realize the difference between solitude and loneliness. Solitude is a delight. Solitude is a pleasant healing joy. Loneliness is something forced on you, not your choice.

And now I'm going to go and be with people again.

Jan on June 18, 1976

In my twenty-fourth daily newsletter today, I reproduced Becker's letter to his union members, distributed it throughout the hospital—and helped the media talk with appropriate hospital representatives. Even *Bay View Times* printed the letterhead and half of the front page of Becker's letter; its front-page headline read, "Charges traded—Local 100 rift deepens."

Becker, head of the statewide Hospital Employees International Union with 7400 members, offered a second ballot to Lakeshore Med's striking union members, now less than 282 (according to the union) because 28 quit (according to Schuster) the union and returned to work.

"Let's face it," Becker wrote. "Schuster and Biggs have made fools of all of us…Only an amateur or someone who has never negotiated a hospital contract would try to make you believe that you could get a $1.25 per hour increase. This hasn't happened at a hospital in the United States, let alone in Wisconsin."

He brought out the fact that Biggs works full-time at Lakeshore Bay's county hospital and halftime at a private nursing home. Of course, Schuster gets his salary from his many legal ventures "…and you continue working without a paycheck."

He wrote that Schuster will not be part of any future Local 100 activities. Becker apologized to everyone for the "uncouth and unbelievable antics" and Schuster's casual attire. Becker described how he "lay in his chair with both legs (not just his feet) on the negotiating table…Schuster's language was filthy, unbelievable, and disrespectful. I especially apologize to the ladies on our negotiating committee who were supposed to laugh (but didn't) when Schuster used such words as S.O.B., pimp, and the unprintable word, f- -kers. In my 22 years as a Union Representative, including five years with the rough, tough teamsters union, I've never witnessed such crude behavior at a bargaining table.

"The result of all this is not that hospital management dislikes the employees, they dislike Schuster and are not about to grant him anything, not even another meeting. In fact, the mediators haven't been able to get one for him…"

So, Becker sent out another ballot with the offer for strikers to receive back pay to May 2.

"VOTE," he urged. "Your ballot is your voice. Use it. Whatever the majority of employees tell me to do by their vote is what I will do.

"Please vote and vote as YOU please."

Bay View Times reporters Dick Wallace and Sean Dennis ran a story with reactions from all sides. Schuster said they were going to ignore the vote and ignore Becker if he signed an agreement. Union leaders were attempting to collect the ballots before the members mailed them and held a ballot count of their own at Schuster's Lakeshore law office. They wrote that by 10 a.m., they'd collected 108 ballots showing 104 for continuing the strike and four for Becker's proposal. Becker charged that they had obtained the ballots through coercion: "They've been using scare tactics on these people saying 'your house will be next' and threatening that they will be fired by the hospital if they accept the agreement."

Each union faction accused the other of ballot fraud.

June 19, 1976

Included in the daily newspaper's many letters to the editor, which I reprinted in our newsletter, was a surgical clerk's letter. She had resigned from the union and went back to work. She wrote, "My reasons for writing are to express my pity and anger to those who are still out there picketing and also to hopefully 'open the eyes' of some of them."

She couldn't get over the violence, such as throwing roofing nails into the entrance driveway and pouring molasses all over the hospital's front entrance. "Ray Schuster," she wrote, "says he likes the violence because it's good for publicity." About the strike, "I don't think many of us thought it would ever get to that point, (striking) and even if we did, I was told 'Don't worry. It shouldn't last more than three or four days.' It's now into its fourth week.'"

I identified with her letter and her sympathies in many ways. I never expected to have to fulfill my promise to write a newsletter every day for this long. Also, the bi-centennial 4th of July parade was rapidly approaching. Where will I get the time to decorate all those floats? And Bea's and my three-week trip to Europe was to start on July 13th. "What will happen if the strike is still on?"

I asked Randy King and he said that I should plan to go no matter what happens. They'd think of something. Perhaps they'd hire an outside firm to carry on my part of the campaign as they hired companies to slip in, one person at a time, like visitors, to do laundry, food service, and other tasks that volunteers were doing. I took photos of volunteers working, including Randy King's mother, sorting laundry, and Pat Marvin cleaning a bathroom. Julia Douglas, the delivery room supervisor, had her retirement party in her unit, and right after that, I photographed Julia holding a wet floor mop over a bucket to clean one of the delivery rooms.

Volunteers and non-striking employees continue to work long hours. We are veterans together as our camaraderie grows.

June 26, 1976

Three days of my newsletters to employees and patients (and even those on the picket line) have been filled with articles on voting conflicts, federal mediation activities and legal implications. Picketers are outside, patients and staff inside and beyond the hospital area and charges of ballot tampering, election rigging, accusations and intrigue continue to frustrate all concerned.

First, the union voters' envelopes were separated according to levels of acceptability. Properly mailed and unchallengeable envelopes totaled 198. There were 22 envelopes other than those provided by the union and 12 that had been opened and then resealed with tape, making the total 232. According to Becker, about 250 members received ballots.

They counted the acceptable ballots first, with 106 votes to return to work and 90 to continue to strike. Striking members could return to work with a 90-cent-an-hour pay increase over a three-year period if Becker would sign the contract. This was when the Swartz/Biggs faction turned on the pressure to get Becker to open questionable envelopes, especially when the Schuster group collected 112 ballots in his office from individuals and tallied a vote of 108 against settlement and four in favor of settlement. Schuster and Becker knew they had 108 'no' votes, yet Becker decided to open that batch of 22 ballots.

Lakeshore Med's settlement was still ahead with 110 to 106.

The pressure increased as six Schuster disciples badgered their state union president to continue the count. Becker opened the taped, resealed envelopes and the final vote changed the results from 111 to settle and 116 to continue the strike.

Exhausted and running out of ideas, I dipped into my history file again and found a June 24, 1872, newspaper article reproduced in my *Lakeshore Medical Center's Centennial News* when Lakeshore officially submitted its articles of incorporation as a "General Charitable Institution of the Protestant Episcopal Church organized for the support, care and medical treatment of the sick, aged, inform and indigent."

Meanwhile, a *Bay View Times* editorial summed up the situation. "The community also has been a loser. It's been on the scene and witness to vitriolic diatribes by spokesmen for the picketers and a prolonged strike that could have been and should have been settled weeks ago. Unfortunately, the entire community must now wait for Local 100 to clean its own house. Then hopefully, it will be able to bargain with the hospital to settle this everybody-is-a-loser strike."

I copied editorial items plus *Lakeshore Labor Weekly* articles emphasizing that the hospital strikers received no union strike benefits since they began picketing on May 24. The labor paper with its limited circulation was not readily available to all. Reprinting some articles and posting all of them on the employee and cafeteria bulletin boards gave employees, volunteers, and patients a revealing point of view about the personalities and issues as they were presented in this labor-focused publication.

Bea on June 27, 1976

I met Jan at the hospital for lunch. I gave her the new song I wrote and we made plans with Marge to see *Murder by Death* to cheer us up. She came about 6 p.m. after working for several hours decorating floats, she needed to change her clothes, a shower to wash off the dust and sweat and a shampoo. We never made the 7:30 show because we shared an intensely beautiful shower together. We called Marge and said we'd be late, but we never picked her up for the next movie at 8:45.

I worked at Emerson House on Friday, but Betty and I went to lunch at the Hub, where we had several drinks. Then we went to Betty's house for supper and after that, Marge and her Tommy came over. We played the piano and violin and belted out a grand old sing-along. I woke up on my couch the next morning and didn't remember driving home. Luckily I made it.

Jan on June 29, 1976

In a letter dated June 24, but printed on June 27 and 28 with its ramifications and qualifications, Andrew Anderson and Dan Becker signed a contract "in the best interest of the members of Local 100 and the employees of Lakeshore Medical Center, Lakeshore Bay. This contract is being signed, providing the signing in no way violates the restraining order now in effect."

Yet another legal obstacle, a temporary restraining order obtained by Bart Biggs, will be tested to be sure that Becker has the power to sign the contract.

As I was leaving the hospital at 5 p.m., I heard my name being paged again on the hospital's public address system. I never anticipated what I would find as I approached the switchboard at the front entrance to be greeted by a process server who presented me with a subpoena signed by Schuster. I was one of five who were to appear as witnesses in a court action on the restraining order to prohibit Becker from negotiating with the hospital without the Lakeshore Med's unit bargaining committee. The others subpoenaed were Anderson, Nick Dixon, former chief steward Al Hart and Local 100 business agent Bill Jacobsen.

I felt queasy when I anticipated being cross-examined by the irresponsible Schuster. What information would he want to find out from me? Practically everything I knew about the strike was printed in my daily strike bulletins, and he could read them at will.

Our attorneys made ready affidavits to present to the court that would protect us from testifying under Schuster's interrogation. It stated that three hospital management employees have no relevant information on the matters at issue and it concluded by stating, "The sole purpose of the subpoenas as issued is to use the processes of this Court as a means to impose unreasonable and oppressive burdens of the said Nick Dixon, Andrew Anderson and Jan Carnigian as management employees of Lakeshore Medical Center, Inc."

I described what happened in my newsletter: the judge saying that employees should get back to work; that Schuster asked for "four or five days to prepare a brief;" that the judge didn't want people "getting kicked around" while these issues are being settled; that the contract is binding and unless union members follow procedures to return to work "we cannot be responsible for what other people tell them."

Today Andrew Anderson mailed a letter saying that the remaining strikers should wait to be notified by Personnel or department heads to avoid confusion and prevent double scheduling.

They must contact their department head by noon on July 2nd. "Bargaining unit employees who do not…will be subject to termination."

CHAPTER 19

June 30, 1976

Several days before, I arranged for a secret meeting in the basement maintenance shop with *Bay View Times* reporter Ben Daniels and four union men who had returned to work plus Frank Rossi and me.

Two men, including Al Hart, wanted to tell what they had experienced, but two of them did not want to be identified; they said they had enough threats of violence. The others didn't care who knew how angry and frustrated they felt.

Daniels hesitated. He didn't want to print any story without full use of names, but he stayed and talked with the men and took notes. When all four men agreed for their names to be used, the reporter wrote the story for today's front page.

One of the men's quotes called the strike a power struggle among local union leaders and recalled a meeting attended by Jack Porter, executive director of the Lakeshore Bay's Education Association, Joe Hunsel, president of the League for Labor, and Lynn Hansen, president of Local 100, and Schuster. "Everybody was so worked up, they couldn't care what happened as long as they got the power they wanted."

Today's tedious but satisfying challenge is to explain the provisions of the new contract where bargaining unit employees receive an immediate hourly wage increase of 40 cents an hour minimum or 12 percent, whichever is greater, for the first year with seven and one-half percent increases for the second and third years of the contract. Andrew Anderson said the total wage increase over three years will amount to a minimum of 90 cents an hour but wage and fringe benefit costs together will amount to $1.26 an hour or a 29 percent increase. It took two full pages to complete the details.

In addition, but not included in this newsletter, letters dated June 29 were sent to Union Stewards Bart Biggs, Helen Vanik, and two other women "Are hereby notified that your employment at Lakeshore Medical Center is terminated. Charges for Biggs and Vanik included pre-strike work stoppages and all four were for picket line misconduct."

Randall King on July 1, 1976

Randy King summarized Lakeshore Med's strike by writing his take on the situation as well as the wage losses for six weeks of the strike that he estimated at $204,000.

Today's newsletter headline read:

Today's newspaper headline read:
"Randall King Observes Strike's Impact."

"One fortunate aspect of this strike is that it has involved few life-support personnel. Because most of our strikers are service employees, the effect of the strike on the community has been more of an inconvenience than an injury. But will the community be as fortunate in the future?

"Ray Schuster discussed some of his long-range labor objectives and strike strategies with me in conversations we had together before the strike. I'm personally skeptical of any success for some of his dreams. (His belief that our new contract with 100 is invalid is another of those dreams.) However, other aspects of his goals are, in my opinion, quite possible.

"It is Schuster's objective to organize St. Agnes Hospital and to take control of our union, Local 100. These two unions would then fit into a larger coalition of area unions that would essentially be comprised of public employees.

"Public employees are the workers who have the most to gain from a strike and the most impact upon operations during a strike. In today's world, the strike in private industry is losing much of its effectiveness. If the UAW strikes an automaker, consumers buy foreign cars. If the steelworkers strike, the industry finds German and Japanese suppliers. Strikes against the railroads help the truckers. However, this situation isn't true for public employees. As long as a source of money is available, public employees can hold the citizens of the community as hostages until their demands are met. This power to hold citizens as hostages is an effective weapon for striking hospital employees.

"The strength of the non-striking employees here at Lakeshore has undermined Schuster's present objectives. Our conversations revealed that he did not expect the dedication, loyalty or overwhelming desire to care for the patient that was exhibited by Lakeshore Med's professional staff during the strike. I'm confident he did not anticipate that 100 union members would cross the picket line to come back to work. Much of his error lies in the fact that his assessment of the level of pride and dedication of Lakeshore Med's employees was based on the feedback from his hand-picked insiders; not the majority. He has lost control of our union for at least the next three years, and St. Agnes has made many recent efforts to keep him out of their hospital. St. Agnes' success will be known as time passes.

"However, precedents have been set. Our operation room technicians, and trained life-support personnel, withheld their services. With this act, they denounced the special obligation accepted by healthcare employees not to walk off the job and leave the ill and infirm unattended and in danger.

"Some other precedents by public employees have been the slowdown of police to enforce federal, state, and local laws against our picketers and the refusal of some rescue squad members to bring some injured people across the picket lines. Other actions included the intimidation of persons in need of our emergency room. They were turned away from our door by picketers and they went to St. Agnes. And, of course, the bomb threat occurred in the midst of tire slashing and picket line violations.

"What about next time? The above activities may be increased and expanded. Will the community be harmed by the lack of working healthcare employees? It is naive to believe that laws can be expected to remedy this threat. One can only appeal to all members of Lakeshore Medical Center staff to remember the special obligation to the patient that you have all accepted. Let that guide you when you are asked to vote on a contract, asked to walk on the picket line, or find that you have to cross a picket line to fulfill your obligations to the patient and the community."

Jan on July 2, 1976
"Lakeshore Med's walkout over"

Reproducing *The Journal's* headline and story, "Lakeshore Medical Center's walkout is over," Dave Franklin, the paper's major business and labor reporter, had Schuster saying that after he had unsuccessfully sought amnesty for strikers disciplined by Lakeshore for picket line incidents and that those grievances will be filed in the hospitals firing of chief steward Arthur Biggs and three other union members, including Helen Vanik, a steward and bargaining committee member.

I also printed

> ### *"A Quiet Victory"*
> by Jan Carnigian
> No cannons roared at this strike's ending.
> No church bells rang.
> No troops paraded back with banners flying
> to be greeted with welcome and waiting arms.
> Fantasy? Exaggeration? Yes.

Our hospital family is but a small part
of events that fill the news in a world
where hostility flares with fury and intensity
to end "not with a bang, but a whimper."
Today's conflicts drag out to infinity.
This hospital strike is officially over.
The contract's signed; return to work.
Yet pickets still gather to litter the grounds
while most return to their time clock
ticking the days away since the strike began.
No cannon roared at this strike's ending—
Hardly even a hurrah. A sigh of relief,
disbelief, apprehension—
When will the last picket throw away the tattered sign
and leave behind the empty promises of misguided
leaders?
When will it truly be over?
For some, it will never end as bitterness prevails.
For more, internal wounds will heal in this hospital setting
and "scab" will have its proper meaning.
No cannons. No, just people quietly caring.

Thank you for reading these daily messages. Your work and your response have been an inspiration that kept challenging me to meet the daily deadlines. In the future, issues will be published again with dates marking the important days when events determine publication rather than the tyranny of time.
(signed) Jan

CHAPTER 20

Bea on July 3, 1976

The damn strike is finally over and Jan will find time to be with me again—after the 4th of July time.

Jan on July 6, 1976

The strike could not have lasted another day for me. I shifted energy and immersed my family and me into finishing the patriotic floats in time for yesterday's bicentennial 4th of July Goodwill parade. Thank Heavens that this holiday landed on a Sunday, giving us an extra day to work on floats with the parade held on Monday.

Of course, we all worked until we were so tired that we couldn't make another decision about what to do next. My dad directed our activities as he stood bent over his elevated table for hours, sketching out words with charcoal on thick double sheets of heavy-weight showcard, and then, resting gently on his forearms with his hands guiding his treasured Cuttal tool, he'd carve out two sets of each float's theme and sponsor's name. We had the kids brush color-coordinated paint on each cutout letter and when all was dry, they'd staple matching-colored floral paper to the bands connecting each letter. They helped me a lot by stapling paper fringe on the bottom of the frames crawling under and into tight spaces and pushing long, steel bank pinpoints back through the paper and chicken wire to me, as I'd done decades before with my mother, our fingers capped with protecting masking tape.

Alex and Matt worked with my childhood neighborhood and old-time tennis friend Rick Nelson, our carpenter who created our basic forms out of lumber. I'd add the curves and shapes with chicken wire, securing the pedaled paper to the structure with pins and staples of varying widths and depths.

This year, Matt would also ride the length of this parade inside a ten-wide by twelve-foot-high Uncle Sam's hat that he would spin by "boy power" as the band, on both sides of the hat, played on.

Uncle Sam's hat appeared on a smaller scale for the last float we constructed for my father's career. For his retirement parade, when he was elected honorary parade marshal as Mr. Goodwill, we covered a golf cart base in white, topped by a tipped Uncle Sam hat about a third of the size of the big one that Matt had to spin. Somehow we found the time to get that finished so Barney Anthony could ride in his parade and get deserved acclaim from the tens of thousands of people who cheered our floats this year and for so many years before.

In a newspaper reporter's interview on Carl B. (Barney) Anthony, the reporter described him. "…a float builder for hundreds of floats for area parades, Anthony feels that floats first came into their own during Labor Day parades. He said 'that years ago, every union had its own float and everybody marched in the parade, or else.' Anthony started his profession, that of a sign painter, in a small shop in Milwaukee where he had the prestigious job of "sweeper— but I learned.'" He admitted to the reporter, "I'm not that well, but I'm proud to be named Mr. Goodwill, believe me."

He never asked anyone to suggest what he should wear on his red, white and blue honorary parade marshal float. I would have suggested perhaps summer lightweight dark trousers, a white shirt with an open collar and a red baseball cap. He chose brown and green plaid trousers, a Hawaiian floral shirt with a red background, a red and yellow baseball cap, and white socks with white and brown wing-tipped shoes. And, I almost died when I saw that he had Chico with him to ride on his lap plus Chico's water bowl.

Var and Sona, as always, picked up my mother at Ridgewood County Hospital because she was well enough to be with us for the parade. We stood in my old front yard, her house actually, my mother and I with our family and friends as the sirens from every piece of fire-fighting equipment from the city and county units shook the wax from our ears, then came huge tractors, military trucks and tanks that ground across the concrete. The first of fifteen marching bands raised the hair on our necks as we choked back the tears from our tired eyes. While our hearing recovered, politicians, dignitaries and beauty queens riding in convertibles waved at everyone in a quieter line that was led by Carl B. Anthony, proudly holding his Mexican Chihuahua, my insufferable sibling rival.

He smiled broadly and waved at us, my mother and me, standing in our front yard, and he reveled in his well-deserved accolades as we stood watching from the sidelines.

Our float team had two traditions, even when we had to work all night before the parade. The kids, Rick, Alex and I would meet for a dawn-breaking breakfast at George Webb's before we directed the floats out of the building area and onto the line of march. Then Dad, Alex, Rick and I always gathered together in my dad's kitchen after we finished the last minute touches on each float, including helping the beauty queens, cartoon characters or patriots onto their places before the parade started. Dad would reach into his cupboard and get out his Kraft pimento cheese glasses and pour us a hefty brandy, which we'd raise in a toast for another Goodwill parade year. This year, he may have had his snort before he met us at his float, but that didn't stop Alex, Dick and me from pouring us a traditional brandy while the sirens were blaring.

Somehow Bea, Marge, Nina and Tommy took me up on my invitation, drove through the traffic, moved barricades along the parade route to park in our backyard off the alley and joined us to watch the parade, but they kept to the other side of the front yard while Alex was around. They all visited with my mother, though, and Var and Sona, while our team rested up to prepare to tear down the floats immediately after the parade.

Bea glowed with sunburn and when I was able to talk with her, she said that Angie Murak and her boyfriend came to her apartment yesterday. She told me that Angie's divorced now and her ex has disappeared. "Angie, her boyfriend and I had a couple of drinks and then we went to the beach and stayed all day. I got cooked and crocked, and I was bored with the two of them. I hate to sit on the beach anyway. There's nothing to do. Then they came back to my place, and Angie and her friend slept in my bed while I slept on the sofa with my sunburn."

I whispered, "With you, Marge and Tommy taking off for Lake Geneva this afternoon, I'm happy that I was able to break away last Thursday for breakfast at your place."

"Ha! Yes! Thursday! And we forgot to eat. But we gave each other better nourishment, didn't we? After you left to do all your jobs, I scoured through our books on Europe again. Jesus Christ, I'm nervous. Being pre-menstrual and feeling goofy and depressed doesn't help. We're going to Europe! My dad actually gave me $500 for our trip! That will more than pay for our charter cost—I'll have about $100 left for us! And we'll be on our own once we land. No tour bus for us! God! I'm so happy your strike is over—too close for comfort to our leaving on the 13th. Holy Cow! Do I love you?

After the parade crowds and traffic dispersed, I drove Mother to the shop where the first floats were already waiting to be torn apart for salvage. We stopped, joked around and stayed out of the way of the many floats' frames with bent nails and staples flying by us. I took Mother home and we ate lunch with Bea, Marge, Nina and Tommy on our porch looking at the lake until she grew restless and I grew even more tired and drove her back to the hospital.

I was able to grab a nap and make some supper for my family before the company started pouring in from the back door and the front so that they could see the annual 4th of July fireworks from our front porch. It helped that they brought snacks and, of course, we had plenty of homemade wine for them to drink. They finally left and Alex and I could fall into bed. With all the windows open, I could still smell the acrid fireworks explosive remains in the night sky.

I certainly didn't expect to have sex with him after all our energies were depleted from our work for the parade. I could rest without concern over how to avert his sexual problems. He wants me and he wants to perform, to satisfy me. And he does, but not as often. Keeping our sexual lives alive requires tender patience in the midst of urgent pressures. As he continues to lose power over me, we're beginning, just beginning, our decline as sexual partners. It's amazing that it hadn't started a long time before.

I try to be sure to satisfy him before he leaves for each of his many business trips around the country. He used to go to New York and Detroit. Now he also travels to Sparks, Nevada, and California. I try to satisfy him when he gets home, too.

Of course, he's continually threatened with my blatant behaviors. Who wouldn't be? The strike lasted for forty days and now I'm leaving for Europe with my lover for three weeks. Who do I think I am, Vita Sackville West? Well, Alex's certainly not the stoic, accepting bi-sexual man like Vita's husband, Sir What's His Name.

Besides parenting, the best activity Alex and I did successfully together was playing singles and mixed doubles games and tournament tennis in city and club leagues—until this year. The competition helped burn off some frustration and we did well together. But as this season developed and work increased, my couldn't take the tennis strain and I asked Sandy Lennen, my women's doubles partner and an excellent tennis player, to help fill in for me while I sat in a chair along the chain-link fences surrounding the courts and watched them play with a thermos of martinis at my side.

Matt is leaving tomorrow as a guest representative for the Japan-Jefferson Medical Company. We've attended orientation meetings and they've given them spending money and blazer wardrobe uniforms for the two-week trip. They're leaving in buses from the company's headquarters. We're so proud of him and his accomplishments. They're even scheduled to stop in Hawaii on the way home.

CHAPTER 21

Jan on July 15, 1976

As Marge backed out of our driveway to take us to O'Hare, Bea and I waved to a smiling group of friends and neighbors wishing us well. Smoldering Alex stood apart, then turned and trod the long path into the house.

Bea said with a grimace, "I'm antsy but calm, I think. We're on our way. I didn't know what would happen back there."

I stopped hunching my tense shoulders and let my bones do the job of holding me up and together. I escaped again. Don't even think about coming home. It's worth whatever the price.

Bea's travel journal on July 14, 1976

Our flight was beautiful. The lights of Chicago were magical, like Christmas or Hanukkah, but a little blurred under the wing by the heat from the jet engine. We flew over Lake Michigan and Canada, then clouds obscured the ocean, but not until we saw the coast below as we left the continent. We had cocktails, lasagna dinner, and then got some sleep. I woke frequently to peer out the window and looked out in time to see Greenland below in full daylight at 3:30 a.m. What a sight! Such barren land. No sign of life.

Just mountains and ice that looked like cracked and peeling paint or soured milk with tiny fissures everywhere, then an iceberg.

We landed at London's Heathrow airport at about 1:30 p.m., took our luggage, landing cards, and passports to check out, caught a shuttle bus directly to Victoria Station, then a chugging black London cab that dropped us off at the hotel recommended in Arthur Frommer's book, *How to Do Europe on $10 a Day*. The white-columned Hansel and Gretel Hotel, 68 Belgrave Road, with our pre-reserved room, costs $7.62 including breakfast. The friendly clerk and two golden cocker spaniels, Hans and Gret, greeted us from behind the counter. Behind them, a cheery living room-sized lobby with Swiss frills and furniture, travel posters and brochures would provide us a sitting room should we want one if we needed to get out of our long narrow bedroom with a lavatory sink, a wardrobe closet with wire hangers, and two metal twin beds lined head to foot, adding linear perspective to one window at the end of the sparse room. Surprised by its basic furnishings—hardly a honeymoon suite—we agreed that's what you get when you shop from a book for budget travelers. It would be fine though, but not too conducive for lovemaking without even room to push the cots side-by-side. Jan offered her plan. We could begin our nights wrapped together until one of us had to move and crawl into our own cot.

Jan had been to London and Stratford-on-Avon in the mid-1950s during Alex's Army years and another time chaperoning her Frankfurt Army dependents high school seniors with Alex and other faculty members, so she felt at home. She loved sharing with me now the many experiences that will be unique to me and to us together.

We strolled back toward Victoria Station and found most pubs and restaurants closed for the afternoon, but we bought what seemed like day-old, hard-bread sandwiches with tea served on chipped crockery veined with hairline cracks at a café in the historic, charcoal-dreary station that reminded Jan of the furtive English lovers in Noel Coward's *Brief Encounter* who met secretly between trains. We cued up to get our train and boat tickets for Amsterdam for next week. It was time for the pubs to reopen and we celebrated our first pint in our first pub, St. George's. We took the tube to Soho, and wandered about Drury Lane to check out the theaters, Covent Gardens, and the Strand. We topped it off with a lager at the Nell of Courage in Drury Lane.

We'd been advised to eat at international restaurants for the best food and found the one we were looking for from our guidebook—Roma Santi with scampi, moussaka cannelloni and eggplant. After dinner, we strolled arm in arm down to the Thames to see Big Ben at night, and at 11:45, we caught a cab for the hotel, had some wine in our room and finally, after more than twenty-four sleepless hours, we collapsed into each of our narrow beds.

Bea on July 15, 1976
Thursday. London.
Fair, pleasant weather, and some clouds.

I was up at 8:15 to write in my travel journal. I found the shower on the floor below and nearly scalded myself. We'll have to shampoo each other's hair in the basin in our room if we don't want to boil our heads bald or become brain-dead. The staff in the quaint basement decorated with fake flagstone walls and dusty paper ivy vines served us our first hardy breakfast. After fortifying ourselves and chatting with fellow travelers, we caught the tube for Charing Cross and bought our tickets for a cruise on the Thames. We walked through the gardens nearby, where Jan took some character study photos, including a frail, elderly couple sitting mutely on a park bench surrounded by green foliage in the background and newly trimmed grass beneath them. The woman wore a large-brimmed hat with a huge flower and a floral dress; he wore black with a summer straw hat balancing on his nodding head as he napped with his cane propped between his knees.

"I hear the Beatles going through my brain almost all the time," Jan said as she quietly sang the lyrics and danced gently around me, "She's (We never thought of ourselves.) leaving home . . . (Why would she treat us so thoughtlessly.) She's leaving home . . .

(Something inside that was always denied for so many years . . . Bye, bye.)"

A tourist boat took us to where I've always wanted to be, on board the Chichester's Gypsy Moth IV and then clipper ship Cutty Sark! After Jan took photos of me staring out to the sea at each ship's wheel, we ate steak and kidney pie, beans and chips on shore in the Cutty Sark Pub with bottle-glass window panes curving about our table as if we were eating at the captain's table on board the Cutty Sark itself. We toured the Naval Museum and the Royal Greenwich Observatory and saw the Greenwich meridian, the official standard for the earth's time zones. My long love of sea adventures inspired and reinforced my dream to single-handedly sail around the world as Chichester had done.

The Thames tour boat dropped us at the Parliament and Big Ben. We hiked to Westminster Abbey and saw the Coronation Chair, Stone of Scone, Poets' Corner crypts, and statuary that inspired the writer and poet in each of us.

We're learning the transit system after hiking about for miles around Buckingham Palace and Hyde Park. We queued up for a local bus back to Victoria Station and boarded the 'Round London Tour Bus, where we enjoyed more hours on the open-top deck. What fun guiding with a pamphlet and getting a glimpse at everything. We went back home for a nap after a lime and lager at St. George's.

At about 9 p.m., we got going again. Jan surprised me by taking a cab to a place with my maiden name and nickname, Sherlock⌐— the Sherlock Holmes Pub near Trafalgar Square, where we drank our lagers, ate Scotch eggs, and bought the arch detective's double flap hat for Dad. We milled about the busy Trafalgar Square and stopped at the Pub Silver Cross before we boarded a bus home, had a beer in the hotel lounge, and watched a bit of British TV with Hans and Gret before we went to our room.

Bea on July 16, 1976
Friday. London. Rain in a.m.

I found another shower unit on the floor above ours. The water temperature could be controlled, except when someone else turned on another shower. It's a good thing the hotel doesn't have many floors or the showers above would be freezing. At breakfast, we chatted with a middle-aged Australian couple traveling across Europe for three months. "When you travel this far, you may as well travel around the world." And that's what they intend to do.

We went off to the Tower of London, a delightful tour that included bits of gory history shouted at us by our regally adorned Beefeater guide. (I couldn't help but think of gin.) Intimidating Tower ravens cawed and swooped in the courtyards as we entered the Chapel and the White Tower with armor and torture implements, and viewed the Crown Jewels with the Star of India in the Scepter. (Not really our thing.) We saw the Bloody Tower where Richard III supposedly had his nephews, the two Little Princes, murdered and where Anne Boleyn and others were beheaded—bloody indeed.

In keeping with our literary theme, we lunched at the Samuel Pepys restaurant eating liver, black pudding, bacon, and roast beef while looking out our window alcove hanging over the Thames at low tide. We shopped at Harrods department store, changed money and bought theater tickets there. Jan took more character pictures; she said she's already taken the touristy ones on previous trips. After drinks at a sidewalk café, we ate prawns, biryani and chicken curry at a tiny Indian restaurant before coming back to write postcards.

Bea on July 17, 1976
Saturday. London. Beautiful weather again.

After an early breakfast, I went to the Jingles Salon to get my hair cut and styled while Jan went to the laundromat. Surprised at my hairdo, she smiled. I reminded her of Virginia Woolf at her happiest, loving time.

She wanted me to experience William Blake's mystical paintings hanging at the Tate Gallery but I felt dizzy and unwell and decided to go to our hotel by cab. Jan asked the desk clerk about a physician and made an appointment to see Dr. Woodcock in half an hour, only a couple of blocks away. Just menopausal stuff, he advised, an inner ear balance, and he gave me some pills and I rested a bit when Jan looked out our hotel window and called me over to see what pulled up and parked. A tall, blonde, casually dressed young man stepped out and she guessed our rented car had arrived, a burgundy-brown mini-Austin "and not much bigger than a hedgehog, like Mrs. Tiggy-Winkle," she chuckled.

We signed the papers to take our lives in our hands by driving for the next few days on the other side of the road and around traffic circles, but we decided we'd leave it parked until tomorrow, Sunday, and took the tube for a 5 p.m. late matinee of *Equus* by Peter Shaffer at the Albery Theatre. The drama is based on a true story played by the magnificent National Theatre Company, where cast members in inventive costumes act as horses in their stalls, six horses that had been blinded by a traumatized young man. In the process, the psychiatrist not only aided the boy but also found a deeper meaning in his life. We loved it!

Afterward, we strolled about Bloomsbury Square, where Jan was beside herself, excitedly retelling me all about England's intellectual freethinkers and writers in the Bloomsbury Group, including Virginia Woolf and her Vita. If you give Jan a setting, she'll give you a role to play. I have to be Virginia because of my new English permanent, "And I'll be Vita!" she declared.

We found a delightful Italian outdoor restaurant in the neighborhood where we enjoyed veal with orange sauce, zucchini, and potatoes. Later when we strolled around its corner, The Old Curiosity Shop appeared with Toby mugs, Peter Rabbit, and Beatrix Potter trinkets and books in its windows. It was closed or Jan would have spent hours absorbing its atmosphere.

Descending down the maze of underground tubes that left us breathless when we turned and stepped on another long, multi-tiered, wooden-treaded escalator, we boarded the trains, ascended, and were surprised when we emerged to the top by the lighted signs as we circled and shopped about Piccadilly Circus. On to Trafalgar Square, we stopped at a pub before boarding a bus for our last night for now at our London home.

CHAPTER 22

Bea on July 18, 1974
Sunday. Stonehenge, Salisbury.
Beautiful day, misty in the evening.

After breakfast, we packed our mini car that filled up fast, even with our conservative amount of luggage. I navigated and Jan held her breath as she drove. Our watchwords were "Think left!" and we did fine in Sunday's early morning traffic.

On the way out of London, we stopped at Petticoat Lane, an eclectic market where Charles Dicken's Oliver Twist and Fagan could have traded their stolen goods. We bought several gifts and Jan took more pictures. With all the East Indian sellers around, Jan told me she heard Ravi Shankar and George Harrison playing the sitar in her head even though Cockney button-costumed street musicians entertained the crowds around the market stalls.

We drove into Salisbury around 2 p.m., parked the car, and headed toward Salisbury Cathedral, down charming streets with, of course, the English houses we had imagined, as well as shops with Tudor architecture, wooden beams, and stone; and on the roofs—chimneys and more chimneys. We walked under a stone arch into the cathedral close, then the cathedral. Its size and scale were awesomely magnificent. Construction began in 1100 or 1200 AD; it wasn't finished until 1375.

The spire, at 404 feet, is the tallest in England. While looking at the history on the wall chart, the organist began and the choir sang to us as angels on high from its vaulted ceiling niche. We smiled in delight. After all, it is Sunday. Returning to the car we drove around town looking for a B&B consulted our tour book and found a sweet little place on Trinity Lane near Love Lane.

After checking in, we headed out for Stonehenge with our excitement intensifying as we grew nearer. And there it was, standing in the midst of acres of green land with sheep grazing about. It was after 5 p.m. with its shadows long and dramatic. Jan squirmed with delight as she drove closer, but I was frustrated by not being able to capture the experience with my camera.

Stonehenge was like a dream and we were high priestesses worshipping the sun, the moon, and the genius of the builders who created this temple of Nature from the dawn of ancient times. We took pictures and touched, even leaned against the stones. We planted ourselves directly on the encircling Aubrey Hole stones and soaked in the electric energy to worship, to honor the earth and the sky and the changing of seasons, celebrating the spiritual potential and the mystery of it all.

Truly, the wonder of Stonehenge.

Years ago (Would it have been 1966?) Jan asked me to create a church school course on Stonehenge. She handed me Gerald Hawkins' new book, *Stonehenge Decoded,* and I went to work on it right away. I'm happy that I remember the details and have done further research speculating on how it was created. Jan appreciates my knowledge. She told me I make a remarkable and intelligent personal guide. Here we are in 1976, now together in Stonehenge, in love, in joy, in England.

The pubs were closed again for an afternoon break. Why do they do that? We came back to our room to rest a bit before we set out in search of dinner. We found it at the Wheat Sheaf, but we became a little nervous when we found we only had 4£ left and they couldn't cash an American Travelers check on Sundays. So, we asked the waitress to advise us as to what we could afford to order for our supper for under 3£. She brought each of us plaice (fish) with chips, peas and biscuits and a half-pint of lager with cheese for dessert.

After we left the warm pub filled with cheerful patrons at the bar and around the tables near the burning embers in the fireplace, we saw the cathedral spire in misty orange clouds. Yes, orange! Salisbury was ours as we headed together along the empty streets to find the cathedral illuminated in the fog. Except for the dark brown eerie shadows on the grass of the church and its spire, the moist, orange luminescence enveloped us as we held hands. Jan actually put her arm around me and I put my head on her shoulder in this public place. But we were alone.

After the misty dampness reached our bones, our appetite called for whatever grog our last English pound of the day would buy for the two of us. Out of luck again. We missed the pub for the second time today. It closed at 10:30.

Jan on July 18, 1976

A soft, late afternoon English sunlight filters through the starched crochet curtains of the one window on the gabled wall of our cozy, low, vaulted-ceiling room—vaulted because we're in an attic under the roof of this B&B just off Love Lane. Other than the ivory-colored curtains, two floral slip-covered chairs, a matching fabric skirt hanging from a small vanity, and a lavatory basin, an aged, gravy-shaded floral wallpaper envelops the room. Two primly made, three-quarter beds with barely adequate mattresses and pillows stand against each side of the lower roof edge where it meets the four-foot-high walls. A ruffled lampshade on a translucent plastic lamp adorns the vanity, and a floor lamp leans at a slight angle toward one of the armchairs. It's one of the most beautiful rooms I've ever slept in. I'll remember it forever.

Our nap after Stonehenge is our sanctuary for a secret ritual of muffled yet unrestrained rapture that transports me back to ancient pagan times as well as beyond time to the unknowable. We two, coiled together as one on the bed under the slanting roof or ceiling or shelter or tent or hut or cave or subterranean cavern, delve deeper and wholly into my soul with my soul's mate returning my fervor, filling my spirit and my mind, my body and my heart with reverent, astounding, intensely passionate energy, hushed and hidden by our self-enforced silence so that our blissful devotions will not be detected.

Bea on July 19, 1976
Monday. Salisbury, Bath, Wells, Glastonbury.
Cloudy to rain.

After eating our breakfast in a tiny room with four empty tables, we had a moment of worry when we couldn't start the car, but I lifted the bonnet, wiggled a couple of wires and it started. We drove into the center of town, cashed traveler's checks, purchased a battery for my camera and bought a blue-black, full-length leather coat! Lovely bargain. Jan thoroughly approved.

We drove to Bath, a large city filled with Georgian architecture plus the famous Roman baths from the 3rd Century that we toured after a pub lunch of sausage pastry and chips. The gentle rain hitting the King's Bath surface of the warm mineral springs caused spirals of steam to travel up the copper-toned stone columns and arches. We stopped in the Pump Room to taste its healing waters, but pub beverages taste much better and make me feel better too.

Driving on from there to Wells, we found a bed & breakfast in a more than two-hundred-year-old farmhouse where two determined, dark-haired young men wrestled and lifted brown and white-spotted calves into a truck while hay whirled around all of them.

Centuries ago, the legendary city of Glastonbury was surrounded by shallow, below-seawater levels with magical mists rising around the high ground. The reclaimed land still holds the magic of the Holy Grail as we leisurely strolled the ruins of the Abbey where Joseph of Arimathea, the wealthy disciple of Jesus and the keeper of the Holy Grail, is said to have come to convert the pagans to Christianity. Then and there, monks claimed they discovered the bones of King Arthur and Queen Guinevere and buried them in the Abbey under a worn headstone that we could still read and revere.

We found The George Hotel and Pilgrims Inn built around the 15th Century to house pilgrims visiting the Abbey and we enjoyed lager and dinner in keeping with the spirit of its long-gone patrons from the past. For over 500 years, pilgrims found hospitality here, and we took a step back in time to join them to feast and savor its delights under great oak beams. I ate smoked oysters in a cheese sauce called Deacon's Delight while Jan enjoyed some less challenging fare. We moved from our table to the pub bar stools and drank sherry, then mead. Delicious!

We asked the bartender how to get to the Glastonbury Tor. He described the route around the Abbey and up the hill and warned us to be careful, perhaps because of the dark, narrow roads and high hedges—or because we looked a bit flushed with sherry and mead.

Ha! Glastonbury Tor rose up out of the misty plain. We found it. It was a miracle, especially when Jan kept forgetting to drive on the left after she negotiated turns in the narrow, hilly road spiraling up to a dark, empty car park at the base of the site. We tumbled out of our little Austin and found a path that led us to its base with spotlights at the top shining on the remains of the ancient St. Michael's Church tower. Finding the Glastonbury Tor is a symbol of our search. In the night, we didn't know what road we took, we didn't know what would happen to us, yet we were determined in our quest.

A flash of color flew through the lights on the tower above. Someone was flying a kite up there!

It started drizzling, but undaunted, we'd come this far and we wouldn't be stopped. It was too dark to find any path or stairs, but heady and excited and holding hands like Jack and Jill, we stumbled straight up the steep incline on slippery wet grass. Who knows, with cows and sheep grazing the slopes, what else made it slippery? Ecstatic and cavorting like adolescents in love, we climbed on until we started laughing so hard we had to find a place to pee or we'd wet our britches. Oh well, we tried to get to the top. Anyway, who wants to struggle all the way up there when someone or maybe more are already there? Turning and sliding back down, probably on sheep shit, we reached a hedgerow that blocked our way forward, but it served to shelter us as we both squatted to relieve ourselves. Jan said she could imagine scenes from English movies with a fox being chased by the hounds and hunters on horseback leaping over the hedge and over us.

We made a grubby trek back to the car and Jan spiraled us down and home to our farmhouse with only our headlights to guide us through the narrow hedge-rowed roads. It was a miracle we found our farm. We deposited our muddy shoes near the entrance and went up to what was a children's room, adapted as needed into B&B accommodations for two traveling ladies. Stimulated by our adventures and full of joy, especially at sleeping in a colorful room with whimsical decorations and playful linens, I looked among the many toys and books and found a copy of Kipling's *Just So Stories*. Jan tucked herself among the double bed covers filled with clowns and balloons while I read "The Elephant's Child" with his "satiable curiosity" looking for "the Crocodile at the edge of the great grey-green, greasy Limpopo River, all set about with fever trees" for her bedtime story. As I returned the book to its place on the shelf, I looked out the window over the sheds and out to the English country night sky. I crawled into bed, turned out the nursery nightlight, and cuddled next to her.

Jan whispered in my ear, "High diddle, diddle, the cat and the fiddle. The cow jumped over the moon. The little dog laughed to see such sport and the dish ran away with the spoon."

Bea on July 20, 1976
Tuesday. Glastonbury, Cheddar, Lynton, Exmore, Tintagel (Camelford).
Drizzle, cooler, variable to partly cloudy, and sunny.

What a wholesome breakfast we ate, the two of us in the farm family's spacious dining room. I drove through the spectacular Cheddar Gorge as Jan sang "Rock of Ages, cleft for me." Its magnificence caught us off guard and we stopped to look back at what we had traversed. It's only the first of many surprises to follow as we traveled up and around Somerset, Devon, and the Cornish coastlines. The moors! The hills! The sea! What legends!

Around each turn, on top of each rise, a new panorama of steeply rolling hills and hedge-rowed fields appeared with sheep, ponies, gnarled and evil-looking trees, heather, and high mounds. Then the land swooped abruptly to the sea. I drove up a hill, seemingly straight up for 500 feet and we imagined our little car slipping in reverse downhill! It must have had a 1:3 grade. We drove over the crest of Lynton and down again into the Lynmouth on the water's edge. Tourists thronged the lovely jewel of Lynmouth—English tourists. We ate a sandwich lunch at the historic Rising Sun Hotel Pub and sat in the sun on the rocks along the harbor.

My movie camera again has let me down. It won't run at all now.

Jan took over and we drove on toward King Arthur's Tintagel. The scenery was still beautiful but without the spectacular contrasts. We first found our B&B in the little hamlet near Camelford. Our large second-story room presented us with a four-poster double bed with drapery on the headboard and matching fabric draperies on the windows to help keep out dampness and traffic noise, two tall and stately chifforobes standing against humpy plaster walls of the old B&B standing right against the sidewalk's edge.

After taking care of our elegant accommodations, we crossed the road and made arrangements to pile into a dusty, battered Land Rover that would take us to Tintagel and out to the cliff-top remains where the legendary King Arthur was to have been conceived—directly above and across a sandy inlet leading to Merlin's Cave. We climbed along the narrow path near the ocean where the skeletal ruins of the ancient barrier walls led to the flat green grass top where the castle once stood. Breathtaking! The late afternoon sun shined on us with the ocean waves beating on the rocks below, then returning as waterfalls, Merlin's caves at the base of sheer rises, the vast expanse of coastline stretching off in either direction, the blue ocean waves and incredibly white foam, the wind blowing hard at us.

And the castle ruins! In the center of what could have been the Great Hall or Chapel, a stone altar is all that remains from the fortress that stood for centuries before crumbling into the Atlantic. We were alone under the spell of Tintagel. Jan and I, in one thought, held each other's hands on this rock and secretly pledged to each other our lasting love. In the everlasting spirit of this altar stone, we spoke quietly of our love as endless as the sky, as dynamic as the ocean, as formidable as the earth, and as magical as the energy that drew us together and blessed us.

We hated to leave, but we finally gave in to the chilling wind, boarded the day's last ride back into town and feasted sensuously on roast duck, potatoes, peas, cauliflower, and cream tea with scones! We also sampled the ingredients of our first bottle of mead.

Impetuous Jan! While driving back along the shore road to our B&B, she caught sight of a narrow dirt lane with a mile of trees creating an arbor of green leading to who knows where away from the ocean. She remembered seeing something on the map and she swerved to drive our little car into the dense, leafy tunnel that turned desolate and eerie when the sky opened again onto a bleak plain with the lonely, stony Neolithic Rough Tor towering like the top of an Alpine mountain in the midst of nowhere. We jumped out of the car and swirled and romped about like primitive folk without inhibitions.

Always wary, I made her drive us home before darkness and sipped our final glass from the bottle of mead, the Cornish honeymoon drink.

Bea on July 21, 1976
Wednesday. Camelford, Land's End, St. Michael's Mount, and Exeter.
Cloudy to partly cloudy.

An excellent breakfast: fresh eggs, bacon thick like ham, fried bread, beans, tea, even cereal, as usual, but extra good today in the charming breakfast room where we chatted with a couple from New Zealand.

I drove the first shift. That little car feels so good to drive, like a wrap-a-round car or a fun one like Dodgem cars at a fair. We wove through many small villages and farms with vistas of the rolling hills and ocean to Land's End, with its impressive panorama of cliffs, rocks, and the Atlantic Ocean. We had a drink in the pub and waved goodbye to the lighthouse on a rock far out in the ocean with nothing but water until you reach North America 3000 miles away.

We pushed on for St. Michael's Mount, an island with an imposing church reached by ferry at high tide or a path at low tide. Strolling along the beach, we took pictures of families sunning on the beach while Jan sang "Every summer we can rent a cottage in the Isle of Wight, if it's not too dear…Grandchildren on your knee, Vera, Chuck, and Dave….Will you still need me? Will you still feed me when I'm sixty-four?" We found a garden café overlooking the beach, watched pilgrims trooping across the sand to St. Michael's, and devoured the delicious tea with strawberries, clotted cream, and biscuits. Lovely. Who could ask for more?

On through the wild country of Bodmin Moor, we stopped at a weather-beaten blackish coach house called Jamaica Inn after the Daphne Du Maurier novel of cutthroat pirates and ladies in distress. I drove on to Exeter, where our B&B served our breakfast table in our room. We parked the car on a hill so we could coast down to get it started. We ate a terrific Chinese dinner in the city center, then drank a beer and brandy at The Ship with its black-beamed, head-denting ceiling and galleon-style bay windows; the same pub where

Sir Francis Drake, the Elizabethan sea hero, drank his grog with his seafaring mates in about 1590.

Bea on July 22, 1976
Thursday. Exeter, London.
Fair to partly cloudy.

It took us over fifteen minutes to start the car and it wasn't until I monkeyed with the carburetor by screwing out a central valve, at least that's what I think it's called, that it caught at last. Jan drove the first shift and we had first-rate motorways with six lanes and could drive at 75 to 80 miles an hour. We left Exeter a little after 9 a.m. and returned to London at 12:30. I drove the second shift into London and we turned the car in at Kemming Car Hire.

We had driven 844 miles! We hoisted our bags and boarded the underground for Victoria Station, ate a tasty pub lunch: beef stew, beans, and potatoes, and returned by bus to be greeted by our Hansel and Gretel hosts. After a bath and a respite, we did some laundry so it would be dry when we were ready to pack our canvas bags for tomorrow's journey. Then we dressed for the Strand Theatre, made our way to King's Cross, and ate a snack at the Eliza Doolittle. Our 1£ ($2.30) seats in the front row gave us a great view of two short Peter Shaffer comedies, *White Lies* and *Black Comedy*. After a farewell drink at The Mabel, we took the tube home for our last night in London.

CHAPTER 23

Bea on July 23, 1976
Friday. London. Amsterdam.
Light haze, sunny.

We hopped out of our separate little beds early so we'd be sure to make our train and boat connections to Amsterdam. Carrying sandwiches and a bottle of mead along with Jan's red and my brown canvas bags, plus my new leather coat and non-working camera in its case, we hopped a cab for Liverpool Street Station, found our train, and nestled into the seats, sharing the spaces in our typically British compartment, as in Alfred Hitchcock and Agatha Christie movies. It pulled out of London at 7:45 a.m. with us hanging out of the open windows.

We read newspapers and enjoyed the two-hour train ride to Harwich, where we boarded the Kaingin Wilhelmina for a beautiful five-hour crossing on the flat calm English Channel. (When Jan crossed with Alex from France to England twenty years back, a rough Channel made her terribly seasick. With vivid memories of that crossing, she positively imagined smooth sailing for our trip.) We sat on the lower deck facing the window and were lulled to sleep several times by the pulsing engines. We woke up to stroll the decks, eat sandwiches, and drink mead and beer.

Landing at the Hoek van Holland, we boarded the train carrying us across the bucolic countryside to crowded Amsterdam. A few actual windmills turned and green polders reclaimed from the sea and protected by dikes contained grazing cattle and sheep amidst the vast expanse of new buildings. The Dutchy old windmills had been largely replaced by giant cantilevered cranes and pumps.

In Amsterdam itself, we boarded a three-car trolley to find our tall and narrow Hotel Welcome across from a canal with houseboats moored at the sidewalk's edge and moving craft loaded with freight maneuvering up the watery roadway. Yes! It's Amsterdam, the Venice of the North.

After our gasping climb clinging to the inner column of steep, narrow stairs, we finally reached our fourth-floor room. We gasped again when we looked out our window to view the beautiful Priningract Canal with a lesser canal cutting across it. We were on the top floor and the characteristic outside furniture hook hung above our swing-in window. It most likely was used centuries ago to haul up the heavy, sculptured wooden double bed filled with a heavenly soft mattress topped with freshly aired, feather-down covers and pillows.

After celebrating our personal passion for Amsterdam in the blissful bed, we dressed, descended down the stairs, and walked past the Rijksmuseum to find the Hoffman restaurant. I had steak and mushrooms; Jan had veal and mushrooms. We walked a different way to our hotel, passing the lovely, softly illuminated canals. Modern, almost silent boats toured tourists, easing them under low, narrow bridges lit all around with cheery yellow lights.

Jan on July 24, 1976

Last night we cleaned our well-traveled bodies in a roomy bathtub and shower down the hall. Bea's delight that she wasn't scalded included her discovery that the showerhead comes off the wall-hung, hand-held fixture to refresh and warm all the body's nooks and crannies. Our bath was also a spiritual ritual before we melded together into the yielding soft comfort and pillowed clouds of white Dutch linens.

Her bare body's fresh fragrance inspired vivid images of our walking past hundreds of flower stalls filled with dense clusters of every color blending into each other in rowdy, radiant rainbows. My mouth, finding her neck and smooth shoulders, sensed curving petals, open and trusting, to be cared for tenderly as a lover brings a bouquet to a beloved.

Her breasts next to mine, rising and falling with one heartbeat, is Mother Nature's rhythm bringing the seasons of ripeness and the harvest. Each stamen, ripe and ready for the gentle arrival of a pollen-swollen bee, grows to its energy's potential, and when tension is released, succulent mouths reach for each other again and we fall asleep with lips and bodies bonded.

When I awoke and felt for her in the fluff of our billowy bed, I raised my head and gazed at her, soft and supple in her yellow blouse, sitting as if in a Vermeer painting, only she is my woman with this morning's light illuminating and warming her. She's writing in her travel journal at the lofty open casement window letting in brightness from pure white, puffy clouds above and sweetness from Dutch air scented with freshly baked pastry drifting up to us with the muffled noises from bicycle riders, market wagons, and canal boats below.

Bea on July 24, 1976
Saturday. Amsterdam.
The morning sun turned rainy to partly cloudy.

I awoke to the raucous squawks of gulls and the chattering of small birds. We two must have been a bit raucous as well during the night because our woman concierge gave us strange looks when we tumbled down the stairs. Oh well. I considered Amsterdam a freethinking city with the Zee Dike and all. But that doesn't guarantee that all of its citizens are broad-minded.

We ate breakfast next door at the Hotel Weikman and gobbled up delicious bread, cheeses, a soft-boiled egg, and coffee at the café tables. To Central Station by trolley, we got our money exchanged and brought our tickets for Paris. We then took the trolley to the Van Gogh Museum to celebrate the finest and largest collection of his paintings. We ate a fabulous lunch there: herring, shrimp, raw oysters, potato salad, and pickles. Jan skipped the oysters.

Impressed by the craftsmanship of the great Dutch painters, including Rembrandt at the Rijksmuseum, we searched out the pub that had been Rembrandt's hangout centuries ago.

Boarding a canal boat tour where the guide spoke in several languages, we circuited the inner city and went out beyond the Central Station to the harbor and pulled up alongside the quay to let off a tour of Spaniards who had to catch the boat for Norway. We saw *The Deutschland*, a cruise ship from the Rhine River, narrowly miss an ancient Dutch sailing boat with gaff head, sail and leeboards.

Coming home to change clothes, we headed out to eat at Holland's Glorie, a fine Dutch restaurant where we had cutlet Suisse filled with ham and cheese covered by a mushroom sauce, tiny browned potatoes, salad, and of course, wine. Next, we had a drink at the Jerusalem of Gold but it was too early for entertainment so we strolled to the Elides Plain, past the Rembrandt's Plain, where, instead of a fountain, they had a forest of torches blazing at the sky. We sat under a canopy of yellow light bulbs, drank beer, and watched people. An old man and his harmonica, a young man and his guitar entertained us all.

Bea on July 25, 1976
Sunday. Amsterdam.
Drizzle & partly cloudy.

We built up our courage to go to the Anne Frank Haus and the unforgettable Secret Annex—a moving experience with displays of the Netherlands during World War II and the persecution of the Jews—to stand in the actual rooms of those who helped the Franks and others hide from the Nazis for two years! Jan and Alex had seen the play when it first opened in New York in 1955 with Susan Strasberg and Joseph Schildkraut. Jan also had read the book and used it when she taught high school English and later, as a Unitarian Universalist church schoolteacher. She cried when we went through the building. I couldn't help myself and cried too. I bought the paperback of Anne Frank's Diary. It's a true miracle that her diary, waiting in this dusty attic, was found after the horrific years of The Holocaust and WW II.

To Central Station again, we boarded bus #87 for Nieuwendam Noord, a suburb across the harbor, then changed to Bus #30 to Holysloot through a dike town named Dergendam on narrow little roads with a small canal on either side, twisting across the polders on what used to be the Zuiderzee, passed small boat harbors on the Ijsselmeer and farms and brick houses bountiful with flowers, but we didn't see a single windmill. At the end of the line, we shopped about in Holysloot, drank a genever (Dutch gin) and beer at a café, and headed back.

Back in Amsterdam, we were surprised to find a folk fair at the Akenaton Street market with hippies, a variety of young and old characters, people with kids on their shoulders or dogs on leashes or dogs on the loose, barefoot girls, and booted boys. All, except the dogs, wore various outfits from ragged jeans to pinstripe suits with vests. Live music kept everyone jumping. A rock group named The Carlsberg and then Black musicians with their steel band called The Invaders vibrated the atmosphere clouded with cigarette and marijuana smoke with smiling people sitting at tables or milling about. We drank three beers and Jan had a ball taking human-interest shots.

We strolled over to the next street and found the Lyn Fa Restaurant we were looking for. The once Dutch-governed colony of Indonesia imported glorious Indonesian food for us to eat, first with prawn crackers, then a tray with about sixteen dishes filled with different delights like pork, beef, fried banana, rice, veggies, oranges, pineapple, peanuts, and lots of hot and spicy sauces.

Jan had been to Amsterdam with Alex in the late 50s, so she had no worries about taking me toward the Zee Dike with sex shops and all in its Red Light District. She said she expected me to be interested in seeing how open the sex trade is with prostitutes in window booths, but I revolted and we quickly turned around and found a quaint old hidden street of homes on a square down a little alley where Jan spied an old woman staring down on us from an upper window embellished with a flowing flower box. The woman never moved, even when Jan took her photo. We finished the evening with a drink at a sidewalk café and made our way home.

Jan on July 25, 1976

"Jesus Christ!" she said to me after she saw a man relieving himself against a Zee Dike wall. "Where are you taking me!"

Shocked and surprised at her reaction, I sputtered, "Hell, Bea. Men pee all over Europe. Just stop your car at a train crossing and men jump out of their cars to pee. At least this guy's got his back to us."

"Why did you think I wanted to see this kind of crap! Who do you think I am?"

"Well, I'm not thrilled seeing a guy peeing either, but I figured the Zee Dike would be interesting and it's still afternoon so we've lots of daylight left. Tourists come here all the time. You've caught me off guard with your overreaction—just because a man pees against the wall."

"I'm a Chicago girl. I know what can happen, and I don't go to places like this." She actually shouted at me. "You don't even care about my safety, let alone yours!"

Flushed, stunned, and speechless, steam almost blew out my ears. I couldn't believe this shocking attack after all of our tender times on this trip. And after her many escapades with men to prove she was not a lesbian. She started to move away from me. Hell. I can play that game too, and I crossed the street and started walking swiftly away from her to release my actual physical and emotional pain with the flow of overwhelming adrenaline. My eyes got blurry.

My heart pumped fiercely. What a fiasco! So sudden! No conversation. No questions. Just blurt out your anger and attack me—for nothing.

I paced up the main shopping street for quite a while before I realized I was so upset that I didn't have an idea of where I was going—and I couldn't remember the name of our little hotel. Great! Now I'm lost. Devastated and lost in Amsterdam. Do I find a police station? What a fool am I!

I grabbed a signpost to steady myself and clear my mind. I felt like throwing up. Then I saw Bea across the street. She had followed me. Now I could find the name of our hotel at least, but I'd have to swallow my pride and let her rescue me.

Why did this happen? For what? For nothing. Shit!

Bea on July 26, 1976
Monday. Amsterdam.
Fair to partly cloudy.

After we ate a delicious breakfast at a bakery with saved leftovers for later, we caught a tram for the deMopes Diamond Cutters, toured the factory, and I tried on expensive rings even though I don't like diamonds. We bought souvenirs for our families at the vast Albert Street market, took a tram to the Mint Tower, and walked through the canal-side flower market with greenhouses floating on barges. After a beer at a sidewalk café, we wandered around the market Waterloo Plein and through the Rembrandt Huis, its low ceilings held up by heavy dark beams. Back to Spvi, our neighborhood, we had another drink while watching people, including an ancient-looking man playing a bulky street organ.

We ate at our hotel café with its walls and ceilings covered with years of piss-yellow cigarette smoke, played the slot machines, and went upstairs for a nap before going to the Stadsschouwburg Theatre where we sat in front-row seats at the edge of the third balcony at the top of theater to enjoy the entertaining Folkclaristisch Dance Group. We were so high that my altitude issue almost made my nose bleed. Before returning back to the pack, we had another drink at our café to bring closure to our Amsterdam adventures.

234

CHAPTER 24

Bea on July 27, 1976
Tuesday. Amsterdam to Paris.
Fair to partly cloudy.

The taxi was on time and we easily found our train to Paris leaving at 7:50 a.m., rolling through flat Holland, then more windmills through Belgium and over the gently rolling land of France with tree-lined roads and farm fields. With great anticipation, we arrived in Paris at 3 p.m.

Paris is huge. While at the station, I bought our reservations for the next leg of our travels, the train to Heidelberg. Jan appreciated my talent for changing money, navigating schedules, and remembering details. I was pretty confident that I could deal with the language because I had two years of college French, but Jan, after living in Germany and traveling in Europe in the 50s, had more practice in communicating her pidgin English into other languages, especially on the phone; so after we selected the hotels we were interested in from our guidebook, she called from the station for reservations at the Hotel Bonaparte on Rue Bonaparte where we had to take the stairway up one floor to our sixth-floor room because the elevator only reached the fifth floor. The bathroom was down the hall, but there was a wash basin and, of course, a bidet in our room. It seemed clean but seedy to me but Jan looked out the window and said it has a perfect Parisian view—for a starving artist.

After unpacking, we hit the streets, strolled down to the Seine, resting while quenching Parisian beverages at a couple of sidewalk cafés, then strolling back across the Pont Royal to the Arc de Triomphe and down the Champs Elysees to the Louvre. Then starving, we made it to our Rue Bonaparte and the Beaux-Arts Restaurant for boeuf bourguignonne, brochette en rump steak, vinaigrette, celery, Camembert Fromage with wine included, plus the music from a fabulous classical guitarist. All for under forty francs.

After our perfect dinner, we strolled to Pont Neuf and took a night cruise down the Seine past the Eiffel Tower and other romantically illuminated Paris sites.

Later that evening, while the two of us watched passers-by at an outdoor café, an attractive Frenchman sat down next to Jan and we started chatting. Jan said later he sounded like an American down on his luck. Within a few minutes, he asked Jan if she "wanted to make love?" Without any thought or hesitation, she answered, "No, thank you," and turned immediately to me asking, "Do you want to make love with him?"

What was she doing? How naive. I laughed quietly at both of them and declined the offer. Ironically, Jan had bought a package of condoms with her. She's never used condoms in her life and when we were joking about why she bought them for the trip, she told me, "Who knows what you'll be up to when we're there, and I don't want to bring home any sexual souvenirs because we weren't prepared." Naturally, she had picked out a package of various colors.

Bea on July 28, 1976
Wednesday. Paris.
Fair to partly cloudy.

Today's destination was a long walk to the Rodin Museum, a lovely house with rooms of carved wood walls full of Rodin's impressive sculptures and lovely gardens and grounds. From there, we headed toward the Invalides to the Eiffel Tower and rode the elevator to the top. What a view of this magnificent city with the Seine and its bridges like a necklace across her ivory white throat. Paris boasts of its many impressive buildings that seem to stretch for blocks and blocks with pillars, colonnades, and statuary everywhere! Fountains and gardens and esplanades of vast expanses.

We walked to the Arc de Triomphe and down the entire Champs Elysees, the most beautiful boulevard in the world! We people-watched at a sidewalk café and pressed on again through the Garden of the Tuileries, where we saw a ballet troupe practicing for a performance on a vast open-air stage set in the middle of a green-coated pond. Hearing more music, we found a carnival with carousels and rides, then a pond where boys sailed model sailboats, directing them with sticks. At last, we staggered through a small Arc du Carrousel back to Rue Bonaparte, where we had our dejeuner again at our Beaux Art restaurant. This time we ate delicious escargot-parc, some beef filet, French fries and Camembert.

We came home to nap after passing a street jazz band at St. Germain des Pres. I ran down the hall to use the bathroom and when I came back to our room, I found Jan standing in the bidet's running waters. She was moaning, "Oh my balls! My poor balls!"

We woke from our nap, dressed and caught the cab to the Rue Des Invalides, the formidable Hotel des Invalides that houses Napoleon's Tomb, originally built by Louis XIV as a pension house for old soldiers. In the magnificent forecourt surrounded by arches and columns and massive erect cannons, we sat in the dark and saw a fabulous light and sound show covering the history of France from the Revolution to Napoleon and Napoleon's son, the King of Rome. All characters were like the "ghosts" of the men and women who once trod the giant cobblestones of the courtyard. The show ended with the inspiring "Marseilles."

A cab ride back to St. Germain des Pres took us to a succession of street entertainers, including a French clown, an English guitar duo, a Black guitarist who sang in Spanish, a magician in tails and top hat, and even an old beggar lady, all enterprisingly earning a few francs from passing the dish or hat. The man standing next to me, probably another tourist, remarked as he threw in a coin, "It's like we're in a bloody church."

Home to bed at about 1 a.m. I estimated that we had walked over six miles around Paris on this fantastic day and night.

Bea on July 29, 1976
Thursday. Paris and night train to Heidelberg.
Fair.

After breakfast of bread and cheese in our room, we shopped along St. Germain des Pres and St. Michael. We entered Notre Dame Cathedral, lit a candle to Jan d'Arc, and stood in awe of muted, aged darkness contrasted by stained glass windows and lofty spires. We rested at a café outside, looking at the lovely sculptures of the building and bought a Tunisian sandwich to eat in the park. We dared to go underground on the Metro to Au Printemps, the French Marshall Fields, and had a beer at the top where a huge stained-glass dome lined with a blue flower motif vaulted above us. Across the other building, we came out on the rooftop observation deck for a Paris vista. We took the Metro again to the Place de Concorde but discovered the Sewer tour did not leave from there so we searched for it along the Rue de Rivoli to find out the sewer tour was only on Wednesdays.

Catching a cab back to our hotel, we picked up our baggage and went to Gare de l'Est to check it in a locker. We took a bus to Sacre Coeur and Montmartre and drank a liter of "grass" beer at a café in full view of Sacre Coeur, almost the rival of the Taj Mahal. We took the short funicular next to the carousel and the curving steps to the church at the very top where the views of Paris were even more spectacular.

After shopping around Montmartre, we found a charming restaurant seemingly carved out of the chalky white stone under the church—a little, low cave as if we were in a candle-lit crypt that offered all the joys of living—and romance with gourmet food, music and wine. Jan had chicken and I had boeuf-stuffed grape leaves, herring and salad, and we drank a whole bottle of Stadsschouwburg accompanied by singing and accordion music. Afterward, we watched the street artists around the square before we sat on the Sacre Coeur steps, where I fell asleep with my head on Jan's shoulder.

She woke me in time to dash for a cab to Gare de l'Est and board the sleeper car that gave us a surprise—six bunks stacked three to each side of the cramped compartment. We claimed the middle bunks and slept in our clothes, covered with one thin blanket, our valuables tucked under our pillows. Four men in their bunks above and below snored around us. Now I know what it must be like in an Army barracks bed or a submarine bunk, but it wasn't long before we two exhausted travelers were lulled to sleep by the gently swaying train.

CHAPTER 25

Bea on July 30, 1976
Friday. Heidelberg.
Fair to partly cloudy

I changed our money to German marks while Jan phoned our chosen hotel. A cab drove us to a lovely courtyard-guarded hotel. Our room is terrific with another huge double bed with downy comforters and pillows. These Europeans certainly know how to sleep in comfort.

We walked around the red brick and cobblestoned town to orient ourselves! What an awesome site is Heidelberg, set on both sides of the Neckar River between hills like huge green leafy breasts.

The town is full of bells and people. After a bratwurst and sauerkraut lunch, we took the funicular up to the Schloss, the castle, and explored the grounds, drank a beer, and watched the bees and birds. We went to see a movie in German, *Das Ritual,* and decided we probably couldn't understand it in any language. To the Red Ox for a drink, then to a lovely beer garden for a supper of breaded veal, pork, spaetzle, salat and delicious white wine. Back home, we slept like angels in the fluff of feather comforters and heavenly pillows.

Jan on July 30, 1976

After a flash of insight, I dismissed going into Frankfurt even though we went near it while we slept on the train. I'd spent almost three years there. I'd have liked showing Bea the places where I lived, taught in the Army dependents high school, and enjoyed life, but those memories have too much to do with the early years of my marriage and before motherhood. It seemed inappropriate to share that with my lover, especially with my husband at home with our children while we're passionately experiencing our intimate affaire d'amour, a phrase I learned from a Paris newspaper headline.

Even though I lived in Frankfurt for two-and-a-half years from 1956 to 1958, I communicated only with basic hausfrau German. Most Germans understood some English or answered our stammering German sentences spoken in perfectly correct grammar in Oxford English accents.

It was twenty years since I had to speak German again.

Researching German on the train to reserve a room in Heidelberg, I found comfortable phrases in my Arthur Frommer book. From the station phone booth, I called my first choice. After practicing my feeble German, I confidently said, "Ein zimmer fur swei dammen, bitte." (One room for two women, please.) Well, you can practice what you'll say, but you can't anticipate nor will you always understand the response. However, she and I worked through the details and I felt quite accomplished. Then she asked in German, "When will you arrive?" Thinking that I was saying, "As soon as we eat breakfast (fruehstuck)," I had said, "As soon as we eat a pencil (bleistift?)." I didn't hear her laugh, just a tiny twitter; and after I hung up the phone with smug satisfaction, I realized what I'd said and laughed out loud at my blunder.

The clerk welcomed us with good humor and assigned us a cozy room with open cottage windows and crisp, chiffon curtains that gently waved in the heady fragrance of geraniums, petunias, and baby's breath from each window box. I remember when I lived in Germany, the hausfraus would hang thick bedding out the windows each morning to capture the fresh air.

Of course, we needed to be refreshed after yesterday in Paris and sleeping in our clothes on the train with cigarette-smoky men stacked around us. We both needed a bath. The mid-morning sun radiated through the high bathroom window of translucent glass onto the shiny white tiles, the toilet, the deep and sturdy Germanic tub, and all the silvery plumbing fixtures. Unlike most of the rooms we stayed in on our trip, we had an entire bathroom all to ourselves. I opened our bottle of Mosel wine, set it and two glasses on an enamel stool with a white facecloth for table linen, and invited Bea to help the earth save water by bathing with me in the huge tub.

We gently anointed each other with oils and our wine cups almost runneth over—as well as a bit of water from the tub when we slid into the clear warm bath together, cautiously watching that the water would not be so displaced that it would overflow. I took the plumbing end with the tub, enjoying watching my lover lean back and rest in comfort against the towel I folded for her pillow. From my point of view, an Impressionist painter could not have created a more peaceful yet sensuous scene. I covered my chrome fixtures with several layers of towels so I wouldn't slip and slide against the pipes and bonk my body or my brain.

The sweet white Mosel River wine that touched our lips, cleansed the palate, and relaxed the inside of our bodies as we unwound completely from our all-night train ride and the tensions of traveling for two weeks.

Bells started ringing as we immersed ourselves together in the water, the bells that pealed from spires across the city as we soaked our bodies and savored our wine, the bells that tolled twelve from every clock—cuckoos clocks too, as we continued, sometimes spilling over the brim onto towels set on the floor soaking in the moisture until the tidal wave of desire became a calm and serene sea and the bells again chimed one o'clock.

Bea on July 31, 1976
Saturday. Heidelberg, Karlsruhe.
Cloudy, cooler, rain in the evening

Our VW was delivered at 10 a.m. It's bright yellow! After filling out the papers, we took off for Karlsruhe and to my son's Army base. Ah. Yes. We almost forgot the excuse for our trip to Europe—to see my son, Jim.

After we checked in at the military gate, Jim, still in his uniform, zoomed up on his Honda. We waited a bit 'til he got someone to take his duty. He changed his clothes and we three took off for Baden-Baden, where we found another unique guesthouse for the two of us. Jim helped us with our luggage and sat in the back seat while Jan drove off toward the Swartzwald, the Black Forest, with dense green scenery, and spectacular views of dark, pine-covered hills and mountains. We drove back down toward the Rhine River valley with the river winking below every now and again as the sun intermittently broke through the clouds. We got out to appreciate a little mountain lake at Mummelese, one of many small, lovely German towns. We had lunch in Baden-Baden before we went up to the Black Forest Restaurant for schnitzel. About 8 p.m. we got Jim back to Karlsruhe after a lovely day, drank a couple of beers together, and drove him back to camp.

He didn't talk much and he didn't invite us to meet any of his friends or show us where he stays or hangs out when he's not on duty. Nor did he invite us to see him tomorrow. He knew, of course, that we were coming and could have made some plans. We can only guess if he's got a girlfriend. It seems strange that we spent only one day with him, but maybe he didn't want to introduce his mother and her lover to his friends, though many women travel together without being lovers. Maybe he's still mad at me for divorcing his father. Maybe he blames me for his joining the Army, but my husband encouraged him to do that.

Back to the beautiful Baden-Baden, where we stopped for a beer and brandy, talked over the day, and then drove to find this night's featherbedded lodging.

Bea on August 1, 1976
Sunday. Baden-Baden and Schapbach.
Partly cloudy and cool

Our small but elegantly furnished room had two twin-sized sofa beds with formidable oak railings around three sides. From the window as large as one wall, we could look through the filmy screen of snow-white curtains to view a manicured lawn and the secluded, tree-lined road that was difficult to find last night in the dark. I slept late, exhausted from the stress of seeing Jim and trying to make sense of what he wasn't telling me.

I heard a clicking sound, opened my eyes, and saw Jan taking my picture asleep amid the pure whiteness of the fluffy bedding. She had moved a vase with a single red rose into the photo for contrast in the morning light that cast patterned shadows from the long lacy curtains. I lay there as she quietly moved around the intimate space, composing more photos of me lying in soft lily-white linens revealing only my face, hair, and the red rose.

After breakfast, we packed up and drove around elegant Baden-Baden, gassed up the car, and headed into the Black Forest toward Buhl and Aachen, where we found Sasbachwalden, a perfect Alpine picture-postcard town that was having a festival. We followed the sound to where a lederhosen band played German oompah music in a huge tent jammed with people pressed closely around wooden tables, drinking wine and beer and eating wurst and brotchen. The band enjoyed playing as much as the people enjoyed listening. Good feelings! When they played "The Beer Barrel Polka," we joined the singing and the fun!

We looked in the shops, bought some wine, and drove on in our yellow VW Bug. We found a side road that wound and wove through the lovely mountains and valleys—at times with rushing streams in concert, at times shelved into an eighty-degree angle slope and were surprised and delighted to find ourselves in the midst of an MG sports car rally of all vintages around every turn. At about 3:30, we found the gasthof Ochfes Wirts Hof to stop for a beer and brandy and found it had guest rooms. It had a schwimmen hallenbad (swim pool)! We signed up immediately for a doppelzimmer (double room) with a balcony overlooking the valley with a chuckling stream under our old-world casement window. We tested the feather quilts, drank wine, and changed into our swimsuits to discover we were the only two in the pool so we could pull our suits to our waists and frolic half nude in the warm water.

At supper, we ate rippchen, drank champagne, whispered, and laughed together—full of joy. I guess with our playfulness in the dining room crowded with sedate German couples and more congenial MG enthusiasts, we two American women attracted some attention, especially when we left arm-in-arm with Jan's outstretched hand holding the half-full champagne bottle by the neck as we listed in tandem across the public room and up the stairs to our Alpine chalet.

Bea on August 2, 1976
Monday. Schapbach. Rheinfelden. Switzerland.
Cloudy and cool.

The feather quilts were so comfortable we didn't want to get out of bed until we had to. After breakfast, we headed toward Wolfbach and found a famous leaded crystal glass works where we saw glass being formed, blown, shaped, and carved into expensive and artistic objects that we didn't need. We drove through genuine Hansel and Gretel scenery and when we stopped for lunch, I tried Russian egg and Jan savored her favorite: schnitzel.

We drove on to Staufen, the legendary home of Goethe who wrote about the legendary Faust who sold his spiritual soul to the devil in exchange for earthly knowledge. Vineyards hung down its slopes like royal robes, dressing Goethe's lovely Schloss crowning the top of a rugged sugar plum hill. A wine festival was expensive, so we bought a bottle and drove up a hill opposite the castle and toasted Goethe.

Jan had felt the impact of a scene in the Milwaukee Repertory Theatre's production of Christopher Marlowe's play, *Dr. Faustus* written 500 years ago. She researched and memorized the quote that affected her and whispered it to me while making love one afternoon in 1974. "Sweet Helen, make me immortal with a kiss. Suck forth my soul—see where it flies! Come, Helen, come, give me my soul again. Here will I dwell, for heaven is in these lips."

Yes, we've learned a lot of earthly and spiritual knowledge in the interim.

We crossed the German border at Rheinfelden into Switzerland, where the guard was curiously interested in the feather quilt we'd bought in Freiburg. This Swiss city is full of little fountains and all night, we heard the one in front of the hotel; its rippling replaced the sounds of the stream that sang us to sleep at last night's Black Forest inn.

CHAPTER 26

Bea on August 3, 1976
Tuesday. Rheinfelden. Zurich.
Partly cloudy and cool.

The crowded Zurich was a short and hectic drive to find the Hotel Splendid where our intimate room seemed like a European artist's garret with low, dark ancient-beamed ceilings lit by inspiring views from deep-set windows that reminded movie buff Jan of Shirley Temple's movie of Heidi's grandfather's cottage. We drove about a bit and unwound a bit. We even stretched out on the grass in Lake Zurich Park and napped near the water and under the sun until about 3 p.m. before we drove up to Dolder Mountain for the view.

It was time to think of going back home. Our last night of our trip would be here. We repacked, changed clothes, and forayed out for fondue in the evening, eating beef bourguignon cooked on forks in hot fat and swirled in various sauces. Delicious. I burned my lip but ate full to overflowing. We strolled back to our neighborhood, savoring the sights and people, stopping in the hotel bar, then to bed with our hearts preoccupied with anticipation of tomorrow's journey.

Bea on August 4, 1976
Wednesday. Zurich. Chicago. Lakeshore Bay.

Lazy in getting away, we finally loaded our yellow VW with all our gear, including my useless movie camera, but took off on foot for Swiss department stores to finish our shopping and stopped for a Swiss lunch of cheese fondue and an egg-ham-cheese dish that we shared. The wine, as usual, was delicious. After more shopping, we finally drove to the airport and turned in our little VW Bug.

When we got in the departure line, we were told that the TWA charter flight would be delayed for five hours. Our last-minute airport purchases included two bottles of Cutty Sark Scotch and a carton of English Benson & Hedges in tins. The 13-hour flight had us land in a heavy downpour for refueling in Santa Maria in the Azores. Back on the plane, I kept the sound off with Jan sleeping on my shoulder while I watched *Brannigan* with John Wayne playing a Chicago detective in London. The movie scenes there brought me back full circle to where we had begun our escape from reality.

We didn't get into Chicago until 4:05 a.m., but it was 10 a.m. to us. Poor Marge and a friend had been waiting at O'Hare for hours and finally drove home to send her son John and his girlfriend back to find us. We finally connected with them at about 5:45—after they drove past us twice as we waited for them to find us. After breakfast, they dropped us off at my apartment where we reorganized our gifts.

Jan cried when we embraced before I drove her home. She was crying softly until I pulled into her backyard. I watched her every step as she carried her red canvas backpack up the long path to her back door before I put the car in reverse and left. She told me later that she pulled herself together as she entered the back hall with her bag of gifts and called out to her husband, her daughter, and her son eating breakfast together—"I'm home."

Afterward

Jan on June 20, 1980

I heard that Alex and Marge and Pete Kramer and his more-than-tolerant wife Josie took an extended trip together through Aegean Sea countries, including Greece and Turkey. I can just see Pete and Alex trying to relive Zorba the Greek on their travels. Pete probably could—and did. The two men are very close. Perhaps Alex looks to Pete to bring out an uninhabited spirit as he had looked to me even in high school, the extrovert, to draw him out of his introverted nature.

Marge could do that too if Alex expected her to do that, while tolerant, Marlene maintains a quiet peacefulness while she sips her wine and smokes her cigarettes. Pete smokes cigars from the side of his mouth. Marge does cigarettes again, even though she had jaw surgery in 1973—when I loved her, I told her I did, but she said she couldn't be an "intimate" friend.

And Alex doesn't smoke; he just smolders from inside.

Jan on May 26, 1984

Alex and Marge were married today at the 1st Unitarian Society of Milwaukee. I quote Alex who would quote Kurt Vonnegut from *Slaughterhouse-Five*, "So it goes."

Remembering Al Hart

Jan writes October 2, 1979

I had a long conversation with our friend Al Hart, one of the best, kindest, and incidentally, the handsomest maintenance man at

Lakeshore Med. He's one of the early union members who left the picket lines during our six-weeks strike in May and June three years ago. As a widower, Al's been struggling with his schizophrenic adult son who lives with him but won't take his meds—and hospitals won't take him as a patient because his illness can be maintained if he takes his meds.

Al told me, "I'm caught in the middle, and he can turn violent. His frequent mood changes, bizarre behavior or withdrawal from us almost makes us crazy. And it's always tense wondering what will happen next."

"I can understand better than most, Al. My mother was diagnosed as schizophrenic and institutionalized on and off starting when I was ten. They didn't have the drugs for outpatients that they give patients now."

"The thing is," Al explained, "that I can't convince a judge about how dangerous he is so he will be committed. The judge says he's completely normal, but my son won't take his meds and suspects that those of us who are trying to help him are actually wanting to hurt him."

"Oh, Al. How awful. My mother turned out to be what the staff called a "burned-out schizophrenic" with years of electric shock and stupefying drugs to keep her quiet, but I suspect that she'd been misdiagnosed. She was depressed and needed help, and then after being committed and institutionalized for all those years, she just caved in. But she did say weird things, like 'They tore my heart out, you know.' But maybe she had reason to think that. One theory is that schizophrenia is a reaction to stress, and she certainly had plenty of that. Some say it's heredity, and that scares me, but I don't think about it, especially when she was the only one of twelve siblings to have the symptoms. Perhaps what happened to my mother was triggered in her brain by a virus or some chemical imbalance."

With sincerity, Al responded, "I'm sorry you had to go through all that, Jan. I just wish I didn't have to have this to drag me down, especially when everything else is going so well. It's frightening—

those mood changes and his strange responses to everyday stuff that happens around him."

"I always knew my mother loved me," I interrupted. "But when I was young, I believed her behavior was all my fault, that I had misbehaved or disappointed her."

"I felt that too," he empathized, "when I saw it first coming on, maybe I didn't love him enough. But all the love in the world can't protect our loved ones from this terrible disease."

"When I'd go to visit my mother in the hospital, especially with my kids, she would light up with the biggest smile and I knew she loved us." Talking faster, I said, "I was mad at my dad for not going to see her—and for other reasons too."

I changed my tone, "But now I really feel sorry for him, Al, living alone for all these years except when my mother would be discharged from a hospital and come home. Then he, and me too, would be living with a beautiful and talented woman again, someone you love so much, yet you're afraid that she'll lose her grip and leave you abandoned again. But later and before she died, I was afraid they'll close the county hospital and I'd have to take care of her— or she'll run away from us and be a bag lady or become lost and die someplace."

Al paused, perhaps thinking about that happening to his son. "I have my mother-in-law living near me and it is the only way that I can have someone watch after him so I can go to work—and I'd better do just that—get back to work. Thanks for the talk, Jan. I can't share this with too many people."

"I know," I answered. "I'll be here for you. It's difficult for many others who don't understand and can't express how they feel for you and your family."

Al and I had already been good friends, but now that I know this about his family, we are even closer, like kindred souls.

An employee letter, November 20, 1979
"Bulletin: Al Hart is a victim in double homicide"

"There was a lot of heartbreak last night," said Coroner John Nysian, one of Lakeshore lab supervisors, when he described this morning the double homicide of Al Hart and his mother-in-law, Mary Bernay.

Bay View Times sources have revealed that Al Hart's oldest son, Benard Hart, 29, is in custody as the suspect of the double shooting and subsequent fires set in the neighboring homes of each victim.

Al Hart's son Peter, who had been discharged last week from the Ortho unit after knee surgery, escaped from the house through the window during the incident. Al Hart's son John is currently a patient at Lakeshore.

North Grove firefighters were called to the scene to respond to the two fires in the homes of Al and his mother-in-law on Freeman Road near Jensen's Park. After they extinguished the fires, they found the victims in the rooms where the fires had originated.

North Grove police and Lakeshore Bay's County Sheriff's deputies were called. They notified Coroner John Nysian at his home at 1:55 a.m. who came to the scene realizing as he arrived that it was the home of his good friend and co-worker.

"It was like an armed camp when I arrived," he said as law enforcement officers searched the area for the suspect, who was soon apprehended in the vicinity of the victims' homes.

More tragedy involves coroner on November 2, 1979

Coroner John Nysian, Lakeshore Med's laboratory staff member and County Coroner Nysian's duties were not restricted to investigating the deaths of Al Hart and Mary Bernay and notifying their relatives of their family's tragedy.

As coroner, he also had to aid and identify victims of a three-car accident involving two drag-strip racers and a van filled with nine members of an Armenian family who were cousins of the

Nysians. All of the victims in the van were returning from a shopping trip in Milwaukee. Two people were dead and others were severely injured. One is hospitalized at Lakeshore Med. The others were taken to a Milwaukee trauma center.

Al Hart Memorial Fund is formed

"It makes me sad' said Vice President Human Relations Randy King when he heard of Al Hart's death via a long distance call from California, where he is vacationing.

He had called the Communications department today for business matters and was stunned when he heard this news.

A memorial fund was formed. Members of the Human Relations department will accept contributions in Al Hart's name. The funds collected will be used to enhance the environment of the hospital.

Lakeshore Medical Center employees mourn Al Hart

Chief Engineer and Al's supervisor Pat Swinski said, "Everybody knew Al Hart. I feel really bad. I'll miss him. Everybody will miss him." Pat had known Al for 25 years; they'd met when they worked together at Belle City. "He was a very loyal worker, dependable and sympathetic to others' problems. He liked coming to work at Lakeshore Med. He felt part of a big family."

That family feeling was a two-way feeling. "Al was very dear to the hearts of the nursing staff. The whole place is in tears," said Director of Nursing Service Donna Durand. "He was well liked and always pleasant about unpleasant jobs and the immediacy of a problem. He said he 'did it for the patients.'"

Donna continued, "In the winter, the night staff looked to Al as someone you could depend on to get a car going in the morning. He'd get cars unstuck in the snow—he was a fantastic help."

Al was one of the original members of the Hep (Hospital Employees' Program) committee. For the past two years he had his

Salmon-A-Rama catch smoked to share with others at Lakeshore Med's picnic.

Ben Berg of the Maintenance department said Al loved his yard and enjoyed planting and working to make it beautiful. As a friend, Ben liked to tease Al about the jungle that Al had planted.

Coaching Lakeshore Med's women's softball team to a league championship was a labor of love for Al. Last season he coached a winning team, and in 1978, he helped Tim Hogan, Randy King and Chuck McCarthy coach the team to victory.

Each year after the season was over, Al gave a big picnic at his home for the team.

"Al was one of the nicest people I've ever met—this hurts," said Shirley Bowers, a two-year team member. "He always had so much to give."

"Al would do anything for anybody," said Kate Sorenson, another member.

Many attended a dual funeral for Al Hart and his mother at their Lutheran church including the son Benard, the accused, who came with hands cuffed behind his back and legs in irons. He wore informal civilian clothes and was surrounded by armed guards.

Family, neighbors, friends and those of us from Lakeshore Med gasped when he was escorted down the aisle to sit in front of his father's and his grandmother's caskets. The service was touching but traditional in spite of the dreadful circumstances that we "read into" the liturgy.

A Service of Remembrance for Albert Hart

Lakeshore Med's Chaplain Arthur Boulton initiated a more comforting, inter-denominational service in our little St. Barnabas' Chapel on November 30, 1979.

"Dear friends and co-workers, we gather together here informally as mourners who wish to pause in tribute to our friend and colleague whom we called with affection, Al. The sudden and violent manner in which he and his mother were taken from us has left us with a sense of shock, dismay and deprivation. We sorrow with and for his loved ones and we gather to lift before the Throne of Grace our own sorrow. We feel a need for time to repair that which has come upon us so suddenly. That our friend's life should be terminated so inhumanely causes us to feel pain on his behalf, for we would have wished him a long and happy life as a due reward for his pervasive kindness and sense of industry. We gather in the hope that somehow in the Providence of a High Power, Al will be duly recompensed for the good things he has done and the wrongs he has endured."

To dismiss the group, we read, "Al, may the angels take thee to Paradise and may the Lord watch between me and thee while we are absent from one another. Amen."

Four more years of legal wrangling
Jan on February 8, 1977

As the weather warmed a bit, Lakeshore Bay's striking teachers were arrested, fined, and released after sit-down protests began. Ray Schuster represented two schoolteachers in court today. They had landed on the hood of a school board member's car as he drove across the picket line and into the Lakeshore Bay's Unified administrative parking area. Rumor has it that the teachers threw themselves on the hood to stop him. Another rumor is that one of our friends is so caught up in the fight that she's leaving her husband and four children to become Schuster's disciple.

Last week I was asked to initiate a new written communication project for government officials and corporate leaders to strengthen our community support network. We called it a "memo" and used a similar Xeroxed, the immediate format of the employee "letter." Our first issue addressed Lakeshore Med's expansion and renovation plans.

Jan on March 10, 1977

The teachers' strike ended today when Jack Porter, the union's general who believes in confrontational negotiations and demands the respect and loyalty of his troops, accepted the school board's offer.

Of course, with the schools closed much of the time during the 50-day strike, the system was threatened with the loss of state aid—the final clout. Schools reopened and children and their parents who crossed picket lines to enter school buildings became objects of striking teachers' verbal abuse, and those teachers who crossed the picket lines suffered as victims of harassment or isolation from their peers.

Porter, like Ray Schuster, has a contentious personality and irritated people on both sides, yet among his militant followers, 464 persons were charged during the strike for resisting arrest. Three Lakeshore Bay schoolteachers appeared on Phil Donahue's TV show in Chicago today to tell their story of being arrested with eighteen others the day before and being stripped and searched by Lakeshore Bay police.

"Another mess" headlined the March 15 "open letter" to Ray Schuster and Bay View Times Letter to the Editor from Dan Becker, president of Local 100, the official head of Local 100 Hospital Employees Union, headquartered in Milwaukee.

In his original letter, edited by the newspaper, he wrote, "Dear Ray, Got another mess on your hands, right? I bailed you out of your disaster at Lakeshore Med. If I can be of any help in your newest holycost, get in touch, right? At least you're getting famous as the leader of the most fouled-up strikes in Wisconsin. I thought Lakeshore Med was a mess, but your teacher's strike in Lakeshore Bay is worse than the Milwaukee Meat Cutters strike and the Centerville teacher's strike put together. How you goof them up so badly, I'll never know. If the ministers can't bail you out today, let me know. I'll do what I can to help."

Jan on April 1, 1977

On Friday morning, I regaled my Wisconsin hospital PR peers with the conflict and confusion of our hospital's six-week strike. I covered the walls of the room with newspaper banner headlines and front-page articles, set out samples of my newsletters and used the chalkboard to try to illustrate the two union factions with Lakeshore Med's patients and employees in the middle of the chaos. Often they would cringe at the potential for more chaos or laugh at the absurdity of situations that occurred.

I told them I felt as if I were held by a thread of mixed information, the fear of litigation, the responsibility of tearing the whole fabric by one's misquote or another's evaluation. I knew media and powerful people would be judges as I watched, heard, read and anticipated all that could be jeopardized.

I was often told that my daily newsletters helped to unify the team inside the hospital who would know of events before the media reported them. It was in contrast to the confusion on the picket line and within union ranks.

"It would be good to say we planned all this. But much of what occurred from our communications efforts was an immediate and intuitive response to what was needed. The entire hospital supported my requests for information to inform them and the community. People in Office Services moved out of the way to let me print on our Xerox 9200. Accountants and various personnel stopped their work immediately to give me facts and statistical records. The administration responded instantly to whatever was needed. Our legal consultants were seconds away by phone if not on the scene. Hospital employees were aware of news tips and sent them on to me.

"They wanted to know—every day."

My HPRC members empathized with all our efforts and several suggested that I organize my materials and submit them for an award from the American Society of Hospital Public Relations. I decided I would call it "A Year of Union Militancy Challenges a Century of

Caring," and when I finished it, I'd also submit copies of it to our public library and historical society.

Bay View Times Opinion Page on April 17, 1977 "Strike tactics backfire on Porter-Schuster"

"A Lakeshore Bay Unified PTA Council committee has begun a study of this year's seven-week teachers' strike in the hope that future disasters can be prevented.

"Excellent idea. We have a suggestion: Analyze the tactics promoted by the partnership of the teacher's union Executive Director Jack Porter and labor attorney Ray Schuster, not only in this year's strike but also in three other strikes, teachers, City of Lakeshore Bay employees, Lakeshore Media Center employees.

"In each of these strikes, Porter and/or Schuster used community organizer Saul Alinsky's prescription of 'polarize, personalize, publicize and pressure.'

"The tactics brutalized labor-management relations and caused grievous hurt to countless persons. One extreme example: The anguish caused to families by the local's grotesque refusal to bury the dead.

"…Porter and Schuster led the teachers and custodians into an illegal strike this year in which the Alinsky technique was carried out relentlessly. The character assassination dehumanized the conflict, making a settlement much more difficult.

"School Board members—the target of assaults—were alienated by the attacks and not as willing to compromise on an equitable settlement.

"The tactics included picket line disturbances in which 474 teachers were arrested. Strikers pounded on cars, shouted obscenities and insults and there were 'dial-a-scab' telephone calls to non-striking teachers.

"…Scab lists have been posted, and some militants are wearing strike pins and strike signs have been hung on classroom doors. 'It's bitter, it's vicious and it's directed," said School Board member Max Powell.

"What did teachers and custodians gain by all their nefarious activity in the strike?

"The school board granted some concessions in the new contract, but the teachers' pay raise went only a little beyond the 6.1 percent hike implemented by the board last fall.

"…The message for Porter and Schuster should be clear by now. Alinsky tactics are obsolete as far as Lakeshore is concerned. The community wants no more "polarize, personalize, publicize and pressure" in public employee bargaining.

"We hope the PTA committee studying the teachers' strike will take into account the ugly results of the Alinsky tactics and make appropriate recommendations in this report."

Jan on April 27, 1979

"Arbitrator Upholds Biggs, Vanik, Mosier, Sanders Discharges"

"The grievance of the four employees are denied. The arbitrator has found that the Hospital had just cause to discharge Arthur Biggs, Helen Vanik, Betty Mosier, and Beverly Sanders,' states the arbitration decision received at Lakeshore Medical Center at 9 a.m. today.

"This decision was signed on Monday in the Chicago office of Peter Gallaher, the impartial arbitrator who was selected by both Lakeshore Medical Center and the Hospital Employees' Union Local No. 100 to evaluate the evidence placed in hearings held last November.

"The hospital's discharge of Biggs and Vanik is upheld for their part in unauthorized work stoppages. Last year on May 7, Biggs led a walkout by forty to fifty employees during the thirty-minute work stoppage. Following on May 22, Vanik led a sit-down strike in

Central Service, 'the consequences of deciding not to perform sterilizing duties in a hospital setting can be critical,' said the report.

"Betty Mosier's discharge was upheld on evidence that she struck a security guard. Bea Sanders was discharged because of her participation in tire slashing.

"Letters were sent to striking bargaining unit employees on June 29 directing them to return to work by July 2. However, these four strikers received notice that they were being discharged for their involvement in picket line misconduct. The four filed grievances protesting their discharge. After a grievance meeting on July 23 proved unsuccessful, the grievances proceeded to arbitration, which would result in a binding decision for both the employees and the hospital.

"Peter Gallaher conducted hearings in Lakeshore Bay on November 4, 13, and 17.

"Included in the report today were the following statements relating to Biggs and Vanik. 'Union members in positions of authority should work to discourage unauthorized work stoppage…(this) is even more pertinent where a hospital is involved and the lives of its patients may be threatened…Biggs's actions gave the Hospital just cause to discharge him. The record reflects that the Hospital did not discriminate against Biggs nor treat him unfairly because he was a Union Steward…The testimony of the co-workers and supervisory personnel clearly established Vanik's leadership role in the work stoppage…The fact that Vanik was disciplined more severely than the other employee is attributed to her leadership in the work stoppage and not her position as a Union Steward.'

"The hospital terminated Mosier because she struck a security guard on two separate occasions. The arbitrator affirmed the firing and stated, 'Mosier's attacks on the officer were unprovoked. The second attack created an atmosphere of violence because after she hit him, a general scuffle broke out between union and employer sympathizers.

"'This type of behavior cannot be tolerated,' the statement continued. 'It betrays the peaceful protest that unions have a legal right to pursue.'

"Sanders was discharged for the destruction of property and vandalism. Though there was conflicting testimony between Sanders and two security guards, the arbitrator said, when determining the credibility of their accounts, 'It is necessary to consider the motives behind their testimony. Sanders's denial of involvement had the effect of protecting her job. However, the record discloses no motives on the part of the guard to lie about what took place. He had little or no personal gain to achieve through his testimony.' His version of the incident, the statement said, was given 'great weight.'

"Randall King, Human Relations Administrator, said this morning, 'As the strike came to its conclusion, we did what we thought was right when we discharged these people. The arbitrator's judgment conforms to our decision. The strike ended on July 2, 1976. Fortunately, for all but these four people. We came together again to work for Lakeshore and to care for our patients.'"

Jan on May 25, 1977

I've organized my hospital strike materials to submit my 250-page document for a national award from ASHPR, the American Society of Hospital Public Relations. It held, in one volume, most of the information that our department was involved in this labor conflict. I concluded my collection by writing, "When Does It End?"

"The year that has passed has brought new awareness in many dimensions, but especially in the increased importance of effective communications.

"Lakeshore Med's human resources during this six-week strike came from hundreds of dedicated individuals with their varied skills and talents, which ranged from labor relations experts to housekeeping crews, from physicians to volunteers, from administrators to cooks. Our strength of purpose came from our concern for the patient and our century of caring traditions. The factor that seemed to unify this all was open daily communication.

"The experience gained by our immediate and responsible media responses and by our sustained, in-depth strike bulletins have enlarged our entire communications program today. The new Communications Department now has two persons, doubling the publications and tripling our goals. As the director, I'm now responsible for external/community relations. The assistant director is responsible for internal/employee and patient communications.

"Our larger goal is to maintain close relationships with employees, with the community and with decision-makers and other special interest groups. Through new information programs, we plan to build stronger positive attitudes about Lakeshore Medical Center as an employer and as a hospital.

"I've often asked myself if more positive communications started years before could have prevented this strike from happening. I think not. The bargaining unit leaders were setting up a confrontational power play that was revealed in the first negotiating meeting. However, more communications were needed at every level of hospital involvement. The community needed to know more about Lakeshore Med services and more about health and wellness information. Special interest groups and decision-makers need to be informed about community health needs and the hospital's plans to meet them.

"Employees needed to know more about benefits. They needed frequent information about each other and their jobs. They needed a sense of importance and total team effort. They needed to know about hospital policy and decisions before they read about it in the newspaper or hear it on the radio.

"Now, in addition to responding to these communications needs, Lakeshore has also established the position of Human Relations Administrator, an executive position created for and filled by a person whose primary motives are to anticipate and to meet employee needs without the turmoil of labor/management conflict.

"Most hospital employees deserve better wages. They are squeezed between hospital cost limitations, the cost of living and inflation, and their own long-term goals.

"The striking service employees at Lakeshore Med could compare wages in the industry where sweepers and other service employees make more money. Metropolitan hospitals pay more. Yet when individual Lakeshore Med employees at this level quit to work elsewhere, many of them would return disillusioned. Before the strike started, we computed the average longevity of the bargaining unit to be seven and a half years. The turnover rate was only twelve percent a year compared to the turnover rate of twenty-four to forty percent in southeastern Wisconsin in hospitals of comparable size. We concluded that Lakeshore Med was not such a bad place to work.

"However, the union militants created for them even greater expectations that could not be met in our community. If these leaders had won their demands, they would look to other hospital unions to gather stronger forces. They gambled for power, but they used our employees' jobs, benefits, and lost wages for their chips.

"When was this strike actually over? Negotiations began on April 7, 1976. The strike started on May 24. The contract was signed on June 24. The immediate legal complications ended on July 1. Did it end when striking employees returned to work? Did it end when angry emotions were forgotten and employees, together again, worked to care for Lakeshore patients? Was the strike over on April 27, 1977, when all charges against Lakeshore were dismissed as having no merit and our discharge actions of four employees were affirmed by impartial arbitration?

"I hope so. It's been such a long and wasteful process in spite of our new awareness.

"But then a clipping appeared in the *Lakeshore Labor Weekly* paper, and the process continues."

***Lakeshore Labor Weekly* on May 20, 1977**
"Biggs, Vanik turn to NLRB"

"Art Biggs and Helen Vanik have asked the National Labor Relations Board to proceed with an investigation of unfair labor practices against Lakeshore Medical Center."

Will the NLRB ignore and overturn the arbitrator's decision and proceed with its own investigation? How much money has been spent on litigation since the labor strife began and continues?

And the battle goes on.

Jan on November 19, 1978

I was shocked to read about the death of Ray Schuster in today's paper. He died of cancer at the age of 44. I didn't know he had a family, but the obit said his wife, two children, his mother, and siblings survived him. His parents and grandparents were attorneys specializing in liberal and union causes. That I knew, and that he had joined the family firm before becoming a partner with Lakeshore Bay attorney Robert Weber. Weber was quoted saying that Schuster was "the most brilliant lawyer in southeastern Wisconsin," He also said that Schuster was a man who would rather stand on the stage naked than not be there at all.

Another described him as a "defender of the underdog."
No one from Lakeshore Medical Center was quoted.
The article also said he ran for public office as a Democrat several times but never was elected and that memorials should be sent to the Beth Hillel Temple in lieu of flowers.

Jan on December 15, 1979

During the recent Board of Directors annual meeting, Nick Dixon spoke about the successful negotiations made again after the six-weeks hospital strike in 1976. He speculated that the final settlement and appeals will not be determined until the spring; but he warned the group that the National Labor Relations Board probably will force Lakeshore Med to pay $86,000 in back pay to two union leaders who were fired for wildcat strike actions in May 1976.

In recalling the incredible discord we all experienced from that complex labor conflict, Nick actually said that my communications efforts, including a newsletter written and distributed daily during the 40-day strike "defused the power of union efforts to sustain a successful strike."

His acknowledgment of my contribution made me feel proud, but it was the contribution of others; everybody who worked hard and long to sustain patient care and keep the hospital functioning. But my communications efforts of the daily newsletter plus excellent media coverage were the most visible and reliable contributions that unified and acknowledged the efforts of others.

Jan on October 5, 1980

The Bay View Times reported that Lakeshore Medical Center has to pay a total of $87,339 to Art Biggs and Helen Vanik to meet the back-pay terms of the 1978 National Labor Relations Board decision that approved their being fired after the strike. The hospital was ordered to offer the strike leaders their jobs back and pay them back wages, plus interest, for the income that they lost.

"Under terms of their settlements with Lakeshore Medical Center, Biggs was awarded a total of $60,670, including $6,000 in turn for his agreement not to ask for his job back. Vanik's total settlement, $26,669, also was understood to include money in return for her agreement not to ask for her job.

"About $23,000 of Biggs's settlement and about $8,800 of Vanik's was used to pay their attorney, Arthur Heltzer."

Attorney Heitzer said he believes that the payment is the largest of its kind in the history of the state. The ruling ends four years of legal wrangling.

Perhaps now, as the *Lakeshore Labor Weekly* wrote, "The ruling ends four years of legal wrangling."

I hope so.

UPCOMING BOOKS
From Mother Courage Press

Additional Books in
The Whistling Girls & Crowing Hens Series

Books are at many online retailers and can be ordered at any bookstore or library.

Book 1—*Not to be Denied* captures humorous, sad and scary family life between 1900 and 1970: The Depression, war, life at home, schizophrenia; tomboy girls and teen girlfriends, sexual encounters, children, husbands, and individuals' choices that shape them. Passion explodes for two women in their early '40s. Liberal religion and Transactional Analysis weekends bring them together. Their paths meld when these naïve lovers test their magnetic attraction after Jan asks, "What could it hurt if we just let it happen?" (January 2024)

Book 2—In *Gullibles' Travel* (1950, 1975-84), Divorced Bea tries not to be a lesbian and her lover Jan strives to keep her children, husband and Bea happy. Bea and friends test the Sexual Revolution of the '60s and '70s. Jan recalls living in Cold War Germany in the '50s and touring Greece, Leningrad and Moscow with her husband in the '70s. Jan defuses a labor/management conflict and Bea and Jan escape to Europe for a rowdy and risqué three-week escapade in '76. (April 2024)

Book 3—In *Secret Transgressions* (1976-84), Jan's hospital PR job expands with Bea as her assistant. Jan's marriage turns raw. Divorce. Bea is subject to sexual harassment in the workplace, is fired, and Jan is emotionally harassed on the job. Travel helps them heal and they create Mother Courage Bookstore and Press. (July 2024)

Book 4—*Being Mother Courage* (1976-89) embodies a dream come true: creating a feminist bookstore and experiencing historic events and adventures in the women's movement and the gay/lesbian world. They extended their first American Booksellers Association (ABA) trade show in Los Angeles starting with San Francisco's gay scene, on a night unlike any other, and ending by sailing with Seaworthy Women on a 31-foot wooden ketch launched from the 5000-boat Marina del Rey to Catalina Island. Women's spirituality circles and lesbian support groups in Bea and Jan's home inspire and support women. Jan confronts job harassment and Bea faces the bookstore's demise. Their Cancun vacation fun ignores sun-bathing on beaches to explore Mayan ruins. Jan enters the snorkeling world led by scuba-diver Bea. At home, their full moon circles begin with feminist and original rites and rituals. Tension turns to courageous laughter when conflicts are overcome. Bea uses her skills to pioneer Apple's Mac desktop publishing and was a guest speaker/teacher at the International Women's Booksellers Conference in Spain. (August 2024)

Book 5—In *Grit & Gratification* (1979-82), Sailor Bea commands the boat and Jan, her bungling crew. Bea and Jan muster strength after Bea's homophobe father and Jan's supportive father die and they rehab their inherited rundown properties. Their new Mother Courage Press creates a significant, successful book for sexual abuse victims. When their retail bookstore closes, they are free to travel. As lusty lovers, they tow their camper to New York City, Provincetown, America's Stonehenge and Niagara Falls. Then they experience Michigan Woman's Music Festivals. Jan accepts that her lost Door County acres can be found on women's festival land. (January 2025)

Book 6—In *Moving On & Up* (1983-85), Bea rejects joint therapy sessions with their friend. Jan goes alone to heal her stress asking to use her uniquely devised feminist therapy regimen that eventually benefits both women. Jan's boss eliminates her PR department and job, but her reputation earns her a better one at a major metropolitan hospital. Bea and Jan stay strong together. Mother Courage Press begins to thrive. Surviving scuba diving and wild camping trips, sneaking into Disney World, being inspired at women's music festivals and gatherings, traveling through the Great Northwest makes them feel on top of the world. (April 2025)

Book 7— In *Closer to Fine* (1984 to 1997) Jan moves up to the 'Big Leagues' of hospital PR in an exciting but stressful job. Mother Courage Press is thriving and they dare to publish Entity Jeni's channeling via a friend's New Age psychic energy messages. Seaworthy Women sailor friends sail together across the Pacific in a small sailboat and send Mother Courage Press their manuscript so Bea and Jan fly to New Zealand and later to Australia. More fun starts with a trip to guitar heaven in northern California, and at home, Bea starts a woman's kitchen band to entertain audiences and themselves. (September 2025)

Book 8—In *Intimate Passages*, (1984 to 2013) Bea challenges the intimate aspects of their long-lasting relationship, but Jan persists. Friends and family dynamics grow closer. National events honoring women's art, music and culture inspire them. Bea travels to experience England's Crop Circles. Jan guides her daughter and grandson through Paris—on Segways. Bea and Jan's Goddess-searching journeys throughout the British Isles, Mexico, Malta, France and Egypt enrich their lives as health and aging issues evolve and goals are met. (November 2025)

For additional information on the series, contact:
Editor/Publisher Jeanne Arnold
MotherCouragePress31@gmail.com
MotherCouragePress.com

ABOUT JAN ANTHONY

Travel is in my DNA. Like Poet Robert Frost's "The Roads Not Taken," I actually traveled roads taken and not taken. In my small world, I taught, wrote and believed in peace, ecology, equal rights, especially for women, and finally lived on the edge, undaunted by conventional routes. My t-shirt says, "Sweet old lady? More like battle-tested warrior queen."

Mother Courage Press
MotherCouragePress31@gmail.com

271